THE

SHAPE

SHIFTERS

CONTINUOUS CHANGE FOR
COMPETITIVE ADVANTAGE

John L. Mariotti

Van Nostrand Reinhold
I(T)P® A Division of International Thompson Publishing Inc.

New York • Albany • Bonn • Boston • Detroit • London • Madrid • Melbourne
Mexico City • Paris • San Francisco • Singapore • Tokyo • Toronto

Copyright © 1997 by John L. Mariotti

 ITP International Thompson Publishing Company.
The ITP logo is a registered trademark used herein under license.

The ideas presented in this book are generic and strategic. Their specific application to a particular company must be the responsibility of the management of that company, based on management's understanding of their company's procedures, culture, resources, and competitive situation.

Printed in the United States of America.

Visit us on the Web   www.vnr.com

For more information contact:

Van Nostrand Reinhold
115 Fifth Avenue
New York, NY 10003

Chapman & Hall GmbH
Pappalallee 3
69469 Weinham
Germany

Chapman & Hall
2-6 Boundary Row
London SEI 8HN
United Kingdom

International Thomson Publishing Asia
60 Albert Street #15-01
Albert Complex
Singapore 189969

Thomas Nelson Australia
102 Dodds Street
South Melbourne 3205
Victoria, Australia

International Thomson Publishing Japan
Hirakawa-cho Kyowa Building, 3F
2-2-1 Hirakawa-cho, Chiyoda-ku
Tokyo 102 Japan

Nelson Canada

International Thomson Editores

1120 Birchmount Road
Scarborough, Ontario
MIK 5G4, Canada

Seneca, 53
Colonia Polanco
11560 Mexico D.F. Mexico

1 2 3 4 5 6 7 8 9 10 QEBFF 01 00 99 98 97

Library of Congress Cataloging-in-Publication Data available
Mariotti, John L.,   1941–
    The shape-shifters : continuous change for competitive advantage /
by John L. Mariotti.
        p.   cm.
    Includes index.
    ISBN 0-442-02559-9 (hc)
    1. Organizational change.   2. Competition.   3. Business planning.
I. Title.
HD58.8.M2652   1997   97–33630
658.4'063--dc21   CIP

CONTENTS

Delight the mind of the customer and they will show you the money!

That is the basic principle upon which the best of businesses are increasingly building their strategies. How to build an organization capable of delighting customers consistently, however, is the $64,000 or $64 million question for firms facing the hypercompetitive battles of the twenty-first century. You'll be delighted to know that John Mariotti's powerful and practical new book, *The Shape-Shifters*, addresses this critically important question.

I have often wondered how the business books of the future will describe the last two decades of the twentieth century. Perhaps the greatest understatement they will make is that it was an era of change. But change is noting new—it is the rate of change that has sent a wake-up call to business leaders around the globe. And all members of the corporate rank and file, from CEO to assistant manager, are seeking guidance on how to manage the unknown change of the future.

Past experience alone is no longer the only prerequisite for success in the future. In fact, as the rate of change in society and in the business world increases, the more successful a firm has been in the past, the more likely it is to fail in the future. Why? Because these firms, and often the CEOs who lead them continue to do the things that led to their success in the past.

So where do corporations turn to find new ways to do things? More and more are turning to continuing education and business books for guidance on how to manage in the future. Many years ago I discovered that business books are much like business speakers: They tend to be either interesting or motivational or educational and dull. If you have ever listened to motivational speakers at a national meeting, you may have laughed at their jokes and felt inspired to go forth and conquer. Some of the speakers tell the audience, "You're a tiger; go get the sales!" Despite the motivation of the moment, you quickly realize that the speaker failed to tell you anything very useful about *how* to get the sales. No theory. No techniques. Nothing very practical. I heard many professors in undergraduate and graduate school provide theory and techniques that were truly the most important and practical ideas that a person could possess. Unfortunately, many (but not all) of those professors were also experts at putting the audience to sleep.

The same situation is found in many business books. If this dilemma bothers you, as it does me, I believe you will enjoy *The Shape-Shifters*. John Mariotti writes from his own experience that spanned a number of firms and progressed from entry level to president of major corporations. John goes beyond the perspective of the corporate executive to write as a person who understands scholarship and the academic literature. The practical, how-to experience solidly based on the insights of other scholars provides a powerful and provocative analysis of what organizations must do to survive in the twenty-first century.

This book is about how organizations must shift their shape to be ready for the future, how they must evolve in the next century. One of the many valuable topics discussed in this book is the issue of value attributes, and the value pentastar provides an excellent way to understand this underlying reality of shape-shifting. While it is still vital to examine how consumer markets are changing and how power in the distribution channel is shifting, we must not overlook the need for new organizational structures to deal with such changes. Some of the most important ideas in John Mariotti's new book are about the shapes of organizations that are preferred most by consumers.

A very substantial amount of literature on multi-attribute attitude measurement exists in academic journals. Most of the academic literature, however, has not found its way into business practice—perhaps because of the style in which it is often written. John Mariotti has built upon this literature, and made it useful in thinking about business. He gives examples most readers can relate to readily. I believe you will like his combination of very strong concepts and theoretical materials presented in a manner that displays his own practical approach to getting things done effectively. I believe you will especially appreciate the way John relates his own, very practical approach to ideas that have proven so valuable to building great businesses.

I believe there is always a better way to do things—bold ideas that make business sense can lead firms of all sizes to successful futures. *The Shape-Shifters* offers insight into new and practical ways on how to do things better.

Roger D. Blackwell, Ph.D.
Professor of Marketing, The Ohio State University,
and author of *From Mind to Market*

ACKNOWLEDGMENTS

I'd like to thank many people who helped in the creation of this work, but especially my wife Maureen, who gave up a great deal of our time together while I was writing this. Certain people were instrumental: Tom Peters, who suggested the title after reading an abstract of the book before I began to write it; Rick Maurer, whose insightful critique helped me to improve the flow and content early in the process; Raj Aggarwal, Bob Bidwell, Larry Cain, Liz Clark, Doug Dempsey, Sarah Gardial, Mike Harris, Ernie Huge, Mike Kami, and Tony Morreale, for their input. John Willig, my agent, and John Boyd, my publisher, for their encouragement, support, valuable input, and for helping to "shape" the finished work; the people at VNR, especially Angela Burt-Murray, John Garger, and Carl Germann for their help; and last, my son Michael for his valuable suggestion to put more of my own beliefs into the book.

INTRODUCTION

In the world of business, many factors enter into decisions. There are people and organizational decisions, equipment and plant decisions, new product and process decisions, political decisions and, ultimately, strategy decisions. What should we create? To sell to whom? For what? Why should anyone buy ours compared to all the alternatives out there? When we make these decisions, what will determine our success? The answer is: The "configuration" of the chosen business and the *value* it creates and delivers to its customers.

I struggled with these issues as president of Huffy Bicycles for almost 10 years, and then for a couple years more as president of Rubbermaid's multinational Office Products Group. Sometimes I thought I knew the answer. The market usually quickly confirmed whether my answer was right or wrong. Each time the questions arose, another combination of factors — a new configuration or "shape," had to be considered, and a new customer's perception of value had to be understood. Now I am doing it as an advisor to leading consumer product companies, and I find the situation the same.

This book is the culmination of over 30 years of experience, operating in fast-paced businesses, where contemplation lasts only until the phone rings, the next interruption occurs, or the next meeting starts. After all those years business experience in four different industries, and even more research, the inescapable, indisputable conclusion I will try to explain in this book is why and how the "shape" that consistently creates and delivers the best value is the key, *because the best value wins!*

Winning does not mean simply getting the first order. It means fulfilling the succeeding orders and making a profit and return on investment greater than the cost of capital, so there is the opportunity to do it over and over. It means keeping the customer as a long-term partner, too. Understanding and defining value is not the only key, but understanding what sort of value is perceived as better than the competitor's offering allows us to create that value both more effectively and more rapidly. Once understood and created, delivering that value consistently is also essential. It is here that the people issues become pivotal. Developing an organization, leading that group of people, and achieving these goals is what the life of business is all about.

Since the customer's perception of value is always changing, our understanding of value must also be shifting to match or anticipate it. It was with this realization that I thought about the concept of the shape-shifter. In the successful television series *Star Trek—The Next Generation*, a shape-shifter was a being who could alter his or her form at will to the shape best suited for the circumstances or conducive to success in a mission. Thus, *the essence of shape-shifting, is to be able to re-create yourself, your organization, its core competencies, and your business into the shape that can create and deliver what the customers value most.*

The only way to effectively change the "shape of value" is to change what I call the "shape of the business" that creates and delivers that value. Understanding how to continuously shift the shape of businesses to deliver value consistently, when the very definition of value itself is constantly shifting, is the key to long-term success. In *Competing for the Future* (Harvard Business School Press, 1994), Gary Hamel and C. K. Prahalad speak of "getting to the future first." I heartily agree—but only if the shape we get there in (to create and deliver value) is the right one. Make no mistake, getting there first is important, but not only must we get there with the best value, we must also continue to deliver the best value consistently.

Many large companies have dominated markets in the United States over the last four to five decades. They got there first, and grew to incredible size and strength. But somehow the fearsome strength of General Motors, US Steel, even IBM, and Sears are not what they used to be. What happened? Could it be that their shape was no longer the right one for creating and delivering the new customer perception of best value? What will be the future of Wal-Mart, Intel, and Toyota? As the customer's perceived shape of value shifts, will they shift too? Fast enough?

Change is inevitable. But change is difficult. People resist change unless they are part of how it comes about. Then they can actually enjoy it. Capitalizing on change effectively can become the most powerful source of competitive advantage but it all depends on the people and their leadership.

Another condition is just as predictable and inescapable in business as it is in nature: As large organizations grow and mature, they become *less flexible* and are *more vulnerable* to newer, more vigorous, and more adaptive competition. Your journey through *The Shape-Shifters* will help you not only better understand value, but to generate some useful ideas about how to build on that understanding, to capitalize on continuous change, and then to build your organization's success based on that change. But before we begin, let me continue the analogy between change in nature and change in business.

I live on a hill that overlooks a vast expanse of forest. In this forest there are trees of all different species, sizes, and ages. While I looked at this work of nature one day, it struck me that there was a message here that could be applied to organizations, especially business organizations. I began to focus on one tree, great in both height and girth. It was, I assumed very old. In fact, there were no small trees in the shadow of its huge branches. The large tree dominated its part of the forest. Its spread was so impressive that it completely excluded new growth (even its own seeds) from taking root in its shadow.

But all around it, the trees were mostly of the same species, of varying ages and sizes, which obviously grew from the seeds of the great tree. Other plant life, too, flourished outside the tree's shadow, and the diversity was beautiful to behold. As majestic as the large tree was, its setting was only enhanced by the surrounding growth. Alone, it simply wouldn't have been as impressive, because there would have been nothing for comparison.

One day, in the very early spring, a great windstorm swept through the forest. Never before has such a wind blown through this forest. Other strong winds had knocked down the smaller, dead, or dying branches of the large tree, and this natural pruning was healthy for it. But this stronger wind tore at the great limbs and branches of the tree as never before. By virtue of its size and age, the tree was rigid and unyielding, whereas the smaller trees were able to flex in the wind and remain unharmed. As the wind whipped the mighty tree, one of its large limbs broke, with a resounding crack, and fell to the ground. Once a strength, now its huge size and weight worked to its disadvantage.

But soon thereafter, something different and new began to take place on the ground beneath where the large limb had hung: The sunlight and rain fell through and some of the seeds from the large tree that had fallen there began to grow alongside many other plants. This new growth was much different from the rest of the area around the big tree. It was very diverse and flexible; it was also aggressive, growing very fast, often doubling in height in a single year. Still, the large tree continued to dominate its part of the forest. Then another major storm came, and another limb broke off the great tree. It was as large as the first, and it was from a part of the tree near the first break. The very core of the great tree was now exposed.

The first broken branch had lain on the ground for some time, and the burrowing, sucking, and chewing insects had found it. From there they had moved to the healthy trunk of the tree, where they found them access to other old wounds. As seasons went by, some of these infested areas began to rot, and the parasites continued their slow, steady march.

In contrast, the new growth around the great tree continued to flourish, gathering greater amounts of sunlight and moisture. As time went by, the old tree slowly gave way to the ravages of storms and parasites. With each broken limb and fallen branch, more aggressive new growth sprouted around it. The trees that had taken root in the area exposed by the original broken limb were now quite large, and still growing rapidly. They were now competing for the light and moisture with each other and not only the great tree.

Finally, after much of the great tree's strength had been destroyed, it toppled over. Its once proud bulk lay on the ground, in somber, sad repose. A few of its roots remained linked to the soil, and some new growth appeared on its limbs each spring, but most of it was a broken and decaying hulk. The new trees that had sprouted in its space now blocked its meager growth from the sunlight and took the nourishment from the soil. As they grew taller and larger, it became apparent there was no longer room for all of them to become as dominant as the great tree had been. Like their predecessor, they could no longer flex with the swirling, stormy winds. Their upward growth had slowed, too. In such large trees, the sap took too long to get to the top for them to become flexible or grow much taller, although they spread their large, rigid limbs outward in an attempt to grasp more sunlight. Their deep roots had to reach even further down to nourish their large frames and cling to the territory they now claimed.

They, too, were bound by nature to fall victim to the ravages of time, the strong winds of change, and the growth of the young and the flexible. Trees can not grow to the sky, and neither can companies. Their own size, bulk and inflexibility become their limitations. Thus, the "shape" of the forest is constantly "shifting." Old growth matures and dies off, and new growth takes its place. Nature's messages are subtle but powerful. Often, we ignore them. More often, we are simply unaware of the messages because we do not know to look for them. One thing is certain. We can learn from the laws of nature and the story of the forest.

Markets have limits just as the forest does. The wise businessperson picks only a limited area of the "forest" to shape, lest he or she be spread too thin. Like trees, the competitors who can grow yet remain flexible will survive and prosper the longest. Many companies came to mind as I wrote this: Bethlehem Steel, PanAm, US Steel, General Motors, even Sears and IBM, to name some of the best known. These once large and powerful "trees" have met a variety of competition. Some withstood the competition and survived, but not without massive pruning and reshaping. Companies like Nucor Steel, Southwest Airlines, Toyota, Wal-Mart, Intel, and Microsoft are now the large trees in the forest. What will their life cycle look like? When will they succumb to the disease of bigness? How will they have to change, and will they do so? Perhaps the most well known and consistently profitable example of a shape-shift from one area of the "forest" to an entirely different one is provided by General Electric, under John F. Welch's leadership.

In 1981, GE was a behemoth, deeply entrenched in cyclical, big-ticket, heavily unionized businesses. Welch decreed that he would simplify management and stay in no businesses where GE could not be either number one or number two. He bought RCA and NBC, and sold the unprofitable small home appliance business. He sold the consumer electronics business and pushed into financial services. GE currently leads all U.S. companies in market capitalization, and Welch's management has proven hugely successful for GE shareholders. GE under Welch has been termed the world's only $80-billion growth company.

Even as I write this, Welch is reshaping GE again. Instead of depending on any tree to grow to the sky, Welch is constantly and continuously planting new trees and moving to new parts of the forest, while not abandoning the still healthy old parts. Welch is also bundling services around the products like the new growth surrounding the large tree. As Theodore Levitt so aptly described in his book *The Marketing Imagination* (The Free Press, 1986), Welch and GE are creating "...the enhanced product, the expanded product..."

Only through a journey of constant shape-shifting can businesses capitalize on the changes occurring in the natural environment in which they must compete. In the chapters that follow, I will describe *why* the changes are necessary, *what* defines the changes needed, *how* to get started shape-shifting, and then close with some final thoughts on *where next*. Let the journey begin.

PART ONE

Why?

THE WORLD WE HAVE CREATED TODAY HAS PROBLEMS WHICH
CANNOT BE SOLVED BY THINKING THE WAY WE THOUGHT WHEN WE
CREATED THEM.

– Albert Einstein

1.

Value—The New Mantra

If you deliver unmatched customer value, you will deliver growth and shareholder value.
—Michael Treacy, in a speech delivered at the
EFI Forum, February 1996
Strategy is revolution; everything else in tactics.
—Gary Hamel, "Strategy as Revolution,"
Harvard Business Review, July-August 1996

THE REVOLUTION

Your job, your career, and everything you and your company do is judged by a group of stakeholders. These stakeholders may be superiors within the company, directors of the company, or shareholders/owners. You also face a "jury of peers," whose opinions and behaviors will have a profound impact on your professional success and life. Customers, suppliers, employees, and other business partners all influence what matters to you and your company. The thoughts and feelings of all these groups are impacted by the information they receive, much of it in the business press or electronic media. Consider the following example of what businesspeople are reading in the contemporary media. (Throughout the book, I will include additional quotes from a diverse group of leaders concerning these chaotic, uncharted times to help you gain a perspective on what is going on around us all.) This is from the premiere issue of *Fast Company* magazine, in 1995:

Something is happening and it affects us all. A global revolution is changing business, and business is changing the world. With unsettling speed, two forces are converging: a new generation of business leaders is rewriting the rules of business, and a new breed of fast companies is challenging the corporate status quo. . . . No part of business is immune. The structure of the company is changing; the relationships between companies are changing; the nature of work is changing; the definition of success is changing. The result is a revolution as far-reaching as the Industrial Revolution. . . . Create the vocabulary of the revolution. Identify the values of the revolution. Debunk old myths. . . .The revolution spreads.

The word *value* is included in the title of this chapter for good reason: Much of this book deals with value—defining it, understanding it, creating it, and delivering it; but above all this book deals with *the revolution*. More specifically, it explains the why, what, and how of survival and success for the people and businesses caught up in the revolution. The secrets of this survival and success lie in finding how to deliver the best value but especially in determining how to learn, evolve, and adapt to unprecedented change at ever accelerating speed. This is no simple proposition. Much thought and hard work lie ahead. Many fundamental metrics (other than financial measures) determine how success will be measured through this revolutionary change, and the preeminent among these is value.

VALUE: THE MANTRA OF THE NEW MILLENNIA

Efficiency, output, and low cost were the mantras of the 1960s and 1970s, and quality and service were the mantras of the 1980s and 1990s. Value is the mantra of the turn of the century and beyond. Value is the sum of all the parts of a decision to purchase one product or service over another (or to purchase anything at all). Another definition might be that value is the worth of something in terms of monetary or other sacrifices required to obtain its function or appeal. Gary Heil, Tom Parker, and Deborah C. Stephens, in *One Size Fits One* (Van Nostrand Reinhold, 1997), says that value is "... the equation that balances product or service quality and reliability, delivery time, overall responsiveness, and of course, price...." Whatever the definition, whoever can understand value best, and assume the "shape" to consistently create and deliver the best value "wins" in the competition for the consumers' mind, money, and market share.

The challenge for business is to create competitive advantage by continuously changing the shape of a business to deliver what customers value now, and by preparing to anticipate or influence the future direction of the competitive arena, market, and industry. The challenge continues to assume the shape that will deliver what they (most likely) will value next. The problem is that when the word *value* is spoken in a group of people, each person will have a different picture of what it means. There will be as many different mental pictures of Value as there are people. Each will be different, and each person will believe his or hers is the right one. I am not naive enough to think that they can all be made to agree. Remember, the customer's understanding of value is often no better than our own. The difference is that the customer's is the one that matters. We must reshape our own mental picture of value to come as close to the customer's as possible or we will mislead ourselves.

By using the material covered in this book, these differences can be translated into a sufficiently close understanding so that actions can be taken based on a consensus of what value is. My knowledge is a product of my experience and education. So this book is sprinkled with anecdotes and stories I have encountered, uncovered, or experienced. I have successfully managed and led organizations and companies of varying sizes and shapes in four different industries and through four decades. The stories involving other companies both small and large provide a rich set of examples of shape-shifting in many different situations. I chose these examples to provide valuable insights into how real-world business situations relate to the points I am trying to make.

"Best value" is the final measure of competitive advantage, and partnerships are the foundations that enable the creation and consistent delivery of the best value. But finding the right shape of a business to create and deliver this value is a complex challenge. Few authorities dispute this; even fewer have attempted to find the solution in its entirety. It is far easier to work with pieces—but that doesn't yield the whole solution.

LEARN FROM THE PAST; LEAVE THE PRESENT BEHIND

To figure out where to go, it is useful to review where we have been and where we are right now. Going back 15-plus years in major business literature took me on an odyssey that started as American business began emulating the Japanese in the 1980s with their adaptation of 1950's American quality work—and we borrowed the concept of "quality circles." These weren't just about quality, but after a number of false starts, many figured this out, and the name (and shape) shifted into employee involvement or participative teams. This is where the shape-shifting integrative process begins. Lest the reader be confused, this book is directed at a dual audience—both the "bosses" and the "bossed." The direction to the future affects both groups profoundly, and only if examined from a dual viewpoint can the path start to become clear.

Deal with the Whole Thing

For nearly the past three decades, well-intentioned "gurus" have extolled the virtues of numerous good "principles and concepts." Properly applied, they work well, but each in its own little realm. Think of them as minishapes that, taken together, make up a larger shape. Let us review some of them, so we can develop our thinking to deal with the entire business instead of pieces of it.

Materials requirements/resource planning (MRP) emerged as a great resource planning system to help launch orders and production plans. Oliver Wight and his associates, Walt Goddard and Bill Golomski, at Oliver Wight & Associates, started teaching this approach in the 1970s. I remember attending an impressive IBM-sponsored program over 20 years ago at which all the people who became the "legends" in this field were participants. Little did I realize the impact their lessons and thoughts would have on the shape of the business world I was to work in for the coming decades. American business managers immediately seized upon their ideas and with the help of IBM computers and software, we brought our own version of MRP into action. It worked pretty well, but forecasts were always wrong, and inventories were never accurate enough. Over time, the inventories became more accurate, but the customers just would not cooperate and buy what we had predicted. (They still don't!)

The just-in-time (JIT) philosophy is a fine way to tightly link streams of inventory. It followed MRP and worked on a "pull" instead of a "push" process, reducing inventories and improving production flexibility at the same time. Unfortunately, many using it were slow to realize that if one lowered the inventories before achieving good-quality systems and supplier responsiveness, big trouble occurred. The name might as well have been JTL ("just too late"). Production all over the world was shut down repeatedly by shortages of JIT materials, disrupting customer deliveries and creating chaos!

In the early "statistical quality control" days, while I was at Huffy Bicycles, we decided it would be nice if all the parts had drawings, and we made the parts to look like the drawings—as opposed to having two people roving the frame-welding department with lead hammers to bang on the fixtures so the parts would fit! This statistical process control had real potential because it took some of the guesswork out of problem diagnosis and solving.

Computer-aided design/computer-aided manufacturing (CAD/CAM) tremendously enhanced accuracy, speed, flexibility, and precision in product and tooling design and production, especially on new products. No longer were we faced with prototype parts that would not go together, requiring expensive tooling revisions. Today's technology has continued to build on that capability.

Total quality management (TQM) became a wonderful way to get groups of people working together, using refined tools for statistical problem solving. We started using what is now known as TQM at Huffy Bicycles in the early 1980s. We didn't know the name then, but concluded that statistical quality work, team involvement, and processes supported by cooperation were the essence of the concept. The application of TQM yielded many improvements, but it still was not sufficient alone, as a means to get a business in a shape to combat the ferocious competition in the U.S. market from the Taiwanese and Korean bicycle producers. Today, Toyota's application of the principles of TQM is among the most advanced in the world; it takes this concept to its fullest extent. The term *lean production* was coined to describe the Toyota approach.

After blending parts of an old GE concept called *value analysis* with some of Allen Mogenson's *work simplification*, Mitchell Fein's *gainsharing*, then adding what we now know as lean production and Joseph Pine's *mass customization* and seasoning with liberal doses of Peter Senge's *learning organization* theory, the resulting shape helped us successfully defend our market position against the Taiwanese and Koreans.

The next competition promised to come from China and from a couple of rejuvenated domestic players. This business "ecosystem" was getting pretty complicated. Our forest was turning into a jungle, and it was full of predators. Perhaps our shape was not something we could just achieve, and then rest on our laurels. Maybe our shape needed to be constantly changing—adapting and evolving as nature does.

We hired Andersen Consulting to help us with computer-integrated manufacturing (CIM) because it was touted as a new, improved way to shift our shape while linking business needs to flexible manufacturing systems (FMS). Actually, it wasn't, but *cellular manufacturing* came out of that effort, based on Dr. Richard Schonberger's book, *World Class Manufacturing* (The Free Press, 1986), and yielded great results.

Then the customers got into the act again. They discovered JIT, which for them meant pushing the inventory back upstream. The next shape-shift idea was to get the orders to us faster via *electronic data interchange* (EDI), which begat quick response (QR) order fulfillment, which led to *vendor managed replenishment/inventory* (VMR/VMI) and now has evolved to *category management, efficient consumer response* (ECR) in which dominant category suppliers manage the inventory, then create and fulfill orders based on consumer purchases.

Now *reengineering*, as described by Michael Hammer and James Champy in *Re-engineering the Corporation*, is trying to shift the shape of processes by taking apart complex systems that have become overgrown like trees, shrubs, and vines in the forest/jungle, uprooting many, and hacking away at the rest, to give a cleaner, more effective look to the business. If the reengineering process sounds crude and painful, it is, but more on that later.

I could go on, but enough of this litany of buzzwords and acronyms. These quick fixes all have one common feature: They represent and deal only with part of the whole shape. True, they are all interrelated. When used properly, they support each other (at least somewhat). But, what about the shape of the whole "thing"? What does "it" look like? In science, ever since the discovery of the shapes of DNA and RNA molecules that make up our genetic structure, the whole ball game has changed. Similarly in physics, Einstein's theories, with their packets of energy, sent everyone back to the drawing boards, to examine prior theories on the shape of matter and energy. In Einstein's own words, "the world we have created today has problems which cannot be solved by thinking the way we thought when we created them." It is necessary to step back and look at the whole picture before coming to conclusions.

That is exactly what I hope to do here. I don't want to discount the goodness or rightness of all the pieces; they may all be valid subshapes or minishapes in their own right. Nor do I want to discredit a great deal of prior work and knowledge. What I want to do is to talk about the shape of the whole thing. (More specifically, I am referring to the constantly shifting shape of the whole thing.) The shape of all the pieces must be assembled into a coherent strategy and organization made up of core competencies and systems that help people get important work done—work that creates and consistently delivers best value to the customer.

Consider the Whole Business

The past decade's leading business books and contemporary works of many other leading business thinkers—still deal primarily with pieces of the business. Maybe that was intentional. As an engineer, my training inherently taught me to break a complex problem down into a smaller set of problems, solving them and reassembling those solutions into a total solution. Unfortunately, unless there is a systems integrator, architect, or project manager who has "the whole thing" in mind, the piecemeal solutions do not add up to a total solution. In spite of this, many consultants and academics plowed on, solving pieces and selling the piecemeal solutions. Some, in fact many, actually did improve competitive positions—until the competitor bought the same know-how. None (or at least very few) dealt with the whole complex, elegant, and important total business.

A few, notably those works by Peter Drucker, Gary Hamel and C.K. Prahalad spoke to the issue of the total business strategy. The Agility Forum's work and Francis Gouillart's and James Kelly's book *Transforming the Organization* (McGraw-Hill, 1995) make good attempts at considering more holistic approaches, and at least touch on most of the important areas. Prior to these recent works, few had attempted to wrap all the current best practices into an integrated framework to support a specific competitive strategy. This is exactly what I intend to do in the chapters that follow—to help the readers learn about the *shape of value*, the *shape of the business*, and how to start becoming a *shape-shifter*. I will not dwell too long on most individual facets of the entire approach, since there are many fine works covering specific areas; I will simply reference them for you. I will concentrate on an integrated approach, dealing with the whole business and the new concept of "shape."

I use the term shape-shifting because, after considerable thought, it seemed the most appropriate. The term I used earlier in my career at Huffy Bicycles was *reconfiguration*. While original at the time (1983–1984), it now bears a buzzword resemblance to *reengineering*. The essence of shape-shifting is to be able to re-create yourself, your organization, its core competencies, and your business into the shape that can create and deliver what customers value most. While reengineering deals predominantly with process changes, shape-shifting (reconfiguration) deals with the shape and behavior of the whole enterprise, in the context of continuously changing markets and competitive conditions.

This book attempts to offer a series of "ingredients" (the dimensions of the shape of the business) that, when combined with your imagination, knowledge, thought, and action, will yield a "solution" (the attributes of the shape of value)—sort of a "Hamburger Helper" to a winning strategy by using continuous change for competitive advantage. The resultant shapes of both value and the business will help clarify the direction to go and the actions to take.

2.

Genesis: The Shape
of the Future

This is the first time in the history of business that you can be beating your competitors today and be out of business tomorrow. Why? Nowadays the changes are occurring rapid fire—one on top of another. There's no rest and there's no getting ready. In the heat of this chaos, it's hard for people to maintain perspective.
—Ken Blanchard and Terry Waghorn, *Mission Possible*

Never has the world been more hospitable to industry revolutionaries and more hostile to industry incumbents. . . .To discover opportunities for industry revolution, one must look at the world in a new way, through a new lens.
—Gary Hamel, "Strategy as Revolution,"
Harvard Business Review, July-August 1996

COMPETING FOR THE FUTURE—BUT HOW?

Gary Hamel and C.K. Prahalad had as much to do with my persistence in writing this book as anyone. In the *Harvard Business Review*, Hamel and Prahalad have written several important articles on management, and are among the very few worthy successors to Peter Drucker in their breadth and depth of perception embodied in articles including "Strategic Intent" (May-June 1989), "The Core Competency of the Corporation" (May-June 1990), and "Strategy as Stretch and Leverage," (March-April 1993).

Their book, *Competing for the Future,* consolidated many of their thoughts into a coherent whole—with one gap. While I think they are onto something big—they get us thinking positively about how to get to the future—they do not build a bridge back to the present. That is what I plan to do in this book.

In a 1996 speech, Hamel spoke of "industry revolutionaries." His term caught my attention since he further explained that he viewed strategy as revolution. He describes these revolutionaries as young, *subversive*, and/or rule-breaking leaders. I will go one step further. I don't know if subversive is the right word (it has negative connotations), but I know what he means. These are people who can perceive a new shape of value and how to deliver it. And they aren't waiting around for competition to figure it out. As I considered how to become one of these rule-breakers, I realized that there was a large missing link. Shape-shifting provides that link.

SHAPE-SHIFTING: ITS ORIGINS

In the successful television series *Star Trek—The Next Generation* there was a recurring character sometimes called Q. He was a shape-shifter (at least the actor who played his human form was a "he"). As the series portrayed him, a shape-shifter was a being who could alter his form at will to that shape best suited for the circumstances or conducive to success in his mission. What a fascinating concept. Take whatever shape works best! Isn't that what companies must do to survive and succeed in the revolutionary, chaotic, rapidly changing twenty-first century, to become the new shape-shifters?

As I reflected on the concept, I realized that there have been many shape-shifters throughout history and in different cultures. The Native-American legends abound with shape-shifters, those mysterious beings that come at night, usually in animal form and then transform to human shape to achieve their mission, returning to their nearly invisible animal forms to disappear into the night. Indeed, many of the most important beliefs of Native-American tribes go back to stories about people who change shape from animals or birds. The stories' characters evolve into their alternative forms and thus can achieve their destiny. Many other cultures have similar myths or legends. So it should be with companies.

Why do you need to constantly shift your shape to succeed in business? Because the environment in which businesses operate and we all live is constantly changing, faster today than ever. There are an infinite number of examples I could choose from to show how the rate of change is accelerating, but you can convince yourself simply by picking up a newspaper any day and reading.

Shape-shifting in the World of Sports

Although major league sports are a special kind of business, their popularity make them a good opening example of how shape-shifting can really work. The Atlanta Braves baseball team had the worst record in baseball in 1990—not only in losses, but in attendance. They were a laughingstock and the butt of jokes around the National League and the country. Their chances for winning a pennant were so outweighed by their chances of being the first team to be "mathematically eliminated" from the possibility that the *Atlanta Constitution*, the hometown newspaper, favored this entry in a team slogan contest: "Mathematical Elimination Fever—Catch It!" Could this be the same team that won five straight division titles between 1991 and 1996, played in three of the past four World Series, and won the World Series in 1995? Well, not exactly.

The Atlanta Braves organization analyzed what was wrong and set about shifting its shape to remedy its ills. Because the team's player "quality" was not good enough, management invested in better scouting and a rejuvenated farm system—the minor league teams that feed ball players to the major league affiliates.

Realizing years earlier that getting and keeping the best players took money, which came from improved attendance, owner Ted Turner set out to improve both (incorrectly at first). Since attendance would not increase until the team improved, Turner began buying big name talent. Unfortunately, for quite some time, he tried the "quick fix" style of random investing in expensive veterans—with terrible results. After several miscues, Turner discovered that by rebuilding from the bottom up, he could provide the shape of value (I'll explain this term in more detail soon—see Figure 2-2) that would bring fans to the games, increase revenue, and thus provide the money to buy even better talent, thus ensuring more attendance, and so forth.

As this bottom-up improvement program started, Turner was able to use his considerable media empire (especially cable TV) to promote the team's visibility. But without a good team, viewers essentially said, "So what if the Braves are on TV again?" Turner's management organization invested heavily in young talent and the farm system (equivalent to R&D investments), which created the future success they so badly needed—but not overnight. Only through shifting the fundamental "shape of the business" (another term I'll explain soon—see Figure 2-1) was the Atlanta Braves organization able to shift the shape of value for their fans.

When the shape-shift started to really roll, it was a landslide. Improved players created a winning team, which filled the stadium and raised the ratings on TV, all of which provided more money to build a still better infrastructure. New promising young stars could be signed by outbidding rival teams. Veteran stars could be locked into lucrative long-term contracts. And a new stadium promises to keep the cycle going. Baseball fans want a winning team that is exciting to watch and competitive year after year. Is this so much different from what customers want from companies' products and services? It is very similar, and can be achieved only by shifting the shape of the whole organization—and the whole business.

AN INTEGRATIVE APPROACH IS CRITICAL

The integrative approach is critical for dealing with constantly changing circumstances. Whether in business or in competitive sports the structure and processes used can either enhance or detract from the performance of the people and organization, and vice versa. In fact, some may dispute the terms used to describe these in the shape of business and shape of value diagrams. Indeed, they are not pure or indisputable, because in their broadest interpretation, they are all blends.

In order to undertake a shape-shift, it is necessary to make an assessment of where your business stands now. This is the first step required to define the current reality. You must take an inventory of your strengths and weaknesses in terms of the attributes of value and dimensions of the shape of the business. What is your current shape? What do your current and prospective customers think it is? Where are your core competencies now, and where do they need to be? What are your core capabilities now, and what do they need to be? To help clarify your thinking on these "core" issues, treat the competencies as what you are very good at (what the market/customers value) and the capabilities as how you do certain things (create value for the market/customer).

Attribute and Dimensions of Shape-shifting

To provide structure for the process of shape-shifting, I will define a set of attributes of value and dimensions of the business and describe what they have to do with shape-shifting and the creation of best value. Partnerships must come first. In my first book, *The Power of Partnerships* (Blackwell, 1996), I wrote that the formation of partnerships with customers, suppliers, employees/associates, and outside special partners are the foundation of success in business.

Partnerships then allow the business to shape-shift itself in five dimensions, which may require change to create and deliver the best value, I chose these five because they clearly define what I call the shape of the business.

It is important that all dimensions of business be considered even though all may not need to be changed. If parts of the business are found to be delivering best value now and for the foreseeable the future, then the number of changes is reduced.

The following list defines these dimensions and Figure 2-1 illustrates them.

1. *Structure*: The form and organization to meet new markets, competitors, and so on. (restructure).
2. *Processes*: How things are done, often improving many aspects of its value performance (reengineer or redesign).
3. *Culture*: Internal relationships that effectively create an involved, participative learning organization, which is both highly effective and very adaptive in doing whatever is needed (transformation).
4. *Relationships*: External relationships with the extended organization—customers, suppliers, special professional partners, and stakeholders who have the ability and resources to respond to and support change in unity (partnerships).
5. *Purpose*: Defines what the business is all about and why. Acts as the organization's compass over the years and goes far beyond the details described by the other four dimensions into the realm of "why." This dimension should change very little, if ever. Every successful business or organization has a powerful sense of purpose.

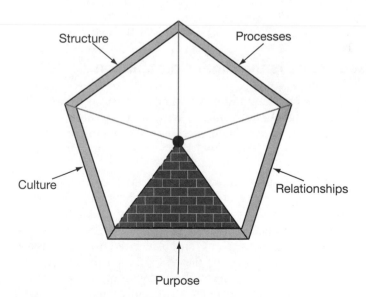

Figure 2-1 The Shape of the Business

The purpose, the guiding compass, is a worthy topic for an entire book, and fortunately Jim Collins and Jerry Porras have already written that book, *Built to Last*. Because of the importance of this dimension, I put it at the bottom of the pentagon in Figure 2-1. It is what the other four dimensions are based upon.

By using these five dimensions to guide action, the business can change to create value via the five value *attributes* of shape-shifting. These attributes are the external manifestation of "things done right" and "right things done" to yield competitive advantage by providing best value. The five attributes are:

Quality
Service
Cost
Speed
Innovation

and the sum total of the right balance or mix of all the attributes is value; or more specifically, when represented in their relative proportions, the *shape of value* (SOV). This shape of value is created by plotting numerical evaluations for the various value attributes on a five-axis diagram like the one shown in Figure 2-2, and then by connecting the values with lines to form a distinctive shape. Ideally, these attributes will be evaluated from the perspective of how the customer would perceive them. Often, this is not done.

Best Value Is the Right Combination

If we can achieve a clear understanding of what mixture of these value attributes create the shape the customers define as best value, then all the resources of an enterprise can be aligned with that shape of value to create and deliver best value, and exploit it for maximum competitive advantage.

To begin shape-shifting requires adequate preparation. Without a clear understanding of value, creating the enabling partnerships and building an involved, learning organization will lead to chaos, disarray, and failure.

To succeed, a sound competitive strategy and effective execution with strong leadership are essential. This strategy must be derived from the mission and vision of the business, which must be driven by the customer's desired shape of value and decisions on what shape of the business the company needs in order to compete in the markets it chooses. The business must understand

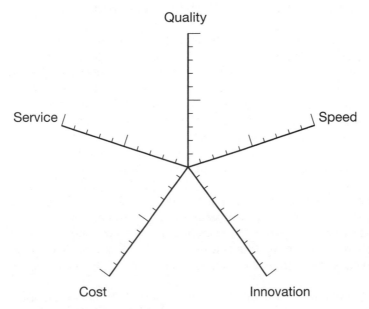

Figure 2-2 The Shape of Value Diagram

why it has a competitive reason (i.e., deserves) to be in this business, which products and market segments are to be targeted, and how to do this.

Many aspects of developing visions and missions, strategies and strategic plans are beyond the scope of this book. But one that is appropriate here is that the mission and vision must be aligned with the strategies and tactics to yield a shape of the business and a shape of value (mix of value attributes) that matches what the customers want. Strategic plans will be discussed in a later chapter. Strategies are mentioned here because shape-shifting must begin and end tightly linked to strategic decisions. It is strategy, with supporting tactics, operating plans, and implementation, that lead to the right mix of value attributes. An accurate assessment of the current situation and this desired mix of value attributes define the dimensions of the business that must be changed and how.

No amount of good work in other areas such as planning will make up for a faulty strategy or poor execution. However, excellence in forming partnerships and the ability to shape-shift to create and deliver the mix of value attributes most desired in the chosen market(s) will enable you to avoid or overcome moderate errors in strategy and execution. In fact, partnerships and shape-shifting will help expose strategic flaws early and also support execution errors through the help of the partners, and the focus on the creation of the right mix of value attributes. Strong leadership is needed for the long-term success of any business, and to reinforce the importance of the purpose.

DIMENSIONS AND ATTRIBUTES: THE HOW AND WHAT

To best remember the components of shape-shifting, refer to the integrated diagram in Figure 2-3. The word "core" in the center refers to the competencies and capabilities of the organization, which is made up of people working in a prescribed manner and relationship with each other. I combined these two terms because while they are different, both are important to succeed. Simply stated, competencies are the "what" and the capabilities are the "how" that enables the organization to excel in its chosen markets and against its competitors. There is nothing other than the leadership, the people, and the environment that links this set of competencies and capabilities to any given business entity.

Around the periphery at the points of the value pentastar in Figure 2-2, are the *value attributes* of a highly functioning organization. These are the attributes that create competitive advantage with the customer/end user, versus alternative competitors. It is the mix, weight, and amount of these five attributes that result from the various dimensions of the shape of the business.

I must add one important point about shape here. Whereas two companies can have the same relative shape of value by having very similar relative competencies in the five attributes, one of the companies may be better or worse overall causing the shape to be larger or smaller. Just having the

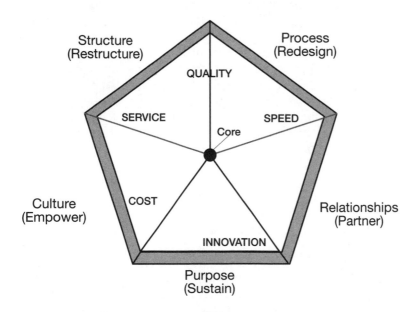

Figure 2-3 Integrative Model of Shape-Shifting

right shape alone is not enough. The "amount" of the attributes (the degree of quality or cost competitiveness, for example) is a critical determining factor. Being equally mediocre in all attributes is as sure a formula for failure as being shaped differently from what the customers and market want.

The dimensions are separated into three discrete groupings. Two of them deal with how assets and people are organized to do things—structure and processes—while two of them deal with the interaction between groups of people in organizations—culture and relationships. The fifth, purpose, is the heart and soul that guides the business. It is indisputable that there is a strong interrelationship between structure, processes, culture, and relationships. Much of the attention in management studies and writing has been given to these dimensions individually or in sets of two, but not collectively. Such works are widely available and will not be discussed at length here, except to tie the concept of shape-shifting together or provide specific examples.

Purpose is different. As I have already stated, it is a guiding constant which transcends the "how" and moves into the "why." It is the dimension of shape that should change little over the years.

WHAT IS "SHAPE?"

Before I go further, let me speak briefly, but more graphically, about another way to depict and visualize the shape I am referring to. I will define shape in considerable detail in the next section, but another image will help. Imagine your hand extended and cupped slightly, with a rubber band stretched around the tips of your fingers. The figure or shapes defined by that band is five-sided—a pentagon. Now imagine the shape of value pentastar in the center of that pentagon. If each axis of the shape of value pentastar were graduated from 1 to 10, it would become essentially a five-dimensional graphical device.

Value can be described adequately in broad interpretations of these five primary attributes: quality, service, cost, speed, and innovation. If each of these were expressed numerically in response to the desires of a given customer or set of customers, a set of points on the shape of value pentastar could be plotted. Joining those points would create a graphical shape, just as the stretched rubber band created a shape around your fingers. Now flex your hand and watch the shape change. You have just created the first visual and tactile representation of what the term *shape-shift* means.

By defining markets, customers, competitors, and your own company in terms of the shape of value desired versus the shape of the business and the competencies and capabilities to provide that shape, this concept takes on life and meaning. A shape-shifter is continuously trying to match what he or she creates and delivers to the shape of value that the customer wants and the market desires, both now and in the future. Flex your hand rapidly and watch how the shape of the rubber band gyrates. This is the symbol of the rapidly changing shape of value in the world of business today.

Figure 2-4 is a very simple example of two similar, familiar products, Rolex and Timex brand wrist watches, shown on the shape of value diagram. Note how highly Rolex is rated for its quality, innovation (prestige or cachet, in this case), and service (warranty and numerous locations for repair at dealers). On the other two attributes, Timex is clearly the winner with its low cost and widespread, convenient distribution through thousands of retailers. Notice how the shapes seem to point to the dominant value attributes. This is a good place to start visualizing shape of value.

Don't Rush Blindly to Change

Noted management professor at McGill University and author Henry Mintzberg has done a great deal of work in this area. He, too, has used pentagon-shaped figures along with other analogies to illustrate forces that shape organizations. In one of his most graphic and humorous examples, he

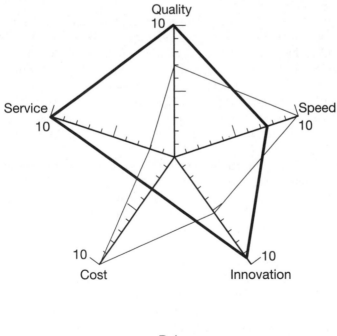

Figure 2-4 Comparing Rolex and Timex on the Value Pentastar

describes many large organizations as like a rhinoceros: large, strong, thick-skinned, and ugly, with poor eyesight, prone to charge full speed at dimly seen, far-off objectives, only to lose interest partway there and stop to graze. The point is, without some concrete idea and picture of the desired shape of value to be created and delivered, what's the rush? Such blind or misdirected organizations will only arrive at the wrong place faster, or expend a great deal of resources to no useful end.

Why not first take the time to define the desired shape of value? Defining strategy is all about products (services are products, too), customers, markets, and value. Moving fast once the objective is defined makes good sense—in fact it is critical. Unlike the rhino that can run fast, but changes direction poorly, moving *fast* and *flexibly* makes even better sense. Distant objectives, sometimes change their position and become moving targets while the journey to reach them is underway.

In many cases, this rate of change is so rapid, it is difficult or impossible to accurately plan the trajectory for the future. Hamel and Prahalad urge what they call "future foresight." While I endorse their intent, developing future foresight is difficult and sometimes unclear, despite the best efforts. The solution is to become quick and flexible enough at shape-shifting to react to whatever or wherever the future (objective) turns out to be.

If this also sounds difficult, it is, but the difficulty is also what makes it a powerful and rewarding capability because few can match it. Being intellectually and organizationally prepared for gut-wrenching, neck-snapping change often gives the margin of victory. It has been said that people do not resist change; they just resist being changed. The same goes for being surprised. Jack Welch, CEO of General Electric, reportedly reminds his organization that, "Change will be so great, we will be surprised, but we won't be surprised we are surprised. Our competitors will also be surprised, but they will be surprised they are surprised. That will give us an advantage." The best way to cope with surprise is to shape-shift to capitalize on it. How? Start with the realization of the need to shift from today's comfortable, successful shape to a newer one that creates the best value.

3.

Status Quo Is Not Good Enough

By the time the rules of the game are clear, the windows of opportunity will have closed.
—Gemini Consulting advertisement
Why your information systems should be architected for change. Find the perfect solution and the problem will change.
—Sybase advertisement

LEADING THE TARGET

As anyone who successfully shoots at moving targets knows or learns quickly, it is necessary to "lead the target." This means making an assumption or mental projection of the path and speed of the target's movement, and aiming ahead of it, so the shot will intercept the target's trajectory when they both reach the right point in space and time. Hockey star Wayne Gretzky described his success this way: "Others go where the puck is. I go where the puck is going to be." In business, changes must be made before the target has moved too far. Setting aside human flaws like greed and dishonesty, the clear theme underlying most of the reasons for business failure is the inability to respond to change, to shape-shift before it is too late.

How, you might ask, can those who have worked long and hard to be successful at what they are; become something different, rapidly. Not easily is the obvious answer. The first criterion for such flexible shape-shifting is the ability to recognize the need, and have the the willingness to change in order to meet the need—to lead the target!

23

Sitting Ducks Get Shot

Tom Peters, one of my favorite writers and speakers, launches tirades, not just quiet arguments. He stomps around and yells at people, telling them extreme and often even unworkable approaches to shake them out of their complacency and make them think and react. In "The Peter Principles," a column he wrote for *Forbes*, he said, "Busy people are smarter and faster than the smartest and fastest machines."

But, people must *want* to do things, and one of the things they least like to do is change. How do we wake them up, inspire, incite, infuriate, and generally stir up people to understand that the only safe thing to do is to change? Sitting ducks get shot. Will Rogers said, "Even if you are on the right track, if you sit still, you will get run over."

We need an integrative approach to use our accumulated skills, core competencies, and capabilities to develop a strategy that can and will win. We must thoroughly understand (or decide) what we want to sell, to whom, how, why, and what there is about that choice that will give us an edge.

At the 1995 Executive Focus Incorporated Forum, Alvin Toffler, the noted futurist,described the problem this way:

> *Our corporations are dealing with the trauma of trying to adjust— an attempt by dinosaurs to become micro-dinosaurs—often without making the fundamental changes necessary to adapt to the new realities. Business is becoming more complex, with rising levels of unpredictability. Predictions tend to be based on linear extrapolation—the notion that current trends predict the future. The problem is, trends don't consider the overall context and what else is happening at any given time. Surprises and upsets can and do occur, particularly in periods of upheaval.*

The approach I refer to as shape-shifting builds on the power of partnerships to do exactly what Toffler describes: adjust.

In fact, the linkages between partners enable the shape-shifting of the business. The business with its four major types of partners, customers, suppliers, employees, and special partners, adjusts in such a way as to utilize its core competencies and capabilities and adapt them to the constantly changing external competitive environment and its "upsets."

A Football Analogy

Another metaphor for the change process called shape-shifting can be found in American football. The coach and general manager seek, recruit, hire, and train talent. This is the way businesses also proceed. A *system* is installed, which is analogous to the *structure*. Within the system, the coach develops a playbook, which consists of plays—*processes*—that capitalize on the talent of the players (*core competencies* and *capabilities*). There are assistant coaches, often dealing in with a wide variety of disciplines from strength/conditioning to execution of specific plays (*functions*). This complement of coaches/players and supporting systems make up the *culture* and *relationships*. The *purpose* of course is simpler: to win.

When all of the ingredients of the team have been brought together, game plans are developed. These game plans must fit the specific competitive situation—the competitor, field conditions, player status (to account for injuries, mishaps, etc.). This is analogous to a strategic and tactical business plan for a given market, time frame, and so on.

As soon as the competition begins, circumstances start changing. The weather turns bad (like market or economic conditions). One of the key players is injured (just as one of the key managers or executives might become ill or be recruited away by a competitor). Perhaps a series of penalties are called (like regulatory changes or product recalls), or even worse, fumbles or interceptions occur (product quality or delivery slips unexpectedly). The opponent shows a new offensive or defensive alignment or adds several trick plays in a new formation. The captain on the field "calls an audible" or "checks off at the line of scrimmage." This is a perfect analogy for one type of shape-shift, which has to happen fast and in the heat of the battle.

It is precisely then that the ability to shape-shift makes the critical difference. Just as the game plan, play selection, and talent are adjusted either off the field, by the coaching staff or on the field by "calling an audible," to adapt to competition and conditions, business must change to meet the needs of the competitive situation. For short-term changes, these shape-shifts might be minor, like "audibles," in the football analogy, but very important and effective ones. Changing the big things, like the game plan or the playbook, are longer-term changes, but even these are often based on the same principle that required the audible. Adjusting to a different talent base is like migrating to some new core competencies or capabilities, without sacrificing the benefits of those already in place.

NOT ANOTHER NEW PROGRAM

Each of the individual approaches or programs discussed earlier may be very effective tools to fine-tune some aspect of the business on a piecemeal basis, but none takes the whole business integration, the strategy/tactics, and the dynamic external environment fully into consideration. But, using partnerships as the cornerstones, shape-shifting does! Two terms have been carefully selected to describe important parts of this issue: *attributes of value* and *dimensions of shape*. The definition of these words is given here to ensure no misunderstanding about the interpretation and relationship of these two terms. Shape-shifting is an integrative way to recognize the mix of attributes that lead to competitive success.

Shape-shifting weighs the proper balance of each of the dimensions to maximize the effect on the most important attributes for a specific customer industry, and competitive situation.

It is very important to emphasize that shape-shifting (reconfiguration) does not necessarily replace or obsolete any of the other programs, processes, or approaches everyone diligently pursues in hopes of elusive success (assuming they were implemented properly and that they are still suitable in the context of the overall business' strategy). Rather, shape-shifting integrates and focuses them on the customers, the competitors, and the market situation. It also does so efficiently, not requiring adjustments in areas that will not affect the competitive outcome significantly. This is not a new name for reengineering—that will be made very clear in a later chapter.

Many other ill-advised change processes have been tried, and the proof of their inadequacy is ever present. Professor John Kotter of Harvard Business School, in the article "Kill Complacency" (*Fortune*, August 5, 1996), wrote, "Whenever a business is forced to adjust to shifting conditions, pain is ever present. But a significant amount of the waste and anguish we've witnessed in the past decade is avoidable." The issue I am addressing in shape-shifting is how to make the change and avoid the worst of the anguish and pain.

Visualize Your Shape of Value

Now let us return to shape-shifting and use the integrative model to test our plans on each of the dimensions: structure, process, culture, and relationships. Do each of these seem aligned to match the needs and wishes of our market and customers? Or, must we change—shift our shape in one or more of these dimensions? And if we should, how, how much, and in which ones? How will such changes contribute to the mix of value attributes?

By using the diagnostic profile and shape of value pentastar diagram, we can map the mix and magnitude of value attributes most desired by our customers and the chosen markets or products. But never lose sight of the customer's view of the shape of value.

The Value Pentastar

I like simple graphical devices, because they help to visualize an abstract concept. I have chosen the shape of value pentastar described earlier and shown in the Figures 3-4 and 3-5 because it is a simple shape to draw and it has the right number of axes for the value attributes. The value of such diagrams is maximized only when they are readily taught, learned, understood, and used. Multipoint diagrams have been used to graphically represent evaluations in the human resources field for years. Usually, however, these contain many points and defy description as a particular shape.

Other diagramming approaches for value, none similar to this, have been used in the past. Bradley T. Gale's diagrammatic approach, a customer value map, is one preferred by many proponents of TQM. In his book, *Managing Customer Value* (The Free Press, 1994), he does a pretty good job of using it to portray "where things are." It is also one of seven graphical tools he prescribes to break down this complex issue of value into actionable pieces. But the map deals only with overall positions.

Quality function deployment is a rich technique, but it requires a complex diagrammatic process, which either intimidates or confuses most participants. Adrian Slywotzky's book *Value Migration* (Harvard Business School Press, 1996) uses three stages of value migration to illustrate where value is moving to and from but not much about what can be done to influence this migration.

There are still other diagrammatic approaches not specifically directed at depicting value such as the "radar chart" used by human resource programs to assess numerous characteristics, or the "Twenty Keys" used in Iwao Kobayashi's work of the same name (Productivity Press, 1995). While these provide useful graphical tools, they do little to simplify or clarify the results of the analysis—they simply display it!

A more recent graphical representation was shown by Chan Kim and Renee Mauborgne in their excellent article "Value Innovation: The Strategic Logic of High Growth," that appeared in the January-February 1997 issue of *Harvard Business Review*. They use a vertical mapping approach which has the advantage of allowing the tracking of more attributes, and the decided disadvantage of resulting in a shape too complex to digest except a piece at time.

Each of these graphic devices have specific advantages, but all fall into the trap of being complex (because value is complex) and difficult to assimilate. Something simpler and easier to understand is needed.

I prefer the value pentastar diagram not only because it is simpler, but because it is more versatile and easier to understand. The mental picture it creates is stronger and clearer. It can also be used for portraying the shape of value from many different perspectives (customer, competitor, product, market) with overlays to see how well they match. The shape of value pentastar is also much simpler to learn and use than a complex set of tables. In workshops, participants pick up on the diagramming concept almost immediately, shifting the dialogue to the definition and evaluation of the value attributes, where it belongs! The goal is to create and deliver the best value by understanding the customer's view of value and by creating a shape of the business that will yield a shape of value congruent with it. The diagram is a means to that end. If a competitor's shape of value is also portrayed in this way, competitive weaknesses or strengths will be graphically evident. Later chapters will go into more detail about constructing shape of value diagrams specifically for customers and competitors.

By using the value pentastar in this way, our two objectives become simple to describe—not to do!

1. Create and consistently deliver value that precisely matches or exceeds the shape of value the customer wants.
2. Provide better value (in each attribute and in shape overall) than the competitors.

The examples that follow in this and the next chapter illustrate simple contrasts using familiar companies with their approximate shapes of value. While the actual numerical values are important, a consistent, consensus-based evaluation is even more important. In another way of saying this, the same levels of attributes must be interpreted and numerically valued consistently for comparisons with customer and competitor shape of value diagrams. This will yield shapes congruent to the customer's when the right value mix is achieved. Remember, the customer's shape is the one to match. If a competitor offers a similar shape of value, but higher levels (a larger shape) then we will lose, but the "gaps" that caused the loss will be obvious. If the shapes are different, then the weight the customer puts on the various attributes must be taken into account. This can be done readily by adding a weighting factor, and plotting it on a normalized scale on the same shape of value pentastar diagram. This weighting process will be discussed later.

In the extreme case of 1:1 marketing, being responsive to exactly the shape of the customer's value desired is the total objective. As information technology and communications speed continues to grow, this becomes increasingly possible. In fact, more authorities are predicting that total customization not only will become possible, but necessary. Perhaps a good way to determine customers' exact shape of value is to ask them. There will be considerably more about "how to ask" in a later chapter. For the time being, dealing with individual consumer's value desires might make the application of this approach overly complex. As we learn to plot on the shape of value diagram, the first step is to complete the diagnostic profile shown in Figure 3-1.

There is an important caution when discussing "asking" and "answering" about the shape of value. Large organizations with strong-willed, dominant leaders, may be sorely tempted to "adjust" the answers to more closely match the shape expected or desired by the boss. This is a sure path to failure! (Been there, done that—ouch!)

Quality: *(Used to be an advantage, but now is just the "price of admission." Think in terms of a broad definition of quality.)*
Very poor 1   2   3   4   5   6   7   8   9   10 Best in class

Service: *(Having what the customer wants, where and when they want it "their way," and knowing the status, and communicating it in a friendly way.)*
Very poor 1   2   3   4   5   6   7   8   9   10 Best in class

Speed: *(Delivering fast, on time, and responding to changes fast and flexibly.)*
Very poor 1   2   3   4   5   6   7   8   9   10 Best in class

Cost: *(Lowest total cost producer of the products or services provided, not just the lowest bid or quote.)*
Very poor 1   2   3   4   5   6   7   8   9   10 Best in class

Innovation: *(Creating innovative or unique products that are highly desirable and using innovative processes to do so.)*
Very poor 1   2   3   4   5   6   7   8   9   10 Best in class

(Detailed definitions of the quality, service, speed/timeliness, cost, and innovation attributes that should be used are listed briefly here and expanded later.)
(The reason the ratings do not—and should not—average to an overall value rating is that they are not all weighted equally in importance. While this might sometimes be the case, it is not normally how a customer's perception of value works. Each attribute must be considered separately, and then value perception in the aggregate.)

Figure 3-1 Diagnostic Profile for the Shape of Value

A Simple Example

To illustrate further how to use this diagnostic profile and apply it to the shape of value diagram, I will use a very simple, albeit extreme example. Consider two alternative modes of transportation: a luxury limousine and a bus. Imagine you are the customer who completes the diagnostic profile by marking the evaluations for each. I have done so arbitrarily (see Figures 3-2 and 3-3) and and plotted the results on the shape of value pentastar diagrams in Figures 3-4 and 3-5. While you may argue with relative values, it is evident that these two modes of transportation have widely different shapes of value. Which one is the better value is not clear without knowing the goals, objectives, and resources of the customer. If the customer is very short of money, the limo may not be an option. If the bus simply does not go where the customer wants to go, the bus may not be an option. The weighting approach described later on will allow certain attributes to be assigned more or less relative importance to deal with these kind of issues.

Quality: *(Used to be an advantage, but now is just the "price of admission." Think in terms of a broad definition of quality.)*
Very poor 1   2   3   4   5   6   7   8   9   **10** Best in class
(The limo takes you there in style and comfort with all the amenities.)

Service: *(Having what the customer wants, where and when they want it, and knowing the status, and communicating it in a friendly way.)*
Very poor 1   2   3   4   5   6   7   8   9   **10** Best in class
(The limo comes to get you and waits to take you wherever you wish to go. The driver even opens and closes the door.)

Speed: *(Delivering fast, on time, and responding to changes fast and flexibly.)*
Very poor 1   2   3   4   5   6   7   **8**   9   10   Best in class
(Maybe a helicopter or charter plane would be faster, but this is pretty fast, and little time is wasted waiting.)

Cost: *(Lowest total cost producer of the products or services provided, not just the lowest bid or quote.)*
Very poor 1   2   **3**   4   5   6   7   8   9   10   Best in class
(The limo is expensive, paying for the vehicle and driver by the hour, but not as bad as a plane.)

Innovation: *(Creating innovative or unique products that are highly desirable and using innovative processes to do so.)*
Very poor 1   2   3   4   5   6   7   **8**   9   10   Best in class
(The limo will take you wherever you want unless it is on water, or too far over water and a plane is required.)

(How this is evaluated depends on your objectives, and your resources)

Figure 3-2 Diagnostic Profile for the Shape of Value for Luxury Limo Service

None of these value decisions is made in a vacuum; numerous considerations influence every such decision. To decide how to shape-shift, we must understand not only value, but discover what influences the decisions of the customers we want to sell to. We must also understand how our competitors are able to create and deliver value better or differently. For that reason, Chapters 10 and 11 will be devoted to analyzing value in this fashion from the perspective of the customer and the competitor.

The preceding example left out one of the most powerful value influences in real life—brand. Value decisions are made for a range of reasons, but brand is a strong factor. A message (information) is attached to every brand, and these messages create perceptions, and until some actual experience or conflicting factual information replaces it, that perception is reality in the mind of a potential customer. Later, we will explore more about how brands can influence value perceptions.

Quality: *Used to be an advantage, but now is just the "price of admission." Think in terms of a broad definition of quality.*
Very poor 1   2   **3**   4   5   6   7   8   9   10 Best in class
(Even the best of buses are not too great.)

Service: *Having what the customer wants, where and when they want it and knowing the status, and communicating it in a friendly way.*
Very poor 1   2   **3**   4   5   6   7   8   9   10 Best in class
(Buses run on their schedule not yours, if they are on schedule at all.)

Speed: *Delivering fast, on time, and responding to changes fast and flexibly.*
Very poor 1   2   **3**   4   5   6   7   8   9   10 Best in class
(Buses usually make numerous stops that slow down your travel, to pick up or drop off other riders.)

Cost: *Lowest total cost producer of the products or services provided, not just the lowest bid or quote.*
Very poor 1   2   3   4   5   6   7   8   **9**   10 Best in class
(Buses are an economical, low cost way to travel.)

Innovation: *Creating innovative or unique products that are highly desirable and using innovative processes to do so.*
Very poor **1**   2   3   4   5   6   7   8   9   10 Best in class

(Buses go where their route is, and stop where their stops are, and nowhere else.)

   (This all depends on your goals, and how much money you have.)

Figure 3-3 Diagnostic Profile for the Shape of Value for a Bus

Who Draws the Diagrams?

A final, but important point here is who should draw the shape of value diagram in the first place, and what this diagram should represent in its most basic form. Since the diagram is intended first and foremost to represent the customer's desire for value, the function best suited to do this is marketing, with help from sales. Marketing's job is "to have what will sell," and sales' job is "to sell what we have." Together they should prepare the first shape of value diagram. But note that I say *first*; there must be others involved. This tool is above all a communications tool to bring about change. For that reason, the general manager, president, and/or chief executive of the business must understand and take ownership of what shape of value is desired and to be attained. The rest of the management team must also understand and "buy in" since they will design the features, buy or build in

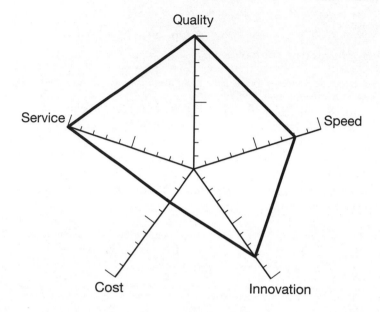

Figure 3-4 The Shape of Value Pentastar for a Luxury Limo

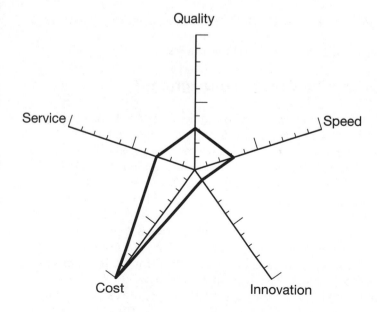

Figure 3-5 The Shape of Value Pentastar for a Bus

the quality, provide the service, and create the organization that can respond with the necessary speed. This must be a total team effort. Ultimately, customers should be engaged to help create their own shape of value diagram!

Later, we will learn how to use this assessment as a platform for determining our own shape of value capability and that of our competitors. More important, we will be comparing that shape to the customer's current and future desired shape of value. But there are some pitfalls in "self-diagnostic" approaches, and I would be remiss if I did not mention one of the greatest pitfalls.

A common human trait is to "listen autobiographically." In this mode, we relate the answers of the respondent to our own experience or to fit our own conclusions. While this is natural, it is also dangerous, especially when doing a self-assessment. When we do this, we tend to respond in one of four ways: we *evaluate*, either agreeing or disagreeing; we *probe,* asking questions from our own frame of reference; we *advise,* giving counsel based on our own experience; or we *interpret,* trying to frame things from our own perspective.

Another common pitfall is denial even in the face of the facts. We may listen only to what we want to hear, and then form conclusions we want to arrive at instead of those we are led to by the actual information! This is why learning how to listen is important. A wise man once said: "Too often we see what we believe instead of believing what we see."

These listening problems are most dangerous when we subconsciously force responses to fit our preconceived patterns. This can badly distort the information and results. Michael Bozic, when he was president of Sears, defined the root of many of Sears' problems this way: "We are trying to sell what Sears wants to sell instead of what Sears customers want to buy."

Such a problem also may occur when we survey only *current* customers. We find out why they are customers, but learn little or nothing about those who are not customers, and who have found greater value elsewhere. Care must be exercised to seek out and hear what the customers *and noncustomers* are telling us. Often, they will be reluctant to tell us the unpleasant truths that will do us the most good in our value determination process. This is the most important reason for hiring outside expert researchers and consultants. It is also easier to determine why customers want certain things now that in the future. They may not even know what is possible or what they will want in the future, yet it is our job to determine that and anticipate those future wants and needs. This, again, is Gary Hamel's and C.K. Prahalad's challenge of "getting to the future first."

Value Is the Goal

Remember, the diagnostic profile and the shape of value are only tools. Value creation and delivery—in the right shape—is the desired result. Competitive success is the goal and an integral part of shape-shifting. Unlike some other writings that claim value to be one of the "dimensions of the means," I contend that value is one of the "ends"—perhaps the most all-encompassing and important one. All of the "pieces" are useful building blocks, but each is only a piece of a giant puzzle (shape) which, when completed, creates and delivers the best value.

Popular concepts like Hormel's and Prahalad's core competencies and Eli Goldratt's and Jeff Cox's constraint management have a place as a part of the solution—as long as they don't make the job more confusing, intimidating, threatening, or "too easy" sounding. Above all, the transcendent issue is what shape do all these pieces need to be in now to deliver the value customers want, now? And even more important, what shape do they need to be next—next week, next month, next quarter, next season, next year, or next decade? The shape will have to be different in the future from what it is now, and whoever consistently delivers the best value wins! Continuous change is the only route to sustained competitive advantage.

The race will be won by the swiftest and the most nimble, who can decide first what is valued, what will be valued next, and what needs to be changed and how. That, in itself, is a daunting task second only to changing shape to deliver this best value consistently and fast—ahead of competitors.

SHIFT CORE COMPETENCIES BEFORE YOU NEED TO

You must view revolutionary change as a wonderful opportunity to shift your shape and gain advantages on competitors. If this is the prevailing attitude, change can be exciting, exhilarating, and full of promise. Otherwise, it can be threatening, frightening, and even paralyzing.

The core competencies (which are inherent in your shape) upon which your current and past successes have been built won't be the same as needed for the future, and once you understand and accept that, then good changes can begin to happen.

Usually, it is not necessary or desirable to abandon everything you have done before (unless there is a discontinuity that totally disrupts your market), but you do need to shape-shift rapidly from where you have been (in core competencies and capabilities) to where you need to be. Just as nomadic tribes move from place to place when their herds have exhausted the food supplies in a given area, or bees move their hive to a new location, companies must move to better value places. A few examples of actual companies may help clarify how this terminology in practice can betranslated into business success.

Huffy Bicycles

A fortunate thing happened to me in 1983. The survival of Huffy Bicycles was at stake. We had to decide whether to continue manufacturing in the United States to fight the imports or "run offshore" and join them. This forced a major decision about the shape our business would take. We decided to stay a U.S. manufacturer and fight. Once we did, another decision became fairly obvious to us. We needed to understand which of our core competencies and capabilities were most valuable (to our customers) and decide if we were (or could become) world-class competitive. We undertook what we called a reconfiguration analysis. I coined the term *reconfiguration* because, at the time, it seemed to be the only word that adequately described what we had to do. Later I concluded that reconfiguration was just a long, technical-sounding word for shape-shifting! We put every dimension of the company on trial for its life against the best we could find anywhere in the world. We also realized that we had to be the best at building the structure of the bike, since that is the foundation on which all the components mount and which determines the shape, size, and function of the bike.

Fortunately, thanks to a legacy of hard-working employees and investments in flexible automation, we were competitive in that area. However, we rapidly outsourced several other processes to suppliers who were more competitive than we were. Outsourcing is another critical shape-shifting decision—one that seems to be very popular these days. Other production processes we brought inside (let's call it "insourcing"), and became the focus of further investment on our journey to become the best value producer. Most important, we learned a lot about ourselves, and what we did that our customers did and did not value.

We learned that even with good technology automation alone would not keep us competitive. We also learned that good, involved, well-trained people without the latest technology would lose to the Orient-based producers where the pay was one-twentieth of ours and the overhead was even lower. This was the beginning of a lesson. The immutable laws of value, like those of science will win out. It was our challenge to figure out how to shape those laws to our advantage! That is what I hope this book will help you do.

Kinko's Shifted To Larger Playing Field

A good case study of a shape-shift is Kinko's. From a simple neighborhood copy center, Kinko's evolved rapidly into a full-service high-technology office center for small (and some not so small!) businesses. Kinko's is a case of a company recognizing that its core competencies could be migrated to a new emerging growth area—serving the rapidly growing number of small businesses and self-employed individuals created by corporate downsizing and outsourcing. In addition, its expanded locations offer highly profitable technology products (on an efficient "pooled use" basis), and sell profitable specialty office supplies on a convenience basis.

On June 10, 1996, Kinko's announced plans to sell a 30 percent stake in the company to Clayton, Dubilier, and Rice, the New York buyout firm for $200 million. This deal forever changed Kinko's from an entrepreneurial, diverse, and loosely managed chain of service centers into a more orderly, structured company. As this shift continues, the question arises whether this growth-related move is for the better or worse. For years, the old system worked. As of late 1996, Kinko's outlets totalled over 850, and its market share of the retail copy market was in the 25–30 percent range.

Clearly, the goal of such a move was to exploit the leverage of size (for low cost) and to enable Kinko's to attract and hire management talent to run the sizable enterprise for improved sevice. The questions is, what impact will these moves have on the shape of value desired by their customer base? Certainly, the size and financial strength will allow broader moves into high technology (for innovation and quality), but the increased size and bureaucracy may also reduce flexibility and agility (speed). Competition has already driven prices down. Some competitors, like franchiser Mail Boxes Etc, are becoming more national in scope. Others are local, and these are more likely the ones to watch, since they are assuming Kinko's old shape! As Kinko's moves to capitalize on its newly acquired size and strength and goes after larger corporate customers, its localized competition will use guerrilla marketing tactics to reclaim the customer base upon which Kinko's built its early success—small/individual businessperson. Clearly, Kinko's has shape-shifted. The question, as yet unanswered, is whether the shift will truly create best value for the customers. What will their next challenge be, and where will it come from?

WHY SHOULD I SHAPE-SHIFT NOW? I'M DOING FINE

The answer, quite simply, is to survive and prosper in the future. In *The Age of Paradox* (Harvard Businesss School Press, 1994), Charles Handy uses a sigmoid curve (sort of an S laying down) to show the ebb and flow, rise and fall of the fortunes of a business or a person. He makes the point that as the peak of a career or an industry-leading position is approached, a new sigmoid curve must be started before the current one goes into decline. Creating this new start is part of a major shape-shift. Unfortunately, it is often very difficult to recognize when this point is occurring, except in retrospect (when it may be too late). Because of this difficulty, we must assume that the peak is occurring whenever we are successful, and shape-shift on an almost continuous basis.

It is interesting to note that if we are not in a successful part of the curve, we are almost certainly trying to shape-shift to become successful. Whether we are in a successful stage or not, we must start planning how to shape-shift. Is it any surprise that the world of business is marked by nonstop change and pressure? Regardless of what point of the curve we are at, we must always be ready to shape-shift. By doing so, we can begin to use this continuous change to our competitive advantage.

Most important, our shape-shift must "lead the curve" by a few months to a few of years, which (in my experience), is a reasonable lag time for the results of changes to impact a business. We must also consider more than one or two areas of the business. To ignore this lead lag time factor and begin shifting too late is very dangerous.

Japanese Auto Makers Forced a Shift By U. S. Producers

To illustrate the concept of shape-shifting in a familiar industry, consider the U.S. automobile industry over the past two decades. Consumers in the early 1970s had been conditioned to await the annual model change which often consisted of little more than cosmetic revisions to the "platform" (although, they did not use that term then. Accessories were added in abundance to enhance the profit per vehicle and allow customers to customize their purchase. This also permitted dealers to make each purchase a unique negotiation in which they could use all sorts of tricks to maximize their profit.

Because gasoline prices had been artificially suppressed since the post-World War II era, gas consumption was not much of an issue. The cars got larger and more opulent. Comfort, convenience, and flashy chrome accessories added thousands to the price and profit, the penalty for this flagrant proliferation was assessed in the quality and reliability of the product. Chrome-plated plastic peeled after exposure to ultraviolet rays of the sun. Vinyl roofs peeled. Glitzy accessories loosened, rattled, or just failed to work properly. But the dealers saw this as yet another way to build their power and profit base—by charging exorbitant prices for repairs that should never have been necessary.

In the face of continued strong demand and record profits, the U.S. auto producers accepted more and greater wage- and benefit-laden contracts with the United Auto Workers to avoid costly production interruptions due to strikes. Eventually, productivity plummeted and costs escalated.

Then a strong wind of change blew through the U.S. auto industry. The first storm came from the formation of Organization of Petroleum Exporting

Countries (OPEC) and the 1970's oil crisis. Gas prices skyrocketed and avail-
ability suffered. Lines of gas-guzzling U.S. autos formed at filling stations. A
"big limb" had been broken off the U.S. auto industry's "tree," but manufacturers were largely unaware of it since their tree was so big and strong. Next,
Combined Average Fuel Economy (CAFE) regulations required higher gas
mileage, and laws requiring posting of mileage on the price stickers were
passed and then tightened at the urging of environmental protection advo-
cates. The "tree" shook from the shock and its roots were damaged. The "big
tree" (or big three—an incidental, but appropriate play on words) did all it
knew how to do; it stood firm, stiff, and unyielding until something "broke."

Meanwhile, Japan had been busy rebuilding its industrial infrastructure
after the devastation of World War II. Since all its fuel was imported, it was
very costly. Furthermore, roads there are narrow and the cities congested.
Small cars made sense for Japan. American quality experts W. Edwards
Deming and Joseph Juran were discovered by the Japanese exactly at the
time that their message was falling on deaf ears in the production-consump-
tion and excess-driven U.S. auto industry. The Japanese began building and
exporting reliable, fuel-efficient small cars to the U.S. market. Initally, this
was viewed as a minor annoyance by the Big Three U.S. auto companies
(GM, Ford, and Chrysler). After all, the low end of the market in small cars
was not very profitable anyway. For example, Chevrolet's Chevette was a
small, unreliable, poor-performing, and unprofitable product. Why not con-
cede that part of the market to the Japanese?

The Japanese learned from and employed Juran and Deming's statistical
quality methods. In combination with the Japanese cultural tendency for fru-
gality, waste elimination (resulting from centuries of living on a barren rocky
island with few resources and little space), and consensus-based analysis
and decision making, the product quality and reliability improved dramatically. As the Japanese auto makers began to tap the potential of the U.S.
market, they created U.S. marketing arms to define products that would
meet the desires of American drivers. Soon, before Detroit knew what had
happened, Japanese cars were coming into the United States with the most
desirable features as standard equipment. This was the second "limb" to
break off the U.S. auto industry tree.

Clearly, the U.S. auto industry should have begun to shift its shape. But
it didn't. Manufacturers simply couldn't see why they should change what
had worked so well for so long. This is one of the worst roadblocks to starting a shape-shift, this natural tendency to practice denial and resist change
in the face of rising competition.

The rest of this story is well known to most Americans. The Japanese
now control almost one-third of the U.S. auto market, and occupy dominant
positions not only in the small and midsize product niches but in the luxury
market. As the Japanese began to understand what I call the shape of value,
they moved their products and production into the "shape" to match it.

Wainwright Shifted To Serve Its Changed Customers

There is an abundance of related shape-shift stories among the companies that supplied the U.S. auto producers. As the Detroit behemoths attempted to change their shape, their suppliers also had to shift. One such supplier that has received wide recognition is Wainwright Industries of St. Peters, Missouri. Wainwright was an old stamping company founded in 1947, with a single-punch press. The company survived and grew for four decades, but the real shape-shift in its success story occurred in 1991. It was then that Wainwright embarked on its continuous improvement process. Having seen the progress of Japanese suppliers and the direction of their industry, management realized that technology alone was not enough to survive and succeed. In the years that followed, Wainwright implemented a shape-shift in its culture, processes, and relationships to such an extent that it was a Malcolm Baldridge National Quality Award winner in 1994, and an *IndustryWeek*'s Best Plants winner in 1996.

Employee suggestions come at a rate exceeding the Japanese average by five times. Cycle times were reduced by over 99 percent, productivity increased over 250 percent, and customer satisfaction soared. Quality improved dramatically, costs were lowered substantially, cycle times dropped to a few minutes, and lead times (speed) were reduced to minutes or hours in an industry that normally functions in weeks of lead time! The result of shifting its shape to a people-oriented, high-involvement culture was the number-one position in its U.S. market.

Wainwright is a thriving example of the power of shape-shifting. Two keys to Wainwright's success were the intensive involvement of its people at all levels in the decisions affecting the business, and an aggressive, frequent surveying of customers to find out what they liked, and did not like, backed by an aggressive service recovery system when there was something customers did not like. This aggressive search for frequent criticism and customer feedback is the mark of a successful shape-shifter.

That the suppliers that were not captive to the car companies made the change faster than those that were owned by auto producers should be no surprise. The inertia of bodies in the natural sciences is proportional to their mass. That inertia keeps them moving inexorably in the direction they are already moving. This phenomenon is only one example of a natural law that can be easily extended to business behavior. Chrysler, the least vertically integrated of the car makers, had less "mass," and thus was able to shape-shift faster than GM and Ford. It was both a culture- and relationship-based shift, driven by need. Suppliers, mistreated by Ford and GM, were quick to come to Chrysler's aid, often bringing the best and newest ideas there first. Thus Chrysler has created the newest and freshest car product lines as the entire industry tries to shape-shift as fast as they can.

In contrast, only the highly original, controversial, and team that developed the original Ford Taurus saved much of that company's auto market share. In addition, the light truck products that were protected by higher duties and subject to less volatile styling shifts protected the Big Three's profits while they *slowly* shift their shape. The major question they should be asking is whether they have already missed "the next shape," and are already late starting another. How has the competitive "forest" changed? What are the new rules of the game? The auto industry's shock at the shifting rules of competition is now being felt in other indutries—especially communications.

Wildfire Communications Is Shifting the Rules of the Game

Now the large trees in the telecommunications industries have yet more dramatic storms to face. Consider Wildfire Communications' new personal electronic telephone assistant. Wildfire takes voicemail to a new level with voice-recognition technology, artificial intelligence, and adaptive interactivity. Speaking with Wildfire is almost like speaking with a live personal assistant. "She" (it is a female voice) will locate you at any of several numbers programmed into the system—home, office, car, portable phone, or take voice messages verbally from its "boss." Not only can Wildfire replace older technology, but it can also fulfill much of the work of an executive assistant or secretary for the management of messages. If executives and managers never learned how to use the time-saving and productivity-enhancing features of their voicemail systems, how can they hope to compete with the managerial and executives who not only use, but capitalize on technologies like Wildfire? (For a demo, simply dial 1-800-WILDFIRE—you will enjoy it!)

Only time will tell how badly these executives/managers and their companies are hamstringed by their inability to adapt and evolve. As much as they have invested in the past, they must leave it behind, indeed destroy it, in search of the new shape of value. If they do not, their competition will do it for and to them.

The typical artifacts of the modern corporation, such as the organization chart, give precious little clue as to what business the company is in, let alone what shape it has chosen (or might choose for the future). Many of these charts can be reviewed through several layers of the management without a single title that describes more than a generic "shapeless" function, and tells nothing at all about what constitutes value in the chosen business. Such charts do serve one purpose clearly, but it is of dubious value: It shows where everyone is "located" relative to everyone else in the organization—hierarchically.

Organization charts and job titles are necessary (I guess) to provide structure for people, but they simply cannot change fast enough to adapt to the market and environmental revolution. What is necessary is a new "team-based" charting process that tracks the roles of the people in their teams instead of their position in the (obsolete) hierarchy.

Nets, Inc. Had the Idea but Shifted To the Wrong Place

There is no doubt in my mind that Jim Manzi, one of the revolutionaries who built Lotus, would have been a misfit in the IBM culture. Now he once again attempted to build a revolutionary idea into a new approach to business. The shape-shifting basis of Industry.Net, later renamed to Nets, Inc., was a brilliant idea. The concept of an industrial shopping mall on the Internet where companies could do one-stop shopping for their supplies and needs redefined the idea of industrial distributors. Unfortunately for Manzi and his investors, he shifted too far, too fast, and committed resources too deeply before the concept has found its proper shape.

I grew up in an era when one reached for the thick yellow McMaster-Carr or W.W. Grainger catalogs for industrial supply needs. If you didn't know where to go, the Thomas Register was the resource. These companies are now scrambling to shift their shape to match the capabilities of the Internet. Nets, Inc. was first, but like many pioneers, it fell to the later, better wave of innovators. All 33 volumes of the old Thomas Register are now fully online (http://www.thomasregister.com), as are W.W. Grainger's (http://www .grainger.com) and McMaster-Carr (http://www.mcmaster.com). Even such an innovative idea requires careful use of resources and a clear understanding of the value equation from the perspective of the customer.

If Nets, Inc. had been more careful with resources, they might have been able to shift again once it became apparent that suppliers would rather pay to put up their own Web sites than to be part of theirs and that customers would pay for the ease and convenience of one-stop shopping and a single huge catalog instead of searching from site to site for what they needed. Such a simple nuance of the value equation was the difference between a successful shape shift and a failure. As Nets, Inc. plunged more and more resources into their venture, others stole the idea, turned it inside out to match the value shape of the customers, and built upon it. As Nets, Inc was failing, GE's Information Services division was shifting from operating the company's huge private telecommunications network, to creating an Internet version of its EDI service called Trading Process Network (TPN). As TPN started to yield large savings inside GE, the decision was made to offer its service to other companies (http://www.tpn.geis.com). This new form of commerce not only saves money but is faster by far than the old processes.

Regardless of the specific company's outcome, this kind of shape-shift created a whole new ball game for everyone in this field. What Manzi started at Nets, Inc. will be finished by others who shifted their shape better and the game will never be the same again!

Such revolutionaries act like Hamel's "rule breakers" to create the new shape of value with energy, creativity, foresight, entrepreneurial spirit, and zeal. Most of the competition in the executive suites of major corporations are limited because they are too invested in the past. After all, they got where they are by behaving the way they learned in the past. Revolutionary behavior is risky for them; it is all new, uncharted territory. Unfortunately for these executives and their companies, they fail to see that maintaining the old behavior and value shape is by far the greater risk.

4.

Visualizing the Shape of Value

A picture is worth a thousand words.
—Anonymous

THE VALUE PENTASTAR DIAGRAM

Earlier, I introduced the shape of value pentastar to help you visualize, depict, and communicate the totality of this concept. Constructing such a diagram can be very fast and simple, but if it is done carefully and thoughtfully, it requires time, research, discussion, and consensus. There is much more to choosing when and how to use this approach most rigorously. As a minimum starting point, three or more value pentastar diagrams should be developed and compared. These can be used to evaluate and then shape-shift based on:

- Target customer shape
- Your own value shape
- Competitor(s) value-attribute shape (the toughest competitor, if only one is the primary threat; several or best-composite competitor, in some cases—more in the chapter on this topic)
- Any combination (compared to customer desires)

Once these basic value pentastar shapes are completed (and this should not take too long the first time—it can be refined later with better "hard

43

data" and more competitive information), the next step in the shape-shifting process is in order.

Remember, the goal is *not* to create diagrams! It is to create the best value and to shape-shift on an ongoing basis to provide that best value even as the understanding and definition of value continuously changes in the mind of the customer.

This next step will help diagnose where our shape and the customer's desired shape mismatch the most, where the greatest competitive disadvantages or vulnerabilities exist. It is also where the greatest opportunities reveal themselves.

In order to begin your assessment of how to shape-shift, a separate set of shape of value diagrams should be done for each dimension, depicting how the shape of the business and its structure, process, culture and relationships contribute to the various attributes (versus either customers' desires or competitors' strengths and weaknesses). The shapes that result from these evaluations should match the shapes of the customers' or market's profiles as closely as possible to achieve the best-value alignment. Remember that different customers within similar markets will still have different profiles.

Familiar Examples

In order to illustrate the concept of the shape of value and the value pentastar, I will use a series of examples familiar to most American (and many international) businesspeople. I have assigned arbitrary value attribute numbers and plotted them on the diagrams. The reviewers of these diagrams agreed generally, although there were some differences over both the definitions of the attributes and the evaluation assigned to each of the examples. This is natural, healthy, and entirely within the purpose of the process, for if these were "real" analyses, there would be extensive dialogue and debate. An actual working group developing the evaluations should be as diverse as possible. Ideally, customers and potential customers should be engaged in the evaluation process.

For our purposes here, let's look at several diagrams to see how the shape of value and the value pentastar help clarify the differences for companies that would aspire to be suppliers or customers of the example companies.

Retailers

As our first example, we'll compare these well-known and successful retailers: Wal-Mart, Nordstrom, and Lands' End. Each has a distinct shape of value that it provides to customers. Wal-Mart's emphasis is clearly on low cost and functional value, and much less on service. Nordstrom, on the other hand, is very quality-, service-, and innovation-oriented. Lands' End has a "middle-of-the road" value shape that balances excellent service and speed of delivery with good-quality, conservative fashion merchandise at reasonable prices. Risky innovation is a lesser element. No doubt the management personnel of these companies would have differing assessments, but remember, the *customer* defines the values. And in this case, as a customer of all three, I have defined them as shown in Figures 4-1 to 4-3. If large numbers of customers agree with my definitions, then they are the definitions for value that these retailers must strive to build upon.

Automobiles

For our second set of examples, we'll consider and compare the Mercedes S-class, Honda Civic, and Chrysler Concorde automobiles. The three manufacturers of these well-known makes of cars provide a clear value shape contrast. Mercedes is the acknowledged high-quality leader, with robust designs, commensurate price premiums, and high-level dealer service.

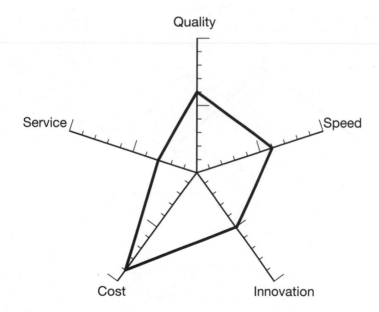

Figure 4-1 The Value Pentastar for Wal-Mart

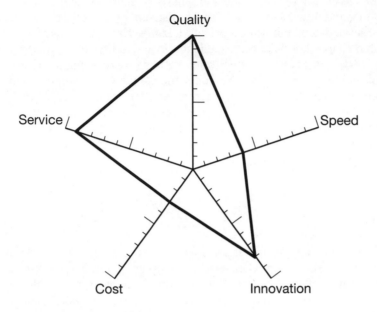

Figure 4-2 The Value Pentastar for Nordstrom

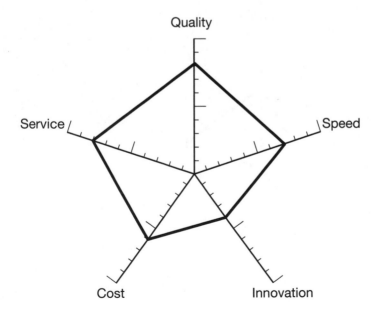

Figure 4-3 The Value Pentastar for Lands' End

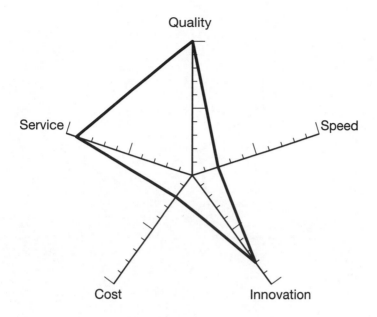

Figure 4-4 The Value Pentastar for Mercedes S-Class

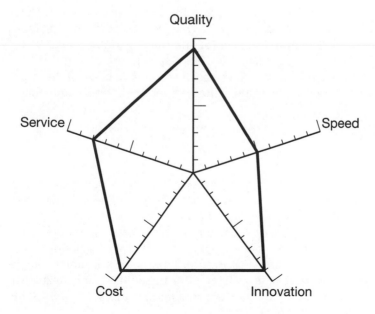

Figure 4-5 The Value Pentastar for Honda Civic

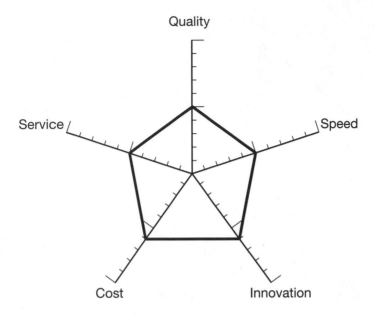

Figure 4-6 The Value Pentastar for a Chrysler Concorde

Honda is known for product longevity, fine functional quality, and techno-logical refinement at reasonable prices. Chrysler has become a styling inno-vator offering good "midlevels" in each of the value attributes (except for some recent quality/reliability concerns). The "speed" criterion in this case is based primarily on how quickly and easily a customer can obtain the vehi-cle. Figures 4-4 to 4-6 show the value pentastars for these three automobiles.

Airlines

Our third example will compare Southwest, Delta, and Virgin Atlantic air-lines, in addition to charter air companies as a group. Airlines all carry peo-ple and cargo from one place to another. Southwest uses low price with minimal service as its primary value attributes. Delta is a full-service provider that offers all basic services and a wide choice of schedules, and destinations, plus some premium features. Virgin Atlantic sells unique, high-service luxury travel; charters, in general, offer the ultimate in convenience and speed with the commensurate price premium. Figures 4-7 to 4-10 show the value pentastars for these companies.

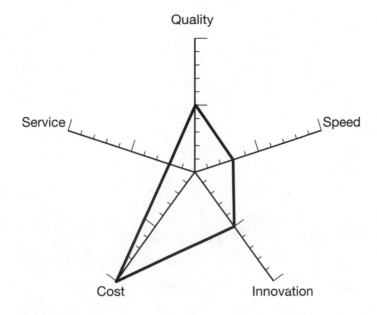

Figure 4-7 The Value Pentastar for Southwest Airlines

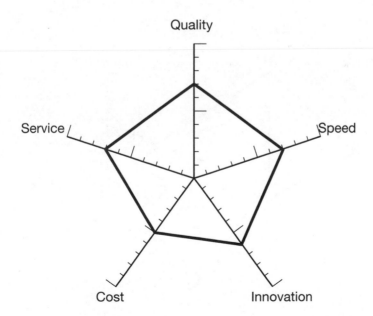

Figure 4-8 The Value Pentastar for Delta Airlines

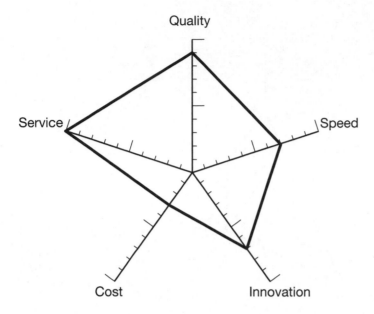

Figure 4-9 The Value Pentastar for Virgin Atlantic Airlines

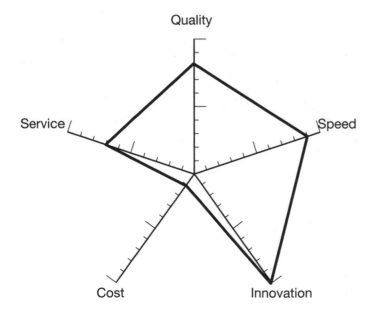

Figure 4-10 The Value Pentastar for Charter Air Carriers

Restaurants

The fourth group of examples we'll compare includes McDonald's, Subway, Chinese restaurants as a group, and "designer restaurants" such as Hard Rock Cafe and Planet Hollywood. For fast food, no company surpasses McDonald's. Quality, while consistent, is not its main value attribute. No one would compare its food—or the prices—to that at a first-class restaurant. Low prices are due to mass production. Innovation is relatively low due to the high cost of complexity in rolling out new items to their worldwide franchise outlets. Subway offers "custom-built" sandwiches and salads only at moderate cost in convenient, but spartan surroundings. Chinese restaurants offer wide variety from a predetermined group of meats, vegetables, sauces, and spices, with take-out services for full meals. Designer restaurants offer a different level of service and cachet—albeit at noticeably higher prices. Figures 4-11 to 4-14 have this group's pentastar diagrams.

One-to-One Marketing from Product/Service Groups

Now consider health care and the shape changes needed based on an individual customer situation. In these markets, the shape of the delivery system must be able to accommodate this variation. Health care is often a

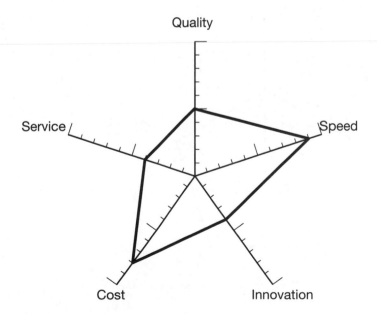

Figure 4-11 The Value Pentastar for McDonald's

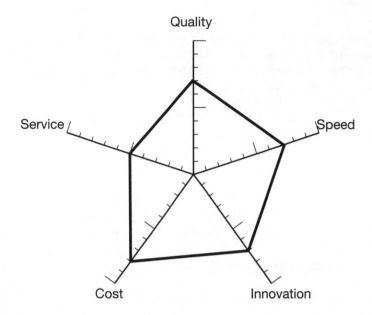

Figure 4-12 The Value Pentastar for Subway

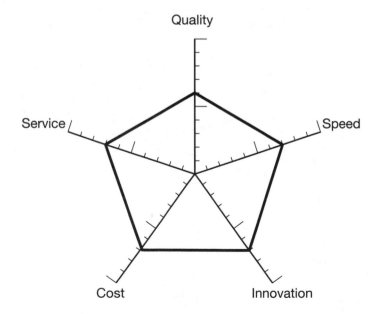

Figure 4-13 The Value Pentastar for Chinese Restaurants as a Group

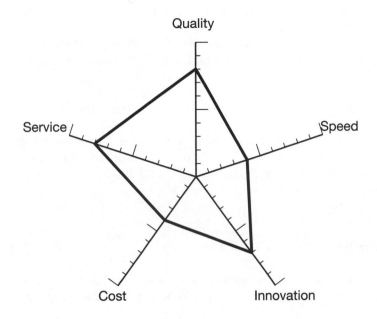

Figure 4-14 The Value Pentastar for "Designer" Restaurants (Hard Rock, Planet Hollywood)

totally specialized one-to-one service, but not always; screening via remote vans for such tests as mammograms is one example of "mass production" in health care; and blood pressure testers in discount stores and pharmacies are examples of "self-service" health care. Still, the majority of medical care is one health care professional to one patient, and the cost attribute is now beginning to weigh in heavily, whereas service and speed (with good quality) were previously the dominant attributes.

Imagine an even more responsive view of the shape of value in the home. Suppose one service provider were supplying all of the home services now provided by utilities companies: water/sewer, gas and electric power, telephone, Internet access, cable TV, and security monitoring. There would be six or seven weighted shape diagrams, since each one of this "portfolio" of value decisions would have different weights on the various value attributes. Then there would be an aggregate shape upon which the individual customer would base his or her decision to purchase combined or separate utilities. This is not just a hypothesis. Leading utility companies like Southern Company, in Atlanta, Georgia, are contemplating such arrangements now. Think about how such an organization must shape-shift to deliver and service these similar but different products.

In *One Size Fits One*, Heil et al. list 10 "customer rules for a one-size-fits-one world." A couple of them are particularly appropriate to mention here:

Rule number 1: The average customer does not exist—get to know us;
Rule number 8: The details are important to us—they should be to you.

The message is that many situations can and must be tailored for individual choice. The shape of value for the individual customer is distinctively different, yet in a large group, many cluster in similar shapes. It is therefore necessary to discriminate between the averages and the details before deciding which customer shape to match. To illustrate this example, Figure 4-15 shows the value pentastar for a medical specialist, and Figure 4-16 shows the diagram for an HMO.

Discount Retailers

As our final group example, consider three very similar but still distinctly different discount retailers: Wal-Mart, Kmart, and Target. Wal-Mart's mantra is

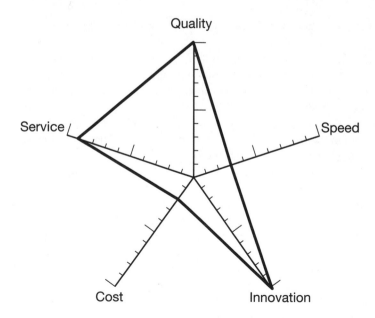

Figure 4-15 The Value Pentastar for Medical Specialist

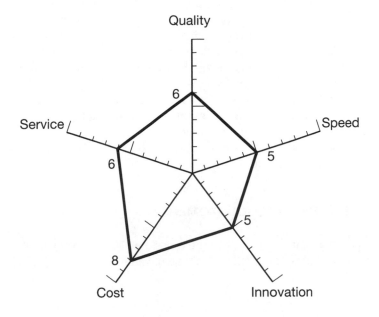

Figure 4-16 The Value Pentastar for an HMO

value based on *everyday low price*. Kmart's mantra is *low price, on sale*. Target offers a slightly more *upscale and style-conscious shopping experience*.

Using the shape of value diagram to differentiate three very similar companies requires a finer resolution of the weight, to differentiate among the nuances of the companies' attributes. (Weighting the diagram evaluations, as described later would help separate the shapes somewhat.) All three of these retailers require approximately the same level of quality, with Target, as noted, aiming a little more upscale, so it would have a slightly higher quality evaluation. All three require prompt shipping service, but Wal-Mart is the most demanding with its three-day shipping service, so it would have a slightly higher speed evaluation. Their service expectations are also very similar, although Kmart sometimes relies more heavily on Vendor Managed Inventory (VMI), and thus may have a slightly higher service need. Since its systems were historically less refined than the other two retailers, Kmart might need a more sophisticated service competency from its supplier. Target's merchandising and style require higher innovation, but its restrictions on supplier point-of-purchase displays require less innovation in that respect. On the cost attribute, all three are tenacious negotiators, and would be rated fairly equally.

Only when all three collide on the same, hard-to-differentiate items (such as toothpaste, tissues, etc.) do they gravitate toward the same price/cost attribute level. While all three participate in the same retail segment and target the same market, to shoppers, they differ visibly. Which one a consumer prefers depends on the weight he or she places on the value attributes, including the shopping experience versus low price.

There is one certainty: All three retailers have minimum levels of proficiency in each value attribute that suppliers must meet to "qualify" for consideration. Knowing what these are and meeting them is "the price of admission" into the competition. Figure 4-17 shows how closely the pentastars for these retailers are drawn.

DIAGRAMS OF SOME TYPICAL CUSTOMERS

In order to compare familiar companies to the types of customers they might attract, consider four different consumers' shape of value diagrams. Each of

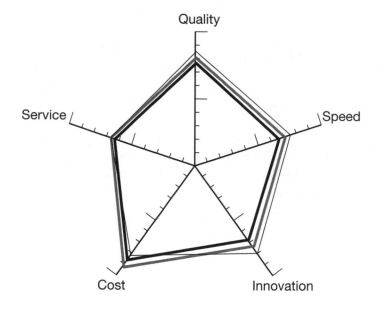

Figure 4-17 The Value Pentastar for Tightly Clustered Shapes

these consumers would make distinctly different choices about where to purchase the goods and services they desired or needed, and these choices would be heavily based on their perception of value.

1. A wealthy *baby boomer couple*, with a six-digit annual income, approximately 50+ years of age, whose children are through college and no longer living at home.
2. A *two-wage earner household* of middle income level ($40,000–$80,000/year) with three preteen or early teenage children.
3. A time-starved, modest income ($20,000–$35,000/year) *single working parent* with one preschool child.
4. A *generation X single*, moderately successful ($30,000–$50,000/year) professional, well-educated, unmarried with no children.

After studying these diagrams briefly, look for the match between shape of value and the familiar companies shown previously. Find clues as to which place consumers would shop, how they might travel, and so forth.

Superimposing such customer value shape diagrams on those of the supplier would reveal a great deal about how to target specific customers. The same approach could be used for suppliers to the specific companies shown in the familiar examples. If the supplier's shape did not match their potential

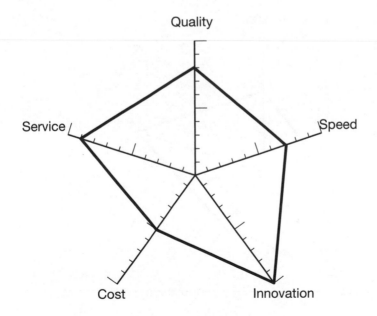

Figure 4-18 The Value Pentastar for Baby Boomers

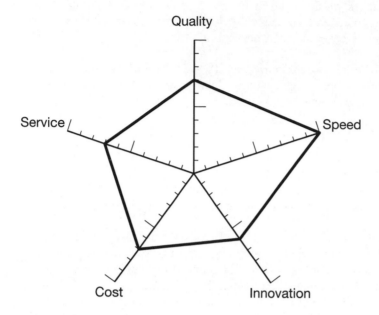

Figure 4-19 The Value Pentastar for Two-Wage Earner Household

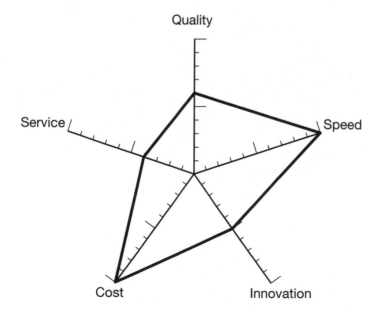

Figure 4-20 The Value Pentastar for Single Working Parent

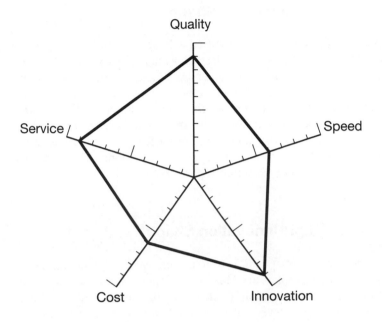

Figure 4-21 The Value Pentastar for Generation X Professional

customer, the likelihood of success in a long-term supply relationship would be small. If the shape did match, the likelihood of success would be good.

Finally, as I will describe in much more detail later, changing the shape of value to match that of the customer is perhaps the most pivotal issue for competitive success in the future.

DISTINCTIVE CHARACTERISTICS OF SHAPES

Before we move on, be sure to notice that these shapes start to become distinctive in their characteristics for specific kinds of shape of value companies. Even so, some companies with similar approaches (such as mail order retailers L.L. Bean and Lands' End) will be difficult to differentiate without weighted diagrams. The fact is few companies can be good at everything. Because of that, each inevitably concentrates on value attributes that are desired most by its target customers and dictated by its shape of the business (call them customer-driven and core competency with purpose if you like). Let's draw some correlations from all these examples.

Low-Cost Shape

Timex watches and public transportation (the bus) are clear examples of
this shape. Wal-Mart's best-value/in-stock strategy also clearly points toward
low cost and excellent service/speed; other attributes are of lesser importance. In that respect, Southwest Airlines shape is similar. McDonald's shares
the low-cost focus but with an emphasis on convenience as well. With the
large number of time-constrained, lower-income consumers in the market,
and the cost-value consciousness of even upper-income consumers, it is not
surprising that these three enjoy strong market positions. The low-cost
provider usually has a strong position in any market.

High-Innovation Shape

Nordstrom derives its market position from an innovation, quality, and service shape of value. Its lookalikes are Mercedes, Virgin Atlantic Airways, and
designer restaurants. All are seeking to attract the discriminating consumer,
who will pay more to be pampered with top quality and service. Nordstrom's
excellent service almost becomes a part of their innovation attribute because
it is so unique.

Balanced Shape

Balanced shapes such as those exhibited by Lands' End, Chrysler, Delta
Airlines, and Subway are more reflective of companies whose target is the
broad market, aiming to service all but the very top and, in some cases, the
very bottom of the cost, status, and service-oriented. The balanced shape is
a challenge in today's divergent consumer environment. The "haves" want
service, quality, and innovation, while the "have-nots" need low cost and convenience (they are usually "time-starved"). As this split grows, achieving a
balanced shape becomes of dubious wisdom. It is difficult, and expensive to
be equally good at everything. To focus on everything may as bad as focus-
ing on nothing!

CONCLUSION

While such generalities are not specifically actionable, they do provide good
overviews of the strategic direction options available to businesses. They can

signal resource waste, errors in marketing strategy, or operational misdirections if a radical deviation from their typical shape is attempted. If one of these middle-of-the-road, balanced-shape companies attempts to go too far upscale (or even downscale) it will usually fail. In moving up, it may lack the necessary cachet and some of the robustness of quality to compete with entrenched leaders. If it goes too far down, it may hurt its image with the broad middle market. Airline wars during which full-service carriers attempted to clone discount branches to compete with Southwest largely failed because it was too radical a departure in shape of value for the shape of the business to support.

If, for instance, Nordstrom or its "shapemates" move too far down, seeking the low-cost consumer with discontinued or close-out goods, there would be grave danger that its current core customers would misunderstand and abandon them for a store more consistent with their image of market target and behavior. Likewise, if its quality or service degenerates, it is also at risk of losing loyal customers.

Experts on consumer behavior such as Dr. Roger Blackwell of Ohio State University believe that the market is increasingly breaking into top and bottom (have and have-not) groupings more than ever before. Assuming that his conclusion is correct, consumers at the top know what they want and will pay for it, although they are also voracious bargain hunters if they believe such bargains exist. Consumers at the bottom have limited resources and hence will shop where they can realize more of the value attributes they consider important, the primary which is low cost. Customers form mental images of their expected shape of value and use them to guide where they shop. This is a very powerful concept!

Remember, there is no such thing as a standard shape. The important principle of shape-shifting is that these shapes will change over time; and to consistently provide best value, you must also change, shifting your shape to stay congruent with that of the customer before your competitors do. Another important point I will make repeatedly is that these shapes should not be developed in isolation. Although I took an arbitrary approach to create these examples, the power of the shape of value approach to shape-shifting occurs as a result of the *collaborative* development of consensus on these shape diagrams.

One of the most valuable uses of the shape of value diagram approach is to consider the likelihood of success in either gaining share or entering a new market against well-entrenched competition. The degree of congruence between your shape of value and that of your desired customer(s) or market(s) is an excellent indicator of success potential. It is also an excellent directional indicator for changes needed in the shape of the business to enhance the likelihood of success.

5.

Understanding Value Attributes

God is in the details.
— Mies Van de Rohe, architect

DEFINITIONS OF VALUE ATTRIBUTES

Because the value attributes can be viewed from very different perspectives, this chapter includes some expanded definitions and descriptors. These will, however, be relatively brief because the contextual and situational definition should be developed by whomever is evaluating the attributes, to fit the business, product, service, and customers in question. I am only illustrating the intent. Naturally, the concepts here were developed based on my own background and experience, which was concentrated in consumer durable products and mass retailing. Other products, services, industries, and markets have nuances and differences that must be considered and accommodated to make this approach powerful and effective in each situation. The definitions that follow are far from complete, but are intended to illustrate the necessity of broad interpretation of value attribute.

Quality

Quality refers not just to "conformance quality," but to quality of performance, specification, and consistency to meet or exceed expectations.

Assume that conformance quality must be uniformly high to have even a chance to compete.

For example, Rolex and Timex watches may have comparable conformance quality, and both may produce products that keep time accurately, but Rolex is widely perceived to be of higher quality. Similarly, Mercedes automobiles are widely considered to be of superior quality to many lower-priced cars because of the robustness of their design, construction, and technology—at a commensurate price premium, like the Rolex.

Service

Service refers not just to on-time accuracy and efficiency, which are assumed to be high just to compete, but rather to the service experience, which includes ease, accessibility, information (status or options), cordiality, personality, intimacy, and consistency.

For example, Ritz-Carlton Hotels and Hampton Inns may have similar conformance quality, and each provides comfortable accommodations, but the Ritz-Carlton services and amenities are perceived to be much better. Likewise, Hertz and Alamo rental cars both offer functional service, but Hertz Number One Gold service offers easier, faster pickup, and drop-off, and shelter from inclement weather during both.

Cost

Cost is not just the first cost or even only the cash cost, but rather the total cost, including the money, and effort (sacrifice) required to obtain, incorporate, and use the product or service.

For example, importing goods from Pacific Rim countries, such as China or Malaysia, usually yields a very low initial purchase cost, but with risks of uncertain quality and delivery and a plethora of ancillary or hidden costs such as handling, damage, ocean freight, port charges, customs charges, taxes, or duties; awkward communications and time zone differences; weak or nonexistent service; problems of warranty or parts supply; and more. Thus, the lowest initial cost may not be the lowest final, total cost.

Speed

Speed means not just on-time (that's service) or normal response time (that's expected), but rather unusual, rapid, convenient, flexible, changeable, and "bonuses" such as special delivery without any added costs.

For example, typical mail order companies deliver within a week or two on a wide range of merchandise, and will provide expedited delivery for an additional charge. Quill and Viking mail order office products are usually delivered within two days or less, at no additional charge. Many mail order computer firms deliver next day at no premium cost. This is clearly better speed, convenience and timeliness.

Innovation

Innovation is not just "new"—that is expected. It refers to the truly surprisingly, unique, creative, fun, exciting, and delightful, with a cachet, uniqueness, style, or status that makes it desirable to acquire or own. Customized products or services on a one-to-one basis are considered highly innovative.

Innovative examples are numerous—custom-made suits, dresses, shoes; original or limited-edition art; designer jewelry, watches, pens; prestige/unique automobiles like the Ferrari, the Dodge Viper, or Plymouth Prowler; customized shopping services; personal/beauty care, unique household or personal care products such as those often introduced on infomercials or video shopping channels; and many, many more.

Now it's time to test your understanding of the process to diagnose and profile the shape of value your company currently offers against that of competitors for specific customers. Using the attributes of value as the headings, as shown in Figure 5-1, assign numerical values for each and mark a "value score" on the scale to indicate your rating. You can later alter the shape diagram by weighting the importance of each attribute to your given customers or markets, to avoid feeling good by being good at things that do not matter much to customers. Mark where your company, products services rate on each attribute the competition.

Be careful not to think in generalities or averages in completing this profile. Averages tend to hide the key differences that influence on individual customer's decisions. Having a specific competitor in mind helps form relative numerical values when this is done for a specific competitor. For now, complete the diagnosis relative to one specific, important customer.

For the time being, ignore on the figure the section that reads:

Structure, Culture, Processes, Relationships. This portion will be used in later expansion of the use of the profile. To change the shape of value and the value attributes in a lasting and effective way, the shape of the business must be altered in one or more of its dimensions. The section showing these four dimensions are to be used when assessing whether a particular dimension contributes to, detracts from, or is aligned in support of the value attribute being evaluated. This is a complicated but very important use of the diagnostic profile, and a detailed example of its analysis and use is included in a later chapter.

Quality: *(Used to be a plus, but now is just the "price of admission.")* Not just "conformance quality," but quality of performance, specification, style, and consistency to meet or exceed expectations. Assume that conformance quality must be uniformly high to even have a chance to compete.

Very poor 1   2   3   4   5   6   7   8   9   10 Best in class

___ Structure ___ Culture   ___ Processes ___ Relationships

_____ **Total Quality Rating**

Service: *(Means having what the customer wants, where and when they want it "their way," and knowing the status, communicating it, in a friendly way.)* Not just the on-time accuracy and efficiency which are assumed to be high just to compete, but rather the service experience including ease, accessibility, information (status or options), cordiality, personality, intimacy, and consistency.

Very poor 1   2   3   4   5   6   7   8   9   10 Best in class

___ Structure ___ Culture   ___ Processes ___ Relationships

_____ **Total Service Rating**

Cost: *(Lowest total cost producer of the products or services provided.)* Not just the first cost or even (only) the cash cost, but rather the total cost including money, effort (sacrifice), cost to obtain, handle, and even use the product or service.

Very poor 1   2   3   4   5   6   7   8   9   10 Best in class

___ Structure ___ Culture   ___ Processes ___ Relationships

_____ **Total Cost Rating**

Speed: *(Delivering fast, and on time.)* Not just on-time (that's service) or normal response time (that's expected), but rather unusual, rapid, flexible, changeable, and even such delivery without any added costs.

Very poor 1   2   3   4   5   6   7   8   9   10 Best in class

___ Structure ___ Culture   ___ Processes ___ Relationships

_____ **Total Speed Rating**

Innovation: *(Creating innovative products and using innovative processes.)* Not just "new"—that is expected. Rather, truly surprisingly, unique, creative, fun, exciting, delightful and with a cachet, uniqueness, or status to make it desirable to acquire/own. Including customized on a one:one basis.

Very poor 1   2   3   4   5   6   7   8   9   10 Best in class

___ Structure ___ Culture   ___ Processes ___ Relationships

_____ **Total Innovation Rating**

Figure 5-1 Expanded Diagnostic Profile for Shape-shifting

VALUE ATTRIBUTE DESCRIPTORS

Having gone through this thought process twice (in the earlier chapter very briefly, and in more detail just now), you no doubt are beginning to realize that defining the value attributes is critical. But although how they are defined is important, how uniformly and consistently they are defined in a series of comparisons is even more important. To assist you in this aspect of the definition, a series of value attribute descriptors are useful. Figure 5-2 lists the descriptors I have chosen. Adapt them to your situation as necessary.

Quality:
- **Specification (Robustness, Refinement):** What is the intended or designed performance level or feature richness?
- **Conformance (Information):** Does the product conform to intended specifications? How well?
- **Consistency (Variability):** Is there a high level of consistency or a low level of variability?
- **Reliability:** Does the product keep doing what it is intended to do, the same way, over and over for a long time?
- **Durability:** Does the product "hold up" or last a long time, and through hard use or even modest misuse?

Service:
- **Courtesy (Intimacy):** Is the service courteous, pleasant, and friendly?
- **Ease (Simplicity):** Is the after-the-sale service easy to get or use?
- **Information:** Is it easy to find out the status of the product or service at any time?
- **Flexibility:** Can the service be accessed and used many different ways?
- **Adaptability (Responsiveness):** Can the service be tailored to specific needs of the customer, and be readily altered as situations change?

Speed:
- **Convenience (Effortlessness):** Is the product easily accessible?
- **Timeliness:** Is the product available on a timely basis?
- **Flexibility:** Does the product arrive where, when, and how it is requested?
- **Throughput:** Is the time from beginning to end of the cycle (of order/production/delivery) very short and rapidly completed?
- **Information:** Is accurate information available quickly?

Cost (Low):
- **First Cost:** Is the first cost low enough to be competitive?
- **Handling and Packaging:** Is little waste in nonvalue-added costs in getting the product where it must be when it must be there?
- **Throughput and Delivery (Information):** Is it possible to determine where/when the product is in its throughput cycle at little or no extra cost?
- **Penalties:** Do requested changes or nonstandard needs cause extra costs and charges?
- **Premiums:** Is it possible to gain speed, flexibility, or other customized changes by paying a modest fee or no premium?

Innovation:
- **Uniqueness (Proprietary or Exclusive):** Can the product be either unique, proprietary, exclusive, or customized/personalized?
- **Cachet and Status:** Does the product convey additional importance or exclusivity on its owner?
- **Technology:** Is there a breakthrough technology involved with the product or some aspect of it?
- **Entertainment (Information):** Does some aspect of the product provide unusual entertainment or informational benefits?
- **Style (Trend or Fad):** Is the product ideal with respect to some current style, trend, or fad that makes it desirable?

Figure 5-2 Examples of Value Attributes Descriptors

I have chosen only five descriptors, to make it easier for those who want to use any of the graphical and mathematical methods described for the value attributes. However, I am concerned about making things too mathematically simple because these are *subjective* descriptors, and assigning numerical values to them can sometimes make them seem more accurate than they actually are. Like the shape of value, the key benefit is the understanding and consensus building that the communication process makes possible.

After you familiarize yourself with these descriptors, we can explore how to use them in conjunction with the attributes of value to arrive at a better, more accurate shape of value diagram. (Note that for simplicity, whenever I refer to *product*, I mean product or service or combination of the two.) Following each of the descriptors is an example question that might be posed to clarify and evaluate that aspect of the value attribute.

For Number-Crunchers

As stated, I am reluctant to use numerical ratings on such subjective terms as these descriptors, because their major purpose is to stimulate thought about the richness of the value attribute being considered, in order to arrive at a better, more descriptive shape of value diagram. But for those readers who need to quantify even the unquantifiable, and insist on numerical analysis, I suggest using a simple scale like this to value these descriptors:

0 = Low, not very important or of secondary importance

1 = Average, of normal or expected importance in this type of situation

2 = High, an important, perhaps pivotal issue

For example, to evaluate automobiles such as the Mercedes S-class, the Honda Civic, and the Chrysler Concorde illustrated in an earlier example on *customer expectations of quality,* the results would be:

Mercedes S-Class: Quality

Specification (Robustness, Refinement): What is the intended or designed performance level or feature richness? **(2)**

Conformance (Information): Does the product conform to the intended specification and how well? **(2)**

Consistency (Variability): Is there a high level of consistency to the product or a low level of variability? **(2)**

Reliability: Does the product keep doing what it is intended to do, the same way, over and over for a long time? **(2)**

Durability: Does the product "hold up" or last a long time and through hard use or even modest misuse? **(2)**

Total = 10

Honda Civic: Quality

Specification (Robustness, Refinement): What is the intended or designed performance level or feature richness? **(1)**

Conformance (Information): Does the product conform to the intended specification and how well? **(2)**

Consistency (Variability): Is there a high level of consistency to the product or a low level of variability? **(2)**

Reliability: Does the product keep doing what it is intended to do, the same way, over and over for a long time? **(2)**

Durability: Does the product "hold up" or last a long time and through hard use or even modest misuse? **(1)**

Total = 8

Chrysler Concorde: Quality

Specification (Robustness, Refinement): What is the intended or designed performance level or feature richness? **(1)**

Conformance (Information): Does the product conform to the intended specification and how well? **(1)**

Consistency (Variability): Is there a high level of consistency to the product or a low level of variability? **(1)**

Reliability: Does the product keep doing what it is intended to do, the same way, over and over for a long time? **(1)**

Durability: Does the product "hold up" or last a long time and through hard use or even modest misuse? **(1)**

Total = 5

With apologies to Honda on "durability," because they do really hold up well, and to Chrysler on most of the descriptors, because they are closing the quality gap, I believe these scores indicate what most customers perceive in their value attribute evaluations. I hope it is now also evident why I prefer not to use a numeric analysis to arrive at the value attribute plotted on the shape of value diagram. The main point, again, is to understand what constitutes value, and to achieve consensus, consistency, and communications during the evaluation process, whether it is internal to a company or external, with customers or suppliers.

Weighting the Attributes

Let us refocus on the value attributes themselves. In many cases one or two of the attributes carry disproportionate importance in the shape of value. For example, price is very important to discount retailers and wholesale clubs, which pride themselves on being low-cost retail outlets, whereas uniqueness is very important to catalog companies such as Sharper Image or Brookstone. And where proprietary features and patent protection may be critically important to a drug maker or a software provider, service would be more important to beauty shops, banks, and the like. Quality would be critical to hospitals, pharmacies, banks, and so on. Clearly, all attributes are not of equal importance to companies, and a means to graphically depict that difference is needed. *Weighting* the attributes enables this to be done fairly simply and effectively.

To use this process to highlight differences in importance of the various value attributes, weight the five attributes relative to each other by dividing 25 points among the five attributes. Note that although the weighting process is simple, the thought involved is anything but. Here is a format and some "thought rules" to follow:

To weight value attributes, follow these guidelines:

9 points or more = very important (the overriding consideration)

6–8 points = above average importance

5 points = average importance

2–4 points = below average importance

0–1 points = not important at all (of insignificant importance)

The diagnostic profile would look like the one shown in Figure 5-3.

To divide 25 points among these five attributes, you must decide the relative importance of each to the customer or market segment to be served. One test of the correctness of such a weighting is to assign points arbitrarily at first and then adjust by asking questions such as:

- For those attributes with higher point totals, ask: Is this attribute significantly more important than the lower-rated ones?
- If the points assigned to one attribute exceed those of two or more combined, ask: Is it more important in the value decision by the customer/market than those two combined?
- Taking two or three together, ask: Are these that much more or less important than the remaining two or three?

Do the weighting several times, since opinions are influenced by moods and recent events, and may vary over time. Ask several people to do this weighting and then discuss (argue if necessary) the results, especially where they differ noticeably. For those attributes with low point totals, determine whether a competitor doing a superb job on these could take the business in spite of being just average on the other attributes.

Quality:
Very poor 1   2   3   4   5   6   7   8   9   10 Best in class
___ Structure ___ Participation ___ Processes ____ Partnerships
_____ **Total Quality Rating** × _____ **Weighting Points =**
Weighted Quality Rating divided by 10 = _____

Service:
Very poor 1   2   3   4   5   6   7   8   9   10 Best in class
____ Structure ____ Participation ____ Processes ____ Partnerships
_____ **Total Service Rating** × _____ **Weighting Points =**
Weighted Service Rating divided by 10 = _____

Cost:
Very poor 1   2   3   4   5   6   7   8   9   10 Best in class
____ Structure ____ Participation ____ Processes ____ Partnerships
_____ **Total Cost Rating** × _____ **Weighting Points =**
Weighted Cost Rating divided by 10 = _____

Speed:
Very poor 1   2   3   4   5   6   7   8   9   10 Best in class
____ Structure ____ Participation ____ Processes ____ Partnerships
_____ **Total Speed Rating** × _____ **Weighting Points =**
Weighted Speed/Timeliness Rating divided by 10 = _____

Innovation:
Very poor 1   2   3   4   5   6   7   8   9   10 Best in class
____ Structure ____ Participation ____ Processes ____ Partnerships
_____ **Total Innovation Rating** × _____ **Weighting Points =**
Weighted Innovation Rating divided by 10 = _____

Figure 5-3 Weighted Diagnostic Profile for Shape-shifting

Finally, ask customers to do this weighting, and see how their perspective differs from yours. Then, ask yourself if there is a significantly different weighting assigned by one or more competitors, and what effect that would have on competitive position. And find out whether there is a trend or direction that would make a higher or lower weighting indicative of future wants and needs.

Delivery Services

Consider several popular delivery services: FedEx, UPS Ground, and the U.S. Postal Service. All three provide many similar services. What would their shape of value diagrams look like? Comparing their services provides a good illustration of how weighting importance alters a shape of value diagram.

Figures 5-4 through 5-9 show the respective calculations of a weighted value shape and a value pentastar for these three delivery services. To graphically illustrate the impact of weighting, I have plotted the unweighted shape in lighter lines and the weighted shape in bolder lines. This kind of situation can occur in services where speed, quality, and service reliability far outrank cost. This also happens where cost/price is the dominant value attribute.

For the example, the three major delivery services will be rated on their handling of perishable medical supplies to a clinic in a major city that is open Monday through Saturday. The clinic director weighted the attributes as:

Quality	= 8
Service	= 7
Cost	= 2
Speed	= 9
Innovation	= 1
Total	= 25 points

It is clear who the loser was in this example. The U.S. Postal Service's (USPS) greatest advantage on an unweighted basis, cost, was weighted so low that it ranked a poor third to the two other services, whereas the tracking ability and consistency of both UPS Ground and FedEx made their competition closer than might have been expected. There was no specification about restrictions on lead time, so FedEx's superior speed, even with the high weighting on speed, did not give it the clear value advantage. (It is only fair to note that if we had compared UPS Next Day probably the results would have been a dead heat between UPS and FedEx (with the exception of Saturday delivery considerations).

Weighting provides an important dimension to using the shape of value diagram in a competitive assessment, because, as noted, all customers do not consider value attributes equally important. Much business is gained or lost because of an imperfect understanding of the relative importance of certain value attributes compared to others. In customer and competitor shape evaluation, this concept must be carefully considered to achieve a true evaluation on which to base shape-shifting decisions.

In an upcoming chapter, I will discuss using the shape of the business dimensions as another aspect of the shape diagramming process. In order to keep this type of analytical/graphical technique as simple as possible, only one of these approaches at a time will be illustrated.

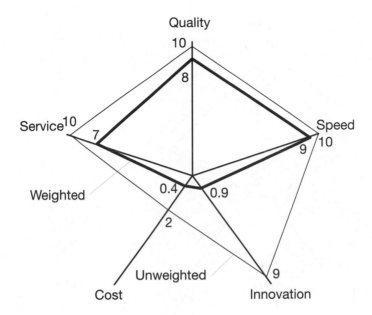

Figure 5-4 The Value Pentastar for FedEx

THE HIERARCHY OF VALUE ATTRIBUTES

When we evaluate the Shape of Value, without weighting, all of the five attributes appear to be of equal relative importance. In fact, they seldom are. The issue of relative importance, weight, or "leverage" requires serious consideration. The numerical weighting approach just illustrated is one time-tested, analytical way to develop an improved representation of relative importance and its impact on overall value.

There is another, more visual and simpler approach to illustrating relative importance which is very much in keeping with the "Shape" and visualization concepts in this book. The essence of it is to create a hierarchy of (value attribute) needs. Most people have heard of Maslow's hierarchy of human needs, but for a refresher, it is shown in Figure 5-10 (page 77).

With a little reflection and questioning, we can create a parallel hierarchy of value attributes for most situations. I had not thought of this parallel approach until fellow author and consultant James Swartz showed it to me recently. His use of this approach to illustrate the relative importance and

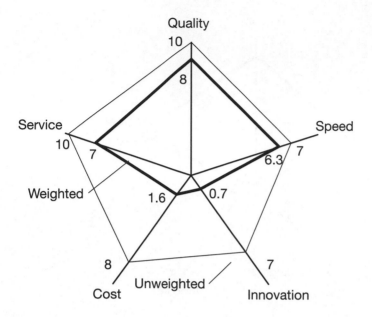

Figure 5-5 The Value Pentastar for UPS Ground

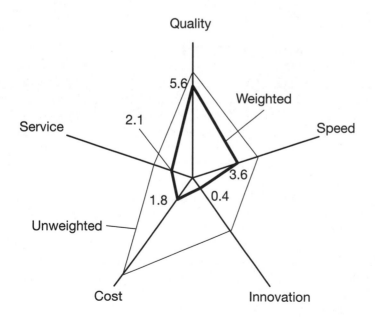

Figure 5-6 The Value Pentastar for USPS Priority Mail

Quality:
Very poor 1   2   3   4   5   6   7   8   9   **10** Best in class
10 Total Quality Rating × 8 Weighting Points = 80
Weighted Quality Rating divided by 10 = 8

Service:
Very poor 1   2   3   4   5   6   7   8   9   **10** Best in class
10 Total Service Rating × 7 Weighting Points = 70
Weighted Service Rating divided by 10 = 7

Cost:
Very poor 1   **2**   3   4   5   6   7   8   9   10 Best in class
2 Total Cost Rating × 2 Weighting Points = 4
Weighted Cost Rating divided by 10 = 0.4

Speed:
Very poor 1   2   3   4   5   6   7   8   9   **10** Best in class
10 Total Speed Rating × 9 Weighting Points = 90
Weighted Speed/Timeliness Rating divided by 10 = 9

Innovation:
Very poor 1   2   3   4   5   6   7   8   **9**   10 Best in class
9 Total Innovation Rating × 1 Weighting Points = 9
Weighted Innovation Rating divided by 10 = 0.9

Figure 5-7 Weighted Diagnostic Profile for Shape-shifting for FedEx

leverage of various aspects of value was such an eye opener; I asked if I could include it here, and he graciously agreed (Figure 5-11).

Consider for a moment a parallel between the hierarchy of needs described by Maslow, and the hierarchy of value attributes in a given situation. A pyramid like the one shown in Figure 5-11 could easily be imagined.

If we imagine any hypothetical situation, we can arbitrarily assign relative importance to the value attributes. In this one, I have set Quality as the foundation (base of the pyramid), and most important attribute, with Service next and Cost third in importance. Speed is fourth—relatively less important in this example and innovation is the least critical. But what if we misunderstood the relative importance, and we thought the order was different? Our diagram might look like Figure 5-12.

The mismatch in the relative hierarchy (importance) of value attributes is immediately and dramatically evident. The "pile" even looks "unstable." Such a misunderstanding could be devastating. The unweighted Shape of

---

Quality:
Very poor 1   2   3   4   5   6   7   8   9   **10** Best in class
10 Total Quality Rating × 8 Weighting Points = 80
Weighted Quality Rating divided by 10 = 8

Service:
Very poor 1   2   3   4   5   6   7   8   9   **10** Best in class
10 Total Service Rating × 7 Weighting Points = 70
Weighted Service Rating divided by 10 = 7

Cost:
Very poor 1   2   3   4   5   6   7   **8**   9   10 Best in class
8 Total Cost Rating × 2 Weighting Points = 16
Weighted Cost Rating divided by 10 = 1.6

Speed:
Very poor 1   2   3   4   5   6   **7**   8   9   10 Best in class
7 Total Speed Rating × 9 Weighting Points = 63
Weighted Speed Rating divided by 10 = 6.3

Innovation:
Very poor 1   2   3   4   5   6   **7**   8   9   10 Best in class
7 Total Innovation Rating × 1 Weighting Points = 7
Weighted Innovation Rating divided by 10 = 0.7

Figure 5-8 Weighted Diagnostic Profile for Shape-shifting for UPS Ground

Value diagram would only provide a part of this information, in the sense that it would provide comparative numerical values. A rigorous weighting such as that used in the earlier example combined with the Shape of Value would reveal the order of importance, but this visual approach is so compelling that it is a worthy complement to use while developing the numerically weighted Shape of Value diagrams. Remember, the mission is to find ways to gain a clear and accurate understanding of value from the customer's perspective and then match it.

The relative amount of mismatch is evident in the relative instability of the hierarchy (pyramidal pile). If we are way off on just one importance understanding, a real problem could be created.

Such a visually impactful method illustrates beyond any numerical approach how important it is to clearly understand the mental picture of value in the mind of the customer. While this hierarchical approach doesn't provide "numerical" relative weight importance, that can be accomplished with conventional weighting as illustrated previously. What this simple and

Quality:
Very poor 1 2 3 4 5 6 **7** 8 9 10 Best in class
7 Total Quality Rating × 8 Weighting Points = 56
Weighted Quality Rating divided by 10 = 5.6

Service:
Very poor 1 2 **3** 4 5 6 7 8 9 10 Best in class
3 Total Service Rating × 7 Weighting Points = 21
Weighted Service Rating divided by 10 = 2.1

Cost:
Very poor 1 2 3 4 5 6 7 8 **9** 10 Best in class
9 Total Cost Rating × 2 Weighting Points = 18
Weighted Cost Rating divided by 10 = 1.8

Speed:
Very poor 1 2 3 **4** 5 6 7 8 9 10 Best in class
4 Total Speed Rating × 9 Weighting Points = 36
Weighted Speed Rating divided by 10 = 3.6

Innovation:
Very poor 1 2 3 **4** 5 6 7 8 9 10 Best in class
4 Total Innovation Rating × 1 Weighting Points = 4
Weighted Innovation Rating divided by 10 = 0.4

Figure 5-9 Weighted Diagnostic Profile for Shape-shifting for USPS Priority Mail

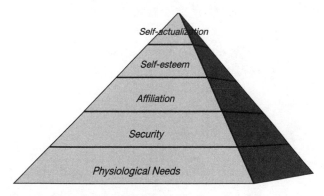

Figure 5-10 Maslow's Hierarchy of Needs

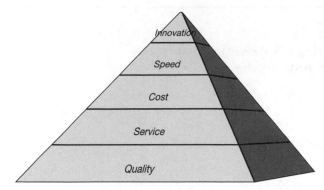

Figure 5.11 Swartz's Hierarchy of Value (value attributes are listed in arbitrary order for this illustration)

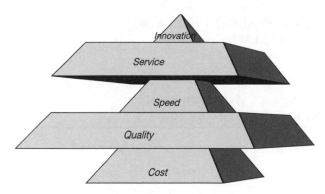

Figure 5.12 An Unstable Hierarchy of Value Attributes

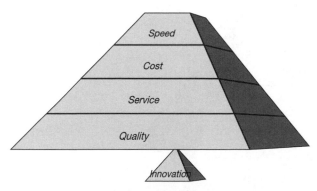

Figure 5.13 An Incorrect Hierarchy of Value Attributes

wonderful graphical approach does is to provide a quick, easy way to rank and agree on the relative importance from 1–5.

Note: This approach would handle even more than five "attributes" if there were more factors and levels to the triangle—but that would become undesirably complex, like large, multiple-factor "radar chart diagrams do—no clearly defined shape emerges! They become "cluttergrams" not shape diagrams!

6.

The Best Shape-Shift Faster

Thriving in the face of an unprecedented rate of change is the biggest challenge (of the next 25 years). . . . So you've got to turn your company from this internal bureaucracy outward to a customer focus. The companies that do it best will win.
—Arno Penzias, vice president, Research,
Lucent Technologies

MAKE HASTE PRUDENTLY, BUT MOVE!

Until now I have focused only on the need for change, and defined some approaches to help identify the nature of that change—what to change and how. Now it is time to address another critical issue: the speed of the change. This time frame will vary considerably from company to company and industry to industry, but one point is certain: faster is better. Changes in the value attributes can be "artificially" supported for a while with no change in the basic shape of the business. Although artificial changes can be supported by spending money and extra effort, this is not the way to make a change that lasts. Temporarily using resources can work and making a series of smaller shifts can throw competitors off balance. But there must be a lasting shift in some of the dimensions of the shape of the business for the changes in the shape of value attributes to stand the test of time and adversity. Also, there must be a clear plan and destination shape at the outset, even though the ultimate destination will be constantly shifting. The "first rule of wing-walking" is a good one to remember here: "Never let go of what you have a hold on until you have a hold on something else!" Then get going, because the competition is shape-shifting, and needs of customers are changing. Getting to the future first is only successful if it is with the right shape of value.

81

Cyberspace Shape-Shifting Opportunities

The explosive growth of the Internet and the World Wide Web has presented both many shape-shift opportunities and an equal number of risks and the necessity of rapid shifts has reached a new extreme. One comment by Marc Andreessen, co-founder of Netscape, emphasizes the cyberspace trend: "Better fast and wrong than slow and right!" Maybe so, but when things go wrong on a large scale and at a high rate of speed, entire companies can be greatly damaged or even cease to exist.

A diagram of the interrelationships between Internet specialist Netscape, service providers America Online and Compuserve, software provider Microsoft, and software/workstation provider Sun Microsystems looks a lot more like a spider's web than the World Wide Web. Not only are the interrelationships complex, but the diagram requires almost daily revision to track the dynamic shifting of positions. All of these companies and many others are trying to keep their options open as to which way they may need to shape-shift. To begin this discussion, we'll focus on one of the most dramatic recent shape-shift cases involving Microsoft and its position relative to the Internet. This will be followed by a series of diverse cases where shape-shifting was either done correctly or too little, too late.

Microsoft Shifted to "Extend and Embrace" the Internet

The most dramatic example of a company deciding to shape-shift and then making the shift fast and powerfully is Microsoft's embracing the Internet. Economist/scientist Brian Arthur, of the Santa Fe Institute, put it well when he described Microsoft cofounder and chairman Bill Gates this way: "Bill Gates is not so much a wizard of technology as a wizard of precognition, of *discerning the shape of the next game*." (My emphasis.)

For the past 10 years, dating back to the establishment of DOS as the de-facto operating system standard for the PC, and progressing through the development of Apple-like Windows software, Microsoft's dominance in PC operating systems and software has been awesome. But authorities such as author George Gilder and Netscape wunderkind Marc Andreessen warned that Microsoft's most important products could become obsolete in the face of Internet and World Wide Web technology.

There are dozens of accounts of Gates' "Pearl Harbor Day" (December 7, 1995) decision to shift immense resources to catch up in this field with the release of Microsoft's Internet Explorer and other applications. After the near disastrous failure of the first version of the Microsoft Network, the pressure was on. Until this point, Gates and Microsoft had been totally focused on Windows products—specifically, Windows 95 and Windows NT. While internally, Microsoft employees were championing the need to shift more attention to the Internet, Gates remained adamantly committed to the next-generation desktop and client/server computer products. Only he knows what finally triggered his realization of the need to shape-shift the company's resources to Internet products. Once decided, however, Microsoft put its formidable economic and intellectual power behind the effort to catch Netscape, at least in technology if not in market share.

Netscape's Navigator, introduced barely a year earlier, had already captured the lion's share of the browser market—estimated at 80 percent or more. Online services Compuserve and America Online were already feeling pressure to abandon their membership and switch to the World Wide Web with Netscape, especially since both were somewhat slow coming up with effective Internet access and browsers for their customers. Perhaps it was the fact that nearly everyone who had been impacted by Microsoft's rise to power in the desktop computer field over the past few years was joining forces against them. Apple, IBM, and Hewlett-Packard among the big-name computer makers, combined with Oracle and Sun Microsystems, creator of the revolutionary Java programming language, to use browsers and the World Wide Web to create a formidable threat to Microsoft's desktop dominance.

After announcing the plan to "extend and embrace" the Internet, Gates shifted at least 500 programmers and committed a reported 20 percent or more of Microsoft's R&D budget to the catch-up effort. Additional resources were devoted to the creation of content for the Internet, and to forming an alliance with TV giant NBC on MSNBC, a cable news channel, in hopes of gaining access to new content for the Internet. Meanwhile, Gates' worst fears about Internet and World Wide Web development began to materialize. Lotus, acquired earlier by IBM, primarily for Notes groupware, had adapted its offering to the Internet in response to the growth of corporate intranets. Corporate intranets using Netscape's newest products were threatening Microsoft's dominance of the desktop market.

While the Internet and Web grew exponentially, Microsoft, preoccupied with the release of Windows 95 and its integration with Windows NT, had no immediate answers. Insiders believed that in 1995 Gates was only moderately aware of the powerful potential of the latest applications of the Internet. Sun's development of Java signaled the first truly effective means for rendering PC-resident application software unnecessary. It was probably this breakthrough that brought Gates to the shape-shifting decision point. The groups within Microsoft that had been arguing (unsuccessfully since early 1994) that Microsoft should take a more aggressive stance on the Internet and Netscape finally saw their opening. Although internal struggles at Microsoft continued during 1994 and 1995, it was not until December 7, 1995, that Gates announced his decision to put Microsoft's full resources behind a major shape-shift toward Internet technology.

Microsoft did not have to change its culture or processes as much as its structure and relationships. The Internet Platform & Tools Division was created in February 1996, and within six months, it had grown to 2,500 employees. Microsoft Network was reformed, and provided as a preinstalled feature of Windows 95. Relationships were formed with Spyglass, America Online, and Sun (as a licensee of Java). Microsoft purchased stakes in UUNET Technologies, an Internet service provider; Vermeer Technologies, the maker of FrontPage, a tool for creating and managing Web documents; Colusa Software, maker of Omniware, which is used to make object-oriented programming for the Internet; eShop Inc., a leader in Internet commerce software; and Electric Gravity, whose Internet Gaming Zone was to be linked to Microsoft Network. These moves all took place in less than seven months! Talk about a rapid, full-commitment shape-shift. A 20,000-employee, $8-billion industry leader took an abrupt left turn while on top of an industry. For a full list of Microsoft's 1996 buying binge, see Figure 6-1.

In spite of this incredible list of acquisitions and investments, Microsoft is still piling up cash, with which they can fund the infrastructure to accelerate future shape-shifts. Most companies could never be so profligate in their use of capital; they must be much more focused in choosing the markets and investments to target, although in this case Microsoft focused on the Internet and its associated infotainment aspects.

January 16: Vermeer Technologies: Maker of FrontPage, a tool for creating and managing Web documents

February 1: Black Entertainment Television: Interactive entertainment and information aimed at the African-American viewer

March 12: Colusa: Object-oriented programming language for the Internet

March 12: Aspect Engineering: Tools and technologies for the Internet

April 8: aha!: Developer of software for mobile computers

April 15: EXOS: Developer of software for game control devices

June 11: eShop: Internet commerce software maker

June 17: Electric Gravity: Creator of Internet Gaming Zone

June 25: Investment in ENTEX Information Services: Help desk contractor

September 9: Investment in Single-Trac Entertainment: Game developer

September 30: Purchased a minority stake in WebTV: Browsing system

October 28: Purchased a stake in VDOnet: Software for compressing voice and video over the Internet

November 20: Purchased ResNova Software: Developer of Macintosh Internet technology

December 10: Purchased NetCarta: Maker of WebMapper, Web site management tool

Figure 6-1 Microsoft's 1996 Buying Binge

Needless to say, Microsoft has not abandoned PC and network software. It is integrating its cash cow, desktop software, with the hottest, fastest-growing new star—Internet products. Windows NT promises to be a more important product than any of the other Windows products in this new Internet-client/server environment. This is what shape-shifting is all about.

Brian Arthur sums it up this way:

You can be smart. You can be cunning. You can position. You can observe. But when the games themselves are not even fully defined, you cannot optimize. What you can do is adapt. Adaptation, in the proactive sense, means watching for the next wave that is coming, figuring out what shape it will take, *and positioning the company to take advantage of it. Adaptation is what drives increasing-returns businesses, not optimization* (my emphasis).

Microsoft not only adapted, it did it fast! It beat Netscape to market with the 3.0 release of Microsoft Explorer on August 13, 1996, and immediately began giving it away—a marketing approach Netscape had used to great advantage with its earlier browsers. On the shape of value attribute list, Microsoft had concluded that price and cost were not significant attributes. Rather, speed, service, and innovation were the ways to the heart of the market.

In a *Time* magazine article written by Joshua Cooper Ramo in September 1996, Gates was quoted as saying, "I don't think you'd be interviewing me on this topic if we were any less nimble. You'd be writing our epitaph." The article ran behind a cover picture of Gates with the headline "Whose Web Will It Be? and subtitled, "He conquered the computer world. Now he wants the Internet. If Microsoft overwhelms Netscape, Bill Gates could rule the Information Age." See Figure 6-2 for the value pentastar for these two companies.

There is, however, one issue that makes this shape-shift model less than perfect. Gates was late starting, and only because he could "throw" people, intelligence, and money at the effort in overwhelming quantities could Microsoft succeed. Microsoft may have been able to shape-shift to catch Netscape, because its resources are so overwhelmingly dominant, (Microsoft's R&D budget alone dwarfs Netscape's total revenue), but it is less certain that they can continue to "outspend" the competition in the long run, especially if strong alliances form between IBM, Sun, Apple, Oracle, and others. If Microsoft's competitors (or the Justice Department) do not successfully "gang up" on Microsoft, then their resources may enable them to continue to roll over all opposition! Only a concerted group effort or an innovative breakthrough (such as Sun's Java programming language and system) could overcome such a dominant yet nimble market leadership. But recent

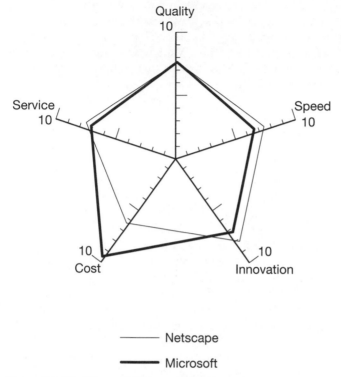

Figure 6-2 **The Microsoft-Netscape Value Pentastar**

agreements between IBM, Sun, Oracle, and Netscape to endorse common object technology for corporate networks pose a new threat to Microsoft's hold on the desktop market.

Java is fast becoming the enabler for a new "open system" intranet/browser-based computing platform. Another shape-shift may be facing Microsoft, and fast, if Java's success continues and grows. Sun's Scott McNealy and Oracle software's CEO Larry Ellison are both champions of the Net Computer, a stripped-down machine that feeds off the Java capabilities and costs about one-quarter to one-half of a current full-function PC. The irony of this shape-shift is that PCs could become dramatically lower in price if the hardware and software producers (heavily influenced by Microsoft and chipmaker Intel) were not artificially holding prices up by adding speed, software, and functionality. The average home user uses less than 10 percent of the capability of a PC. The corporate user may use a little more, but the two to three times cost premium for corporate MIS departments to support networks of full-function PCs compared to simpler Net computers may actually hasten the success of the Net computer in that market.

Another more subtle, but just as profound, "shift" is occurring in Microsoft's position on the Net computer (NC). After taking the stalling tactic that such simpler PCs would be unlikely to catch on, Microsoft is now accelerating their involvement in exactly this type of technology. Like race cars drafting behind a leader only to use the aerodynamic advantage to pull out and pass the other car, Microsoft first denies the viability of such new directions (thus dissuading the unconvinced or less confident from supporting the newer technology) only to later shift themselves into position to not only support the new technology, but to claim leadership.

Microsoft has become a master at "misdirection." Their "denigrate-incorporate-dominate" strategy is proving tremendously successful when backed with their huge market base, technological, and financial resources. Unless Sun can accelerate the use of Java, or enlist the support of another behemoth like IBM to slow Microsoft's progress, another successful shape-shift will go into Microsoft's win column.

In 1997, Microsoft continued its march toward extending and embracing what appear to be competing technologies with acquisitions such as WebTV, a $1 billion investment in Comcast, a leading cable TV company, and its shocking investment in Apple Computer. The simple fact that such a technology application has Microsoft's huge resource base behind it shifts it to a much higher competitve level. When this is combined with ownership positions in MSNBC and cable-related companies, the message is simple—get ready for another shape-shift into easy-to-use video entertainment for the home market.

Microsoft, like the behemoths of the past, IBM, Sears, and GM, is always in danger of becoming complacent because the game has been played according to its rules for so long that it overlooked the customers—who actually write the rules. I must emphasize the need for changing the dimensions of the shape of the business to enable truly effective and successful shifts in the shape of value, which is what Microsoft did.

The application of the shape of value diagram to the Microsoft versus Netscape situation is far from simple. Can a smaller, nimbler opponent survive the onslaught of an industry behemoth, even with the help of others? Can Microsoft maneuver Java to become a semiproprietary piece of its desktop, or will Java enable a new Microsoft-independent desktop-browser combination. Only time will tell!

Speed Versus Size and Strength

A rapidly developing technological environment is one in which helping the customers decide what constitutes best value may offer a real advantage in determining the outcome. It is here that partnerships with customers (and other competitors who share a common foe) give a significant competitive edge. Simply put, companies that can rapidly align their shape to match that of their customers will succeed. Microsoft, to return to that example, should be concerned about a competitor that is faster and more innovative in a market that has brought success to companies with those attributes. In contrast Netscape should be very concerned about Microsoft's major size and resource advantages.

In the words of Peter Drucker, "the best way to predict the future is to create it." That is certainly what Bill Gates is trying to do. He is taking control of the shape of the business and determining how it can create and deliver the shape of value most desired by customers. Doing it again and again are the next steps. But, before proceeding to a deeper discussion of exactly what to do and how, let's consider several diverse examples of successful shape-shifting, along with a few examples of problems experienced by companies that did it wrong.

Making the Right Choices

Apple and IBM partnered with each other and several software companies, and a large semiconductor/cellular telecommunications company (Motorola) to develop a new chip, operating system, and platform. How can a previously unimaginable partnership shift the shape of several major business enterprises? This is becoming commonplace! It often sounds good, but it often fails because the shapes of the partnering companies are too different. Although the PowerPC chip was successfully developed by Motorola, the joint Apple and IBM attempt to create a cross-platform design to use it was a failure. Apple was entrepreneurial and creative but undisciplined, whereas IBM was very structured and organized but bureaucratic. It is no surprise that they had trouble working together. The principles of forming partnerships caution about this kind of classic "misfit."

When the shift can occur within a single company's shape, the chances of success are greatly improved. Motorola's history reveals a dramatic shape-shift over the past two decades, when it decided to stop producing volume consumer electronics and dedicate itself to the new semiconductor and communications markets. This example is widely documented, but it is worth repeating because the retrospective view makes it so clear. Motorola created markets in which they were the first, and thus, the dominant participant. It defined whole new shapes of value, and used its strengths to model them. Only after these markets had begun to mature did Motorola begin to encounter stiff competition.

Hewlett-Packard made a similar but less dramatic shift, in addition to several smaller ones. It evolved from an "instrument maker" to a computer company, and then to the world's leading producer of printers, especially for the personal computer user. HP management took note of the shape-shift into large-scale use of personal computers and acted with great speed to design and build a line of printers that exceeded the value of all competitive manufacturers. It is now considered the "benchmark," nevertheless, it must consider its next shift. It has already reemphasized and reentered the portable and desktop PC business after a hiatus of several years. Although it may be a "late entry," it may also have avoided the period of turmoil and competitive shake-out. If HP can succeed in adding digital photograph printing to their already strong position, they will have made yet another good choice of a shape for their business.

Too Slow Often Means Too Late

For this case study, I return to my experience at Huffy Bicycles. This is the study of our relative competitive competency in the various aspects of bike manufacturing in the early 1980s. At that time, it became essential to "benchmark" ourselves against the best in the world in all aspects of production. In this way, we could decide where to shift our shape or where to invest (insource) and where to divest (outsource) the production operations. This became a test of our shape of success, and it altered our future direction for five to seven years—at which point another shape-shift became necessary. By 1988, the dollar had weakened, and mid-1980s competition from Taiwan and Korea no longer loomed quite so large. Instead, the threat was lower-cost domestic producers. To compete effectively, we decided to utilize our brand name in combination with the benefits of mass customization. This permitted us to leverage the brand name everywhere, yet avoided head-to-head competition with our own products. This shape-shift and concurrent differentiation strategy was effective for several more years, until the combination of a recession and another change in cost competition dictated yet another shape-shift.

At the time I left Huffy, in 1992, the lowest-cost producer in the United States was Roadmaster, a company whose quality had been suspect and whose organization had been slow to develop. As it quality improved, the competitive arena began to change again. At the same time, China began to emerge as a formidable competitor to the U.S. bike market with very low prices and a huge capacity potential. It was time for another shape-shift if Huffy was to remain competitive. Unfortunately, Huffy failed to shift fast enough or in the right ways to maintain its market share and profitability. Failures of this sort are commen when the management group that led a company to a preeminent position leaves and a new group assumes control. A shift in the shape of the business occurs to match the views and wishes of the new management. And whether it is a change in leadership or a difference in shape (strategy or competence) that causes the problem is never clear until after the fact. One thing is clear, however, shifting the shape of a business to meet new competitive conditions is a prerequisite for continued success. The questions remain: How? When? How fast?

Shape-Shifting Before You Have To

Business leaders realize that good execution is good strategy, and vice versa. As a result, companies shape-shift in diverse ways. Take the case of Tenneco Packaging. The Counce mill is the largest of Tenneco's four container board mills. This 1600-acre facility, built in 1961, is located on the Tennessee River, east of Memphis. After almost 30 years of operation, in 1990, this unionized paper mill made a decision to reject its longstanding autocratic management style in favor of an entirely new culture. Mind you, Tenneco was not failing at the time, but the shift led to a surge of improvement in every aspect of the business. Probably the change would have been necessary eventually any-way, but doing so ahead of trouble was a savvy move. To do less would have meant losing ground to competitors. Today, in its unionized facility, 90 per-cent of the workforce participates in empowered teams. Reject rates have dropped by almost one-half, as has scrap. Employees receive an average of seven and a half days of annual training, and are rewarded for productivity improvement via a gainsharing program. Suppliers have been reduced in number, but upgraded in quality; and customer confidence ratings have climbed by 30 percent. Predictive and preventative maintenance have cut machine downtime in half, and raised uptime to over 95 percent. Safety has improved significantly. Could all this have been done without a cultural shape-shift? Maybe, but it is highly unlikely. Incremental change and contin-uous improvement is valuable and necessary.

Milwaukee Electric Tool Shifted Before It Was Broke

Consider the story of Milwaukee Electric Tool Company (METCO). METCO opened its first out-of-state plant in Jackson, Mississippi, in 1973. The com-pany grew relatively successfully through the 1980s using "conventional pro-duction methods," essentially applying the "if it ain't broke, don't fix it" adage.

But when Harry Peterson took over at Jackson in 1990 and considered the new plant planned for Koscuisko, Mississippi, he and vice president of Manufacturing Jerry McCormack decided to do just that—"fix it before it broke." They saw conditions that convinced them to shift the shape to a new paradigm of behavior in manufacturing management, incuding Japanese-based principles of JIT, Kaizen (continuous improvement), and cellular man-ufacturing, which had been in use for several years, and were a well-tested set of solutions. They decided that self-directed teams were the best for implementing these new processes and establishing a new culture. METCO committed to 40 hours (one full week per employee) of training each year. And a pay-for-knowledge compensation system was initiated for the highly motivated workforce. PCs were installed on the production floor to make information easy to access and manipulate.

Consequently, productivity, quality, and sales all climbed rapidly. Lead times dropped from five months to two days! Customer order fill rates improved from 70 percent to 98 percent. And, 100 percent of the workforce participated in the self-directed team efforts, and employee-to-supervisor ratios went from 18:1 to 50:1. They definitely "fixed it before it broke."

Shape-Shift for the Long Term

Under Roger Smith, GM tried to change its corporate shape, but not the shape of their value-creating units (I will describe this term in detail later), by simply diversifying with the purchase of Electronic Data System (EDS), and Hughes Electronics. In doing so it surrendered massive portions of its once dominant auto market share to Japanese manufacturers and U.S. producers Ford and Chrysler (both of whom had been on the precipice of bankruptcy before realizing they had to shape-shift too!). GM had once defined the shape of the industry, and dominated it so completely that to change was viewed as almost heretical. Fearing that it could not change the old shape or structure, it decided to start fresh with Saturn. Saturn was the only new growth it permitted, and it has been hugely successful (although not profitable until 1996). By going with Saturn, GM's dinosaur-like bureaucracy took its shot at shape-shifting. The goal was a car that could compete favorably with the best Japan had to offer. The shape was all new, one based on major cultural, relationship, and process shifts, from a high-involvement workforce in Spring Hill, Tennessee, to the customer-friendly dealer network. Even the new car's dent-resistant plastic body panels sold well when placed on a derivative body design reminiscent of the older-generation midsize platform styling.

The Saturn factory partnered with the United Auto Workers (UAW) and GM to organize teams and change the relationship between the union and the management. The dealer network formed customer relationships that were free of the traditional hassles and haggles of car buying, and in doing so created a fiercely loyal and highly satisfied customer base. The plant became a showcase for high-performance productivity.

However, more recently, the new shape started to shift back toward the old one. As GM tried to expand Saturn's success to other car lines and plants, the old practices and work rule issues with the UAW resurfaced. Ironically, this shining experiment of all GM's profligate spending in the 1980s may yet fall prey to union-management disputes that have marred the GM-UAW relationship over the decades. The point is, a single shape-shift, no matter how successful is no guarantee of continued success or adequate return on the investment.

Shift, But Don't Lose Sight of the Customer

Rapid change brings with it instability and even more rapid change. Life cycles of many products drop from years to months and months to weeks. Retail merchants drive the cycle faster and faster, trying to gain a competitive advantage. Les Wexner and Limited Stores is a prime example of this cycle time reduction. The Limited Stores computer-based inventory and sales-tracking systems combined with nimble Pacific Rim suppliers and a fleet of Boeing 747s enabled the retailer to distribute its fashion assortment in hundreds of stores in a matter of weeks. Suppliers could turn out Limited's "invented brands" like Forenza and Outback Red in a fraction of the time of other designers, and have them in retail stores practically overnight.

Unfortunately, The Limited wasn't paying attention to its customers. After years of record growth and profitability, its most loyal supporters did an annoying and disruptive thing—they got older, and their tastes and sizes changed. At the same time, the new younger buyers shifted their tastes to higher value, lower cost, more basic styling—like that offered by Gap. Gap, too, was able to replenish its stock very quickly, but from more conventional domestic distribution centers, at lower cost.

The speed advantage that The Limited had built became less critical, and eventually was replaced by the dominant attribute of low cost. The Limited attempted to adapt to the style (innovation) shift by modifying its Limited Express stores, which were the trendy, youth-oriented outlets to more traditional products, and by altering the merchandise in the original Limited Stores to more conservative fashions. Unfortunately, the effect of these changes was to confuse the clientele of both stores. When confused, consumers simply do not buy; they look elsewhere. "Elsewhere" was Gap!

The Limited is still a large, viable retailer. The point is, they had to learn a painful lesson by not understanding the mix of attributes that would make up the their customers' next shape of value. Wexner now has created a complete assortment of stores, which leverage both fashion (speed) and operating costs (cost) while freeing them to pursue the appropriate merchandise for the right customer (innovation/service). It has survived, but is a wiser, humbler, and more diverse company as a result.

As a footnote, Gap is now capitalizing on its own design shop to create trends that they plan to be the first to capitalize on. It has also shifted a portion of business downscale to Old Navy stores so it is not tempted to cut quality in Gap stores. By doing this, it is mimicking and improving some of The Limited's earlier actions, but still trying to match the shape of value in the consumers' minds, an aggressive but wise strategy!

Serial Shape-Shifting

Of the trio of department and catalog giants Sears, Roebuck, Montgomery Ward, and JCPenney, the last was the first to realize that it must reshape. In a dramatic move, it dropped many durable goods product lines and redefined itself as a fashion apparel and home products company, selling good, stylish products at moderate prices. This worked for a while, but Penney is once again struggling in the new high- or low-cost versus innovation/service market. ("High or low" here means consumers are prone to seek the highest prestige brand/style or service or the lowest-cost items, shirking the middle as offering no desirable "shape of value" combination.)

Montgomery Ward Montgomery Ward, under the leadership of Bernard Brennan (younger brother of Sears Chairman Edward Brennan, whom you'll meet shortly) redefined itself in the mid-1980s as a "value-driven specialty retailer," offering a wide range of products under the same roof (literally in the old Wards stores), but in a series of specialty shop formats. This strategy had merit because specialty retailers consistently earn better returns than their general merchandise counterparts. Brennan believed that these specialty shops could also be viable as freestanding stores. But after modest success with Electric Avenue, a freestanding electronics and appliance specialty store, the concept stalled. Part of the problem was in weak execution and at least in part was due to the "high or low" consumer selection. Brennan's inability to retain senior executives caused continual turmoil in the management organization with the resultant lack of continuity and erratic execution. Wards dramatically shifted the shape of its stores, but perhaps it did not adequately shift the shape of the business (in this case, corporate behaviors), to support that new shape. At this point, Wards is faltering and seeking a new shape for its future, with new leadership in the person of former Toys 'R' Us executive Roger Goddu. After filing Chapter 11, their future shape and survival is in doubt. Even well-conceived shape-shifts require sound execution and a foundation of purpose.

Sears Roebuck Over several decades leading up to the 1990s, Sears grew to be America's largest retailer by offering broad assortments of popular priced products of all kindds. The Sears catalog and retail stores were institutions of choice for shoppers of all types. Then, in the 1970s and 1980s discount stores like Kmart and Wal-Mart began eroding Sears' base business by offering low prices at no-frill stores in convenient locations. Sears stuck to its old ways and its customers simply quit shopping there in huge numbers.

Change was needed, but Sears, as the "biggest tree" in the old forest, was the slowest to change. Only after Chairman Ed Brennan took many missteps was he willing to turn over the management to former Saks executive Arthur Martinez. Then in the mid-'90s, Sears recovery and shape-shifting really began. While currently, Sears stores are posting admirable comparable store results, its shift is far from over, and Martinez admits it. Its stores still occupy the dominant position in many of the retail malls in America but this may not be the ideal location in an overmalled and overretailed country. Strip malls are creating new forms of speed and service-based advantages, playing to the time-starved consumer. Sears is now attempting a shift similar to the one Wards tried, using smaller-format specialty stores to capitalize on the strip malling of America. The choice of their strongest product brand— Craftsman— is a wise one. Creating specialty hardware stores alone is not the solution to Sears' needs for the future, but Martinez likens it to GM's Saturn strategy. Sears also plans to capitalize on other strong brands like Kenmore appliances and DieHard batteries, taking advantage of strong, embedded consumer relationships. A new dimension of Sears's current shape-shift is to build on their large service business. In this thrust, their effort differs from both Penney's and Wards' past tries. Martinez sums it up very well, in a recent *Fortune* article by Patricia Sellen, when he related that two years ago, he had no idea that small stores and service would become Sears' new growth vehicles. His change of directions doesn't concern him, as he states "A hallmark of great companies is an ability to recognize the game has changed and to adapt." Whether Sears can change its corporate shape to accommodate this shift rapidly and profitably enough remains to be seen. At least Sears, under Martinez's leadership, understands that only in continuous change can it find real competitive advantage.

Kmart and Wal-Mart Kmart, which grew to be the largest discounter in the United States in less than 25 years, also chose to change its corporate shape by diversifying into specialty retailing. Chairman and CEO Joe Antonini led this strategy. His idea of diversifying was not a bad one, but it ran into a roadblock: complexity without flexibility in the core business. Because of inattention to the shape of the basic business, Wal-Mart overtook Kmart in less than 15 years, and today dominates the discount retail field. Kmart's specialty stores generally performed better, but there was no corporate synergy in their shape because they operated independently. To bring them into the Kmart corporate fold would have changed their corporate structure and culture, reduced their flexibility and put them at a competitive disadvantage. To leave them alone worked best, but there were not enough financial resources to keep Wal-Mart at bay in the core discount field. Kmart did the only thing it could: It let its offspring go on their own, and used the proceeds from the sale to attempt to save the "big tree." Only time will tell whether Kmart, one of the pioneers in discount retailing, can find a way to shift its Shape to compete successfully in the future.

Shape-Shifting May Mean Cutting

In order to reinforce the need to shape-shift, and to lead into the next section, it is necessary to consider how to know when to make a radical change. Sometimes the only solution is to "cut down the big, old tree." Consider Promus Corporation, a company that shape-shifted radically in the 1980s. Promus was sort of a conglomeration of unrelated companies. Holiday Inn Hotels was its "big tree"; its Hampton Inns chain was just getting started. The company also owned shipping and transportation companies, all of which were marginally profitable and offered no real synergy.

Thus, it was an easy decision to sell off the marginal companies. The really courageous and far-reaching step led by Chairman and CEO Mike Rose was to "cut down the big tree so the new growth could survive and flourish, and then find a new forest." Promus decided to sell Holiday Inns. The properties were old, some of the locations were no longer prime, and their image was as tarnished as the facilities. In contrast, Hampton Inns were new, occupied better locations, and catered to a new generation of value-conscious travelers with clean, efficient rooms, and "free" continental breakfasts. This was the young part of the forest, and it grew rapidly. Promus branched into a hotel-based business that was a much more profitable (albeit more risky)—casinos. Promus bought Harrah's, a leading Nevada hotel/casino chain and began to expand. The parent company has spun off Harrah's; and, Harrah's is having its own problems due to overexpansion and some miscues. This story is, like all of them, still unfolding.

SET TARGETS WITH TIME FRAMES

Earlier, I commented on the importance of defining a time frame and a destination. A useful time-based tool is to plot a series of shape of value diagrams, to be viewed as "snapshots" taken while the shift progresses. Doing a shape of value diagram for the present and the destination is, of course, essential. And, unless the changes can be made in a fairly short time frame (a few months), doing intermediate diagrams is also valuable. As I've said repeatedly, the customer's future perceptions about value are of critical importance. These are actually the desired target, not those based on past impressions, which are so much easier to analyze.

Intermediate shapes of value also become the vehicle for tracking the changes required in the shape of the business. Even though the destination will continuously shift, that should not deter getting underway or tracking the progress against defined milestones. The key is to adjust, adapt, evolve, and keep moving, always checking to see where you are (in a shape of value context) and reconfirming where you are going.

THE SHIFT THAT CUTS BOTH WAYS

Let us continue exploring the connection between shape-shifting and value. Only if we are mentally prepared to shift our shape can we do so rapidly enough to create the value required to survive and prosper during organizational and business upheaval.

As companies worldwide struggle to improve productivity, U.S.-based companies are holding their own. However, they are seeing the reverse edge of productivity improvement. Because it takes fewer and fewer people to produce goods and services, corporate fat had to be trimmed. The term "lean and mean" takes on a literal meaning. Downsizing has evolved to rightsizing and restructuring to reengineering. The industrial fabric of the country has been cut (and often ripped) apart and is being pieced together into an entirely different shape. This is *not* what I mean by shape-shifting.

Peter Drucker, arguably the most brilliant management thinker of the past three decades, reminded us that the changes in global competition had come about because of the ability to export not only technology, but also managerial know-how. U.S. businesses had to adapt to not being the leading source for most of the world's goods. The shape of the competitive playing field had shifted and would never be the same.

Industrial powers like General Motors, Caterpillar, and Xerox saw their once huge, world-dominant positions deteriorate. IBM got caught, struggled mightily, and is only now recovering. Entire industries (like consumer electronics) "emigrated" to take advantage of low-cost labor, excellent technology, and rapid product innovation and introduction. Still other companies sought government intervention and demanded for a national "industrial policy."

Sometimes a shift can lead an industry or company away from what made it successful in the first place. When People's Express decided to become more than a discount, bare-bones airline, its decline began. The wholesale or warehouse club industry in the United States, now dominated by Price-Costco, Sam's (part of Wal-Mart), and to a lesser extent B.J.'s, is an industry that almost lost its bearings by shifting away from its core wholesale customers and high-volume, low-variety principles. With change comes opportunity—and risk. That is why understanding the customers' value is so critical to choosing the right shape.

Only Shape-Shifters Can Capitalize On Change

Companies like Xerox rediscovered much of its lost excellence, but never recovered all of its market position from Canon, Ricoh, and others! Many U.S. companies changed forever. International Harvester, once synonymous with heavy farm equipment and large trucks, mutated into pieces, changed names, and was digested by competitors and scavengers. Proud names of the past like RCA, Admiral, Frigidaire, Philco and others became just "brands" in a stable of larger (and mostly foreign-owned) appliance producers. Service- and information-based industries sprouted, grew like weeds after a spring rain, and became larger than former manufacturing behemoths. Chips of silicon became more powerful and influential than the largest beams of steel— and far more profitable.

What kept those that survived and prospered from failing with the masses? What they did, above all else, was to look at their enterprise as a whole, not an accumulation of parts. They rapidly and continuously shape-shifted the skills and competencies they had into a competitive, dynamic enterprise. Motorola shifted from the maturing, low-profit business of consumer electronics of the 1970s to the new high-potential fields of communications and semiconductor electronics of the 1990s and beyond. Kodak struggled with a maturing film and camera business (and an ill-fated venture into the drug business) before realizing the need to reestablish its position as a leader in imaging (and not just on traditional film). That delay in shape-shifting is still haunting the film giant.

WHY COMPANIES FAIL

In a *Fortune* magazine cover story in late 1994 titled "Why Companies Fail," author Kenneth Labich identifies six big mistakes that lead to failures:

1. *Identity Crisis.* The failure to understand their own business and ask the right questions about what is core to their business.

2. *Caution: Failures of Vision.* Too many companies are content to prepare only for the likely snags, rather than stretching their imagination to find unexpected threats and successes.

3. *The Big Squeeze.* The pressure of excessive debt load brought on by over-optimism, too-aggressive leverage—or simply greed!

4. *The Glue Sticks and Sticks.* Trying to use old, previously successful strategies and tactics in a new, different, and more competitive environment.

5. *Anybody Out There?* Failure to stay close to and listen effectively to the customer.

6. *Enemies Within.* Cynicism, resentment, and hostilities within the workforce when management says one thing and does something else.

Four of the six items in this list have to do with what I call the shape of the business relative to what customers value and competition offers as alternatives. So if four of the six reasons for failure are related to or caused by the wrong "shape," it seems only logical that learning about shifting that shape is important.

PART TWO

What?

AN INVASION OF ARMIES CAN BE RESISTED, BUT NOT AN IDEA WHOSE
TIME HAS COME.
—Victor Hugo

7.

What Is Value ?

Your competition is coming up with new products as if they lived in their customers' minds.
—Hewlett-Packard advertisement

THE ESSENCE OF SHAPE-SHIFTING

Wouldn't it be nice if you and your company could come up with products as if you lived in your customers' minds? Years ago, a former associate taught me a simple little rhyme about marketing and selling that I have never forgotten: "If you want to sell what John Smith buys, see John Smith through John Smith's eyes." What a powerful thought. If we could see through our customers' eyes and live in their minds, we could better create and deliver what they want.

Like the shape-shifters on *Star Trek*, successful companies will shift their shape to match the needs of today's revolutionary global marketplace. The companies that do not will fall behind or fail. Businesses must learn to be shape-shifters, altering their structure and processes around or from their core competencies and capabilities to respond to customers, to serve new masters, and to capture new markets fast and effectively. Shape-shifters must also continuously reshape their internal culture and external relationships with employees, suppliers, and customers into more powerful partnerships. Maintaining a strong sense of purpose is the guiding force, and the shape of value keeps them moving in the direction in which they must go.

As I have stated, to start the shape-shifting process, it is necessary to discover the "right" shape of value to serve your target customers and markets. It is also necessary to acknowledge what it is your business and organization is good at and what it is not good at doing. Only if the shape of the business is suitable for creating and delivering the desired shape of value can success be realized. Learning to describe these findings clearly and succinctly is important if the changes are to be communicated and understood clearly. Later chapters provide some insights and new techniques to help in this undertaking.

SATISFYING A VALUE-CONSCIOUS PUBLIC

Wally Abbott, retired senior vice president of Procter & Gamble, made an astute observation on today's customers when he said, "[Today], we probably have the most value-conscious public [ever] in America." But what does "value" really mean? And is the definition in the mind of your customer the same as yours? How can you know?

Value is perhaps one of the most useful but also most elusive words in the business vocabulary because its meaning is so subjective; we all have different answers when asked what value means to us. But as business people, unless the image of value in the mind of our desired customer or market matches the one in our own mind pretty closely, we will neither be able to create nor deliver the right "best value." There are many different "official" definitions of value, and much has already been written about them. I have chosen a selection of historical and contemporary views of value for this chapter, because if value is not properly understood, the correct shape of business cannot be understood either.

This chapter sets the stage for you to reach the best possible understanding of value and how to measure it—if indeed it is truly measurable. Succeeding chapters will build the case for defining and forming the new shapes needed to achieve value.

When I talk about the customer, I am referring to either the end user or the intermediate purchaser of whatever good or service is being sold. If the end user or intermediate customer does not view the product or service as the best value, he or she will buy a different one. It would seem that all we would have to do is ask intermediate customers and end users/consumers, what they prefer and deliver it. Unfortunately, it's not that easy, but it's not a bad place to start!

In fact, this approach will work some of the time; and in a fairly stable market, it will work a lot of the time—until someone innovates! But which markets are stable these days? Very few!

What does all this have to do with value? If we are really searching for the best value both for now and the future, we must not only ask customers what they want or like, because their frame of reference is too limited. They will respond only in terms of what they know exists or might exist. In the words of one research team: "[We] must know better than the customer what is valued, and coach them to the right view...." Former Wal-Mart executive Jack Shewmaker put it very well: "Our job is not only to give the customers what they expect when they come into Wal-Mart. It is to surprise and excite them with things they never knew existed."

Does all this mean we should not ask our customers and potential customers what they want? Absolutely not! The value of listening to customers and potential customers is immense. In fact, learning *how* to listen in order to understand value is one of the greatest challenges any organization faces. If an interviewer is not careful, he or she may add bias to their research and inadvertently and incorrectly alter the results.

The Art of Listening

I was working on my own list of reasons for listening to the customer when I found these written by John Guaspari in Rath & Strong's *Leadership Report* (1995, pp. 2–5).

1. *It can inform.* This can help you make more informed choices.
2. *It can energize.* This can make things happen with more energy.
3. *It can align.* This can accelerate and focus change.

There is only one thing worse than not listening to the customer, and that is listening and hearing what you want to hear instead of what they are actually saying. It is also important to engage customers in a variety of ways. Don't assume that ordinary questioning will reveal everything the customer has to tell you. And always, always practice empathy in listening.

I also recommend that you involve nontraditional people to do either or both the listening and/or the questioning in these conversations. A common error is to involve just sales, marketing, and service people, who may be too closely involved in the outcome to listen objectively. Take advantage of skilled researchers—they know what they're doing. The ideal mix would be research professionals and company sales, marketing, or service personnel.

Another useful approach is to frame the issues various ways to uncover unexpected insights. I will add more about alternative ways to ask questions in an upcoming chapter.

The best and quickest way I have found to measure value is to use a simple diagnostic profile like the one shown in Figure 7-1. The simple act of trying to quantify ratings is as meaningful as the outcome. Doing it repeatedly, with different participants, can provide a basis for important future dialogue, too.

Quality:										
Very poor	1	2	3	4	5	6	7	8	9	10 Best in class

Service:										
Very poor	1	2	3	4	5	6	7	8	9	10 Best in class

Speed:										
Very poor	1	2	3	4	5	6	7	8	9	10 Best in class

Cost:										
Very poor	1	2	3	4	5	6	7	8	9	10 Best in class

Innovation:										
Very poor	1	2	3	4	5	6	7	8	9	10 Best in class

(Each attribute must be considered separately, and then value perception in the aggregate.)

Figure 7-1 Diagnostic Profile for the Shape of Value

A TRADITIONAL VIEW OF VALUE

In the 1950s the General Electric Company was deeply involved in professional business management (PBM), a pioneering effort to define and identify "management." Every GE manager was involved, and this created an environment in which many new ideas emerged. One was originated by Larry Miles, who designed a process called *value analysis*. It enabled hundreds of companies to save millions of dollars through the use of this cost-versus-function-analytical-based process. It naturally multiplied (like all anecdotal solutions) into *value engineering* and *value purchasing*. Perhaps most important, it raised the concept of value as an all-encompassing definition of what the customer wanted.

I was first exposed to the concept of value in the value analysis context in the early 1970s when the company I worked for at the time, L.R. Nelson Corporation, retained some former GE managers to conduct a value analysis seminar for us. It was a revelation. The firm, Value Programs for Industry (VPI) was founded by Jack Prendergast, who defined *value* for us as "function plus esteem per unit cost," then expressed it in an easy-to-understand formula: (Function + Esteem)/Cost = Value.

Armed with this information, we formed six teams of four people each from different functional backgrounds and began to break down value into its components and study it from many different directions. First we did a detailed cost analysis. Taking the bills of materials and adding standard (or better yet, actual or current) costs to each part number, we methodically dissected the cost of our products. This served two purposes. It enabled us to focus on the largest components of cost; later it provided the basis for cost analysis on "properties," such as weight, square feet, length, and so forth.

The cost analysis was critical. Finding the largest "chunks" of cost to work on was essential, for two reasons. First, the principle of VA was to strive for large increments of value improvement (in order to look beyond the conventional, small, or incremental improvements), and since cost was the denominator of the value equation, large value gains were often associated with large cost reductions. The second reason can be succinctly summed up in the words of former bank robber Willie Sutton, who, when asked why he robbed banks, said, "That's where they keep the money!" If we didn't operate on areas of large cost content, how could we ever hope to achieve large cost improvements to contribute to value improvement?

We succeeded in the value analysis project partly because we had selected multifunctional teams of people, representing different disciplines and viewpoints, which was, perhaps, more important than the technical skills each of us brought to the process. After beginning with the "costed bill of materials," we moved on to areas such as functional analysis and defined the basic function, where we decided what the product was supposed to do from a function viewpoint. Then we attempted to assign value in terms of cost for achieving this function. We used comparative analysis, comparing similar parts to see how their cost for an almost identical function differed. We also used more creative approaches such as "blast, create, and refine." This involved discarding (blasting) the current product, and creating a new one that captured just the essence of the function previously defined and then refining that creation to provide most of the functionality of the original product. This process was useful in breaking our "functional fixations," which often obstruct true innovation.

Improving on the Old

Lest this chapter turn into a diatribe on traditional value analysis, I will include only one example, that of L.R. Nelson, maker of the control dial assembly for oscillating lawn sprinklers. The dial originally consisted of many parts: a zinc die-cast bracket, a plastic dial with a stainless steel ball and spring detent, and plastic levers that were attached to the bracket and to the gear train of the sprinkler, with thread-forming screws or pivot pins. Grease was added to assure smooth operation, and the four-position selector dial was aligned with a stamped mark and secured to the spray bar with a set screw. Sound complicated? It was!

If the sprinkler were stepped on or dropped, often one of the plastic parts would break or the whole assembly would become misaligned. Although the sprinkler might still operate, the area watered would be far from what was expected! Realignment required a small allen wrench, which few consumers had, and a keen eye to find the alignment mark (which tended to disappear with age and corrosion) Repair, while simple, was a nuisance for consumers who usually just returned the whole sprinkler.

After value analysis was completed, this entire assembly and all of its components were replaced with two snap-together plastic parts that enabled over 50 positions and that were attached and aligned on the spray bar with a detent (bulge), which could be easily snapped back into position after being dropped or knocked out of alignment. The result was the elimination of a handful of small, expensive, or easily broken parts and a complex assembly operation, thus dramatically lowering cost, while providing the consumer with a much more useful, more adjustable, and more durable product. This illustrates value analysis at its best.

In my experience using this process at L.R. Nelson Corporation, Huffy Corporation, and Rubbermaid always yielded substantial savings from ideas for value improvement. Moreover, it changed how the participants thought about and described value, which led to a continuing series of further improvements, often from the very outset of a product's conception. The process is still worthwhile and effective today.

Another factor in the equation, however, created more than a little consternation. It was the numerator, Function + Esteem. This kind of value often goes beyond the definable attributes of the product into murky areas like taste, style, and pride of ownership. The challenge was to figure out how much of the cost was attributable to the functions (basic and secondary) and how much was attributable to esteem. If we could do this, then we could certainly decide how to reallocate the cost to provide better value.

A NEW UNDERSTANDING OF VALUE

Fast forward to the 1990s. Many experts have studied value in all its forms and from many different viewpoints. Knowledge has grown dramatically, but the search for a better understanding of value continues. A group of researchers at the University of Tennessee spent the past five years conducting countless interviews to determine what is value in the eyes of customers. Customers of a variety of products were studied: a beverage (Gatorade), an automobile dealer (Saturn), boats (Sea-Ray), medical services (Fort Sanders Medical), and more. The findings, in a nutshell, indicate that value goes far beyond the physical attributes of a product, although most of us immediately relate to attributes because they are tangible, measurable, easily identifiable, and usually manageable! Furthermore, there are complexities of value that the VA approach ignored. Value is situational; it can change over time. A product can be both satisfactory and unsatisfactory at the same time. How does that factor into the simple VA equation? The sacrifices required to obtain a product or service make a big difference in the perception of value, and price is only one of those (others are accessibility, delivery, setup/installation, learning to use, and many more).

Clearly, value isn't clear after all. And yet it is the ultimate measure that determines the consumer's choice. Value is a complex combination of considerations, attributes, consequences, sacrifices, situations, and higher-order benefits (like esteem, prestige, safety, security, etc.) that must be considered, weighed, and ultimately decided upon by a customer.

Value goes beyond attributes of the product or service. Dr. Leonard Berry, director of the Center for Retailing Studies in the College of Business Administration at Texas A. & M. University, describes additional aspects to understanding value in *Inside Retailing, Special Report* (Leibhar-Friedman, Inc., May 8, 1995). Although Berry wrote in the context of retailing, his thoughts merit consideration in the total definition of value. The better and more inclusive this definition is the more likely you will have the ability to determine "best value," and to deliver it consistently. After stating that retailers must understand that there is a difference between value and price, Berry wrote:

> *Let me just add what I mean by value. Value is the benefits the customer receives for the cost incurred, and the benefits refer to all beneficial aspects of selecting one store over another, product quality, service, atmosphere, convenience and the like. Costs include not only monetary costs but nonmonetary costs.*

What is exciting about of the University of Tennessee research is that it identifies hierarchies of value, ranging from the simple attributes of the purchase, beyond consequences, to the higher-order reasons for choosing one value over another. While attributes may change rapidly, these higher-order needs do not; they provide a more stable base upon which to build a value proposition. Customers may not be able to tell us exactly what they want in the product, but often they can more easily describe the consequences or higher-order benefits they are seeking. Our job is to translate those into products and services.

Berry also discusses retail winners and losers, and it is worth considering some of the factors he identifies for retail success or failure because they are applicable in other areas. His answer to the question what differentiates the winners from the losers are summed up in four points:

1. They compete on value, not price.
2. They have a clear distinction and stand for something.
3. They are time- and energy-friendly.
4. They make shopping more enjoyable.

It is interesting that three of the four address higher-order reasons for retailer selection—a sense of "standing for something," time/energy, and pleasure/fun—none of which has anything to do with price or physical attributes. All have everything to do with less tangible, yet very powerful reasons that influence the perception of value greatly.

To truly understand value, we must go into the realm of the definer of value—the customer. So much has been written about customers, I will not even attempt to summarize or annotate the information. Instead I will cite and discuss several of the more insightful customer value perspectives from a number of different sources.

Using pictures to anchor concepts in the mind is also useful. As you know, I have selected the value pentastar to depict value for several reasons. First, it is very useful to graphically depict the shape of value for a wide range of customers and competitors in each of the value attributes. As you saw in earlier examples, when those value attribute levels are plotted on the five axes of the value pentastar and the points are joined with lines, a distinctive shape results. This is an excellent graphical depiction of the Shape of Value being delivered or received by companies.

Measurement and Brand Are Critical

I have said value is difficult to measure. But that is not a sufficient reason to avoid doing so. The simple act of trying to measure something can add to the understanding, even if the measurement is less than accurate. Our challenge is to measure honestly and take care not to alter what we are measuring unintentionally. If we also keep in mind that the goal is to find measures that put the same shape of value in our mind and that of our customer, we can proceed with optimism about the outcome. If we accept that the source of value influences that value, then certainly other aspects of the purchase decision area are also likely to be influential.

The customer forms impressions about products and services they buy and where they buy them. They assign to these impressions, shorthand names, which are often the brand name of the product, service, store, or the company that provides it. The associated imagery creates what is called *brand image*.

In today's frantic need for more time and information, brands are a source of information about products, services, and purchase alternatives, but the complexity of choice continues to increase. As it does, shoppers (potential customers) look for familiar symbols and signs on which to base their buying decision.

A couple years before I left Huffy Bicycles, customer feedback indicated we had reached an important milestone. It rated "a brand you can trust" ahead of "on sale" as the primary reason for purchasing. Our consumers were responding to the trust we had built.

When the store name is the "brand," the customer trusts the retailer to assure that even another, unfamiliar brand name associated with the retailer's reputation is worthy of selection. When this occurs in conjunction with habitual shopping patterns, it is termed *store loyalty*. In other cases, OEM or industrial suppliers and customers develop strong, familiar long-term relationships that behave like store loyalties. Wal-Mart's choice of Popular Mechanics as a "house brand" for its hardware/tools and Sears well-known and highly regarded Craftsman and Kenmore brands as previously mentioned, are good examples of store brands that capitalize on their shopper's trust and loyalties. Likewise, industrial supplier W.W. Grainger has built a strong, loyal brand image following among its customers. AT&T has done so in long-distance telephone services.

But what really creates this customer loyalty and makes up brand image? In Bradley Gale's work in 1994 with Perdue chickens, brand image carried the highest weight of all the factors. This is not always true. Brand image is a very complex mixture of attributes, perceptions, and situational feelings about a given company's products, service, quality, prices, and much more. How was Perdue (and many others) able to create a brand image that translated into better value in the eyes and minds of its customers? Both advertising (communication) of the image desired and performance by the product were necessary to build this brand image. If the promise of the ads was not delivered by the product, the consumer's expectation would not have been met.

Frank Perdue elevated the chicken from a commodity to a differentiated product, and used the premise that value is in the eye (and mind) of the customer to build an empire. Gale analyzes some of Perdue's successful approaches to understand how the customer perceives value. He defined an acronym, GASP, which stands for Generally Accepted Strategic Principles, to explain how customer value is at the heart of a company's strategy. He states simply, "...companies succeed by providing superior customer value." His next sentence, however, "And value is simple quality, however the customer defines it, offered at the right price," is an oversimplification. The customer defines value, although not always as consciously as we would like. And while price and quality have a lot to do with value, there is much more to it than that.

Gale advises that to find out what goes on in customers minds, we should ask them to weight the various factors. We can then construct many comparative, quantitative analyses upon which to base decisions. This approach is both logical and useful It is especially so if competitors are evaluated at the same time and under the same (controlled) circumstances.

Myths can sometimes develop from a value image. The Maytag repairman's lonely existence carries a mythical message of legendary reliability to potential customers. Only years of consistent advertising and product performance can build and sustain such myths, but once built, they can sustain customer preference for decades. Only a dramatic failure to perform will destroy the myth. Schwinn bicycles came dangerously close to destroying its image (I'll expand on this later in the chapter). Often a mythically powerful brand conveys a distinctive "shape of value" for the company that owns it in the mind of the consumer. It is important to recognize and portray the brand image impact on the shape of value by assigning higher evaluations to those value attributes where its influence is strongest.

Is Brand Loyalty Dead?

In their report "Marketing with Blinders On" (1993), Kevin Clancy and Robert Shulman attempted to explode several myths about marketing that relate closely to this discussion of value and customers, especially in the area of branded products. One of the most important myths they attack is that "brand loyalty is dead." I agree that it is far from dead. Clancy and Shulman cite, "As consumers streamline their lives, branding becomes a dominant factor in consumer decision making (that is, where brand is a factor at all). Brands offer consumers a shortcut by which to identify products and services worth high value—hardly a new idea" (*Across the Board*, October 1993). Their research shows that 7 of 10 American consumers buy the same brand over and over without really thinking about it, and 6 of 10 "don't have time to investigate the quality of different brands, so [they] usually just buy the same brands [they] bought last time." Three-quarters of all consumers agreed that once they found a brand they like, "it is very difficult to get [them] to change brands." Does this leave any doubt that there is a strong linkage between value and brand? In fact, in today's information-dominated, fast-paced, time-constrained, and brand-proliferated world, those brands that survive will emerge stronger than ever, and will provide invaluable consumer information about what value is best.

Extending a product line is not the least risky way to introduce new product value. It is easier to do than to develop a new brand, and this is very tempting to product and marketing managers. The danger arises when the new item potentially damages the brand by failing to live up to consumer value expectations. Line extensions can also fragment the brand value position in the market, exposing it to attack in relatively weaker areas, leading to erosion of the overall brand dominance. This is where Rubbermaid has suffered in recent years.

When done carefully and with proper concern for the brand and its image, however, line extensions make a value perception portable and transferable to a new product. Soft drink marketers Coke and Pepsi have been the most successful with extensions, but as the New Coke debacle proved, it too is not infallible. Line extensions can benefit from a clearer understanding of the shape of value the competition has taken, but they must be implemented with extreme care until this understanding is very clear. Jack Trout, author of *The New Positioning* (McGraw-Hill, 1997) has warned against overextending brands and product lines to their detriment. Remember, we are looking for the shape that delivers best value, so all of these factors are important and must be considered.

Changing Value Perceptions

Customer value perceptions vary with time and situation. Numerical ratings are a snapshot in time, and can show only the current situation. But, and this is a big but, situations in the real world are constantly changing. To improve on attributes of the product (specifications, content, features, etc.), we can use these weightings to help us rank their relative importance, but only as long as no one has altered the competitive arena by providing some new, better value solution (or until everyone provides that feature or benefit, at which point it becomes the price of being part of the competition). For example, in Gale's research on chickens, "no pin feathers" was a very highly ranked quality/value aspect. This remained true until all competing chicken suppliers had also achieved the ability to deliver chickens with no pin feathers. Then it was simply a requirement!

Remember, the customer's understanding of value is often no better than our own. The difference is that the customer's is the one that matters. We must make our own mental picture of value as close to the customer's as possible or we will mislead ourselves.

Using Brands to Convey Extra Value and Price

Consider brands like 3M or Rubbermaid. 3M's innovative products are legendary, and Rubbermaid enjoys a brand image and recognition most companies envy. What created those brand images? In short, they were the result of accumulated impression over years of favorable experiences, with good-quality products that performed beyond consumer's expectations and were priced fairly. Part of Rubbermaid's brand image had to do with creating a better and more innovative solution to some basic household storage needs. More recently, Rubbermaid has been suffering in the marketplace because other companies have copied their designs and features, and Rubbermaid has not been able to match the low prices of some of these new competitors.

As a market strategy discipline, product leadership (through innovation) can be lucrative, but also risky, since a few stumbles allow competitors to copy and catch up.

Is product innovation a consideration in a customer's value perceptions? Of course. Jack Shewmaker's comment about "surprising the consumer" with something they didn't know existed was a part of both 3M's and Rubbermaid's brand image success stories: lids that fit tighter, yet opened easier; Post-it Notes, Scotch Brand Magic adhesive tape, and many more.

3M and Rubbermaid both enjoy brand image advantages built on a combination of value attributes, which after time become valued aspects of the product. Good brand names "live" a long time, unless the owner abuses the consumer trust/franchise by producing poor quality or charging too-high prices. A strong brand can help companies survive difficult times with greater success than their performance might warrant. The years of consumer value "goodwill" is like a bank account. Only after repeated heavy withdrawals is this account depleted or overdrawn.

Too Little Too Late

One excellent example of a legendary brand that nearly destroyed its image is Schwinn. The premier U.S. bike maker for years, the product began to fail to deliver on the excellence expected by consumers. Its product image deteriorated from the best you could buy to heavy, clunky, and old-fashioned. Other, newer brands like Trek, Cannondale, GT, and Specialized eroded Schwinn's consumer franchise.

Schwinn changed its shape in a negative way, and almost destroyed a mythically powerful brand. The full story of Schwinn's decline was documented in the book *No Hands: The Rise and Fall of the Schwinn Bicycle Company* by Judith Crown and Glenn Coleman (Henry, Holt & Co., 1996). Schwinn repeatedly refused to recognize and react to major shape-shifts in the industry, until it was too late. Today, however, the Scott Sports Group is leading the ailing company's shape-shift recovery, and trying to sell the rejuvenated bicycle business at a handsome profit.

DON'T REST ON LAURELS

Human beings long for something stable upon which we can stop for a while to catch our breath, but when we do in business, the competitor passes us. A phrase I like to help keep this in mind is "success is the enemy!"

I want to return to Gale's work as an introduction to this section. He wrote:

Note that there is nothing "subjective" about a customer value analysis, when it is properly conducted. Any market research firm should be able to determine, objectively, whether or not the opinions of the panel...were correct. If market researchers do their jobs well and the definition of the market served is held constant, then a market-perceived quality profile and a customer value map produced by one research firm will be essentially the same as a market-perceived quality profile and customer value map produced by another. Thus, a *properly calculated market-perceived quality profile provides an objective, impersonal measure of how the customers in any given marketplace really judge and select products.* (My emphasis.)

I strongly disagree with Gale here. I only wish it were that simple. I have already defined and encouraged the use of diagnostic profiles, shape of value pentastars, weighting, and so on. Valuable information and communications come from such analyses, so my criticism does not mean such assessments, graphical devices, and value maps should not be done. Means of depicting the comparative value versus competitors are very useful. The danger is the sense of "accuracy and constancy" portrayed by any such graphical technique.

Quantitative, well-conducted research is essential in most value determination processes. But research alone is not the whole answer. The research methods used and the interpretation of the results is also critical. You must realize that such information is perishable, especially as change accelerates. Changes in consumers' options, and the competitive business world are accelerating at an unprecedented rate, making the consideration of how value perspectives change a critical factor in understanding value.

I do think Gale's final observations are useful. "Very few companies have market-perceived quality profiles and fewer still have customer value maps." Sad, but true. Without some good baseline information, the understanding of the finer points of value may be irrelevant. The article closes with another worthwhile observation: "An income statement looks at the past. Customer value maps and market-perceived quality profiles look to the future." With this sobering admonition, let us move on and consider what creates value in the future.

VALUE DISCIPLINES HELP STRUCTURE THINKING

In their best-seller *The Disciplines of Market Leaders* (Addison-Wesley, 1995), consultants and authors Michael Treacy and Fred Wiersema describe "value disciplines." I paraphrase them briefly here. In what may be an over-simplification of a complex topic, Treacy and Wiersema believe that performance in only three value disciplines is the determinant of success:

1. *Operational excellence*, which means the lowest-cost, most highly effective, and/or best middle-of-the-market service or products with the fewest inconveniences (or sacrifices as I called them earlier); for example, Wal-Mart.
2. *Product leadership*, which means offering products and performance that are at the innovative forefront in their markets, year after year; for examples J.&J., Nike, Rubbermaid.
3. *Customer intimacy*, which means delivering not what the entire market wants but what specific customers want, and cultivating relationships, and satisfying unique needs; for examples: Cable & Wireless, Nordstrom.

Treacy and Wiersma also wrote:

> *Customers today want more of those things they value. If they value low cost, they want it lower. If they value convenience or speed when they buy, they want it easier and faster. If they look for state-of-the-art design, they want to see the art pushed forward. If they need expert advice, they want companies to give them more depth, more time, and more of a feeling that they're the only customer. They know they have to redefine value by raising customer expectations in the one component of value they choose to highlight.*

Although this is a worthy and credible assessments it lacks one rather important consideration: While extolling the importance of capitalizing on the value discipline in which a company is strong, the authors overlook the need to understand the mix of value attributes (shape of value) a company must use to create and deliver the kind of value and in the mix desired by the customer. Treacy and Wiersema contend that it is necessary to "hit a minimum" (of competency) is the other two value disciplines (in which they choose not to be exceptional).

Major imbalance in value discipline competency manifests itself in an erosion of market leadership position. As I've noted, Rubbermaid is suffering from this problem right now. Its phenomenal growth in the 1980s under Stanley Gault was fueled by product leadership, and this is still its driving force. However, management let their operational excellence lag too far behind competition, and now they have problems in cost competitiveness, service delivery, and information systems (not to mention that the phenominal growth and the loss of key managers along the way has depleted the organizational bench strength). The result is that competitors that are "fast followers" in product development are "knocking off" their best products rapidly and eroding its leadership position, especially at its largest customer, Wal-Mart.

Similarly, the vacuum cleaner industry is currently suffering turmoil because Eureka, backed by Electrolux AB's deep pockets is using a fast-follower product development strategy and undercutting the other two large participants, Hoover and Royal, on pricing. This is reminiscent of Panasonic's tactics against Sony in the 1980s. Such a strategy can be effective in the short term, but usually burns out as the shape of value provided by competition changes over several years. It is not sustainable because the leader of an industry drives the shape of value competition with a clearer understanding of value. The low-price copy cat simply follows, often blindly, and is not aware of missteps until they have cost them market position.

It is also critically important to decide which kind of customers you intend to serve and how they define value. To learn this, look *outside* your company, not inside, for that is where the "truth" lies. Many large company's failures are rooted in excessive internal focus.

In 1996, Michael Treacy confirmed the validity of value as the ultimate criterion for success. He said, and I agree, that:

> *There is too much emphasis on shareholder value and too little emphasis on customer value. . . . I believe shareholder value is a consequence of (delivering superior) customer value. The only thing that keeps you there [viable, profitable] is better value every year.*

"VALUE MIGRATION"—BUT TO WHERE?

Like many consultants, Adrian Slywotzky does an excellent job of constructing both a visual and verbal model to describe where businesses are in their industry and life cycle. In his book *Value Migration* (Harvard Business School Press, 1996) he uses the term "business design" to help form a mental image of the choices available: products, markets, and methods of producing and delivering. He describes three phases of value migration. (My unanswered questions/comments are noted in italics).

1. *Value inflow:* The initial phase, which absorbs value due to a superior business design. (What does "absorb" mean?)
2. *Stability:* When business designs are matched to customer priorities and competitive equilibrium exists. (He says this can vary in length. I say it is constantly in flux, and to think otherwise is to invite disaster.)
3. *Value outflow:* Value starts to move away from an organization's traditional activities toward those with better business designs. (*I concur— call it shape-shifting.*)

These are not much different from the growth, maturity, and decline stages of any product or business life cycle. Later, he advises to "anticipate value migration":

One of the most valuable skills has been the ability to detect the first signals of value migration and anticipate its trajectory. [E]xacerbating an organization's natural tendency to focus inward is the fact that value migration is a complex process...The identity and priorities of customers can shift in ways that may not be immediately apparent to the incumbents in an industry.

These are excellent points. I close this section with one more quotation from Slywotsky:

What is the changing pattern of what customers need, want, and are willing to pay for, and what business designs respond most effectively to this changing pattern? To answer these questions, managers must first create a moving picture of their customer— one that is strategic, accurate, and actionable.

A VALUE RECAP

Let us review what we now know about value:

- Value is complex to measure since it depends on the situation and context.
- The attributes of products or services that make up value are easier to relate to the definition because they are usually either measurable or tangible.
- Cost, quality, service, speed (or timeliness), and innovation are the attributes of value embedded in of a product or service in broad connotations.

- Finding the shape of a business that will create and deliver the right mix of these attributes of value is the key to success.
- Shifting the shape as the customer and competitive environment change will ensure long-term success against erosion by competition.

To understand value you must realize that consequences of the value matter more than a specific attribute. In an automobile, antilock brakes are valued only because they promise the consequence of safety in slowing or stopping the car in a controlled manner. An airbag promises the consequence of protection against personal injury in a collision. Absent these consequences, or in the presence of other, more effective ways of providing the consequences, antilock brakes and airbags would have little value as attributes.

Think about the implications of such consequences in the area of personal or business communications. The U.S. mail suffers greatly in speed compared to: telephone, fax, FedEx, UPS Next Day, or e-mail. When cost is factored into the equation, speed versus cost versus convenience versus reliable service versus flexibility become the primary attribute trade-offs, and the desired consequences rule the value decision. Fax is instantaneous but it is not the "real thing"; it is a facsimile, and requires equipment on both ends. E-mail is even faster and cheaper, but (at present) less commonly used, perhaps less reliable, and requires more expensive/special equipment (a computer). The telephone is more personal, but cannot be used for a "document," and requires that both parties be at prescribed locations with equipment at the same time; however, the equipment is inexpensive and widely available. A cellular phone and a personal digital assistant may be able to do all of the proceeding, but at a sacrifice in cost and complexity. What are the desired consequences and benefits versus the sacrifices? The answer governs the value decision.

Now consider an even "higher-order" consideration than the consequences. Neither safety in slowing and stopping the car nor protection in a collision are really the higher-order goals of antilock brakes and airbags. These higher-order value considerations are personal safety and security for self and passengers. This is what really drives the value decision.

In the mail example, is it important to hear the recipient's voice (or even see him or her via video conference)? Only the telephone (or video teleconference) permits this. Must the document be a "signed original?" This precludes fax and e-mail. If either an emotional bond or legal one is the higher-order end state, then these will drive the communication mode value decision. When several options fulfill the consequence and higher-order needs, then attributes such as cost (and the old VA equation for calculating value) once again become the determining decision criteria. The proper "bundling" of attributes is what ultimately yields the shape of value advantage based on the understanding of consequences and higher-order end states. Finding a shape of the business that will deliver this shape is critical. The word shape in this context involves all aspects of the business—its structure, processes, culture (internally), and relationships (externally), as well as its underlying purpose.

Even when this approach to value is well understood, it is not enough. There are "honeymoon" periods, after which the value perception will change, sometimes for the better, but usually for the worse. Recognizing that what was once a superb value may become less valued over time is important. It is also possible for both satisfaction and dissatisfaction to exist at the same time! Different aspects, attributes, and consequences can contribute to both positive and negative feelings. A customer might like the way the car rides, but not its acceleration, or vice versa. When a sound understanding of value is in place, these anomalies can become new sources of opportunity, rather than "problems." With this platform for understanding the many aspects of value and how customers perceive it, we can proceed to the issue of how value perceptions change, and how we (and our organizations) must change (shape) if we are to deliver value consistently and at a high level.

THREE STEPS OF SHAPE-SHIFTING

In conclusion, let us recall the result we are trying to achieve: best value. We must shift our shape to change, but how and how fast be determined only if we stay customer-connected. In this way we have the greatest chance to make the right change. As discussed in the first chapter, we must understand how the *customer* is doing, and not just the traditional how *we* are doing. Then we must take the three steps of shape-shifting to produce that change.

1. Hear and understand what the perceived need for change means, primarily from the customer, but also from our other partners.
2. Help the organization and our partners internalize the need to change.
3. Act to bring about that change in order to consistently create and deliver best value.

In 1532, Niccolo Machiavelli wrote in his masterpiece *The Prince*:

It should be borne in mind that there is nothing more difficult to arrange, more doubtful of success, and more dangerous to carry through than initiating changes. The innovator makes enemies of all those who prospered under the old order, and only luke-warm support is forthcoming from those who would prosper under the new.

Creating an institutional will to change is one of the most difficult, yet most essential steps to successfully reconfiguring any business, and yet it is often skipped in our haste to respond. Change is always difficult to bring about. Later, we will consider how to make this change happen, and enjoy it to a successful outcome, but first we will consider some of the recent, flawed approaches to change, so we do not fall prey to the same mistakes.

8.

Shape-Shifting to Integrate and Revitalize the Business

[R]eengineering is disruptive, painful, and typically results in layoffs and downsizing. By some estimates, 70 percent of the companies which adopt it will fail to reap significant benefits."
—Michael Hammer, in "Reengineering:
Changing the Global Competitiveness
Equation in Significant Leaps and
Bounds," 1994

THE ONLY CONSTANT IS CHANGE

To this point, I have spent a lot of time and words to demonstrate the need to become a shape-shifter. Change is difficult to do, and even more difficult to convince others to embrace. Only when there is a near desperate need will people embrace change in the hope that it will make a bad situation better. The key is to make the changes before a crisis requires it. Knowing when to change, what to change, and above all how to change are some of the largest inhibitors to change.

Unfortunately, modern management and business leaders seem to grasp desperately at new concepts that will make this change process easier. Like fitness equipment that exercises only one or two parts of the body, "quick fixes" produce distortions at best and injuries at worst.

That said, many of these new approaches are valid and valuable, but only if used in moderation and integrated into an overall shape that creates and consistently delivers the best value. That is why the understanding of value is so critical. In later chapters you will read about some of the problems caused by using misguided or piecemeal approaches, and you will also learn the way to find an organization structure able to shape-shift successfully. That many companies have failed to accomplish this should not dissuade anyone, because we can learn from failures as well as successes.

Some companies realized they had to shift their shape, and shift they did. Motorola, Hewlett-Packard, Ford, Texas Instruments, Harley-Davidson, and Chrysler (twice!) decided they could and would compete, even if they had to do it in a very different shape. Costs had to be reduced, not just in labor, but in corporate overhead, through the use of technology and with dramatic product design innovation. Service had to be dramatically improved, and innovation and speed had to become major parts of their capabilities.

Superior quality, a benchmark set by Japanese auto manufacturers, went from a competitive advantage to the "price of admission." The ingenious, independent, competitive American workforce had to learn to go beyond the individual contributor stage and work in teams to create value demanded by the more sophisticated consumer of the 1980s and 1990s. The "good enough," "make all you can" 1960s were gone forever.

Unfortunately, the improvements in productivity resulted in repeated downsizing; and new markets struggled to grow fast enough to replace jobs lost in the old ones. Lucrative factory jobs gave way to lower-paying service sector jobs or private employment (and early retirement). The best new jobs being created in information technology required an entirely different set of skills, so the displaced factory workers remained in trouble. This was a shape-shift in the entire economy.

American management had to learn to empower and enable the remaining people to work collaboratively, in teams, and to really compete. Concepts such as TQM were named, studied, and implemented. Lean production described how Toyota had become the benchmark for efficient, flexible, high-quality, low-cost automobile manufacturing. It, too, was widely emulated to the benefit of many American businesses. Competing in time (speed) was rediscovered as a powerful competitive weapon.

Many U.S. companies realized that markets had globalized while they were fending off foreign competitors. Unions discovered that it was better to join forces with their employers to compete, than to spend their time and effort struggling to gain an ever larger piece of a disappearing pie.

SHAPE-SHIFTING IS NOT REENGINEERING

Before going any further, le me clarify that shape-shifting is not just a new word for reengineering. Reengineering deals with the processes by which things get done. Shape-shifting deals with the entire business—its structure, culture, relationships, and processes. Shape-shifting goes to the heart of the business, its strategy, the value it is delivering, and how.

In writing this chapter, I intend to make liberal use of *Reengineering the Corporation* by Champy and Hammer, *Reengineering Management* by Champy, and *Reengineering Revolution—A Workbook* by Hammer. (I intend to use them to hold down my papers so they do not blow off the table as I write this on my screened porch.) If more executives had used them for such practical and effective purposes, American business would probably be better off and a lot of pain would have been spared millions of workers.

Do not misunderstand me. The fault did not necessarily lie with the authors. Their original *Harvard Business Review* article was superb. It took on the topic of people who were automating antiquated, inefficient processes using computers to do work more efficiently that should not have been done at all. I read it, loved it, and passed it around to my organization, exhorting them to rethink their processes totally. The concept is truly good. Times change. Situations change. People change. Markets change. Technology changes. Why shouldn't the processes used to do business also change (and radically)? But then the management intoxication with the "quick fix" took effect. Reengineering became the magic pill, that would make everything better—well almost everything. The fault lies heavily with the desperate management who tried to use reengineering to remedy a multitude of past sins and errors in one quick fix!

Reengineering, as described by Hammer and Champy is a dangerous "magic pill," which, like chemotherapy, is often as likely to make patients very sick or kill them instead of curing them. Chemotherapy, when used in the treatment of cancer, is intended to attack the diseased cells, but it attacks the healthy cells, too. Reengineering can be applied in similarly indiscriminate fashion. Only with the deftest of touch by the leaders and managers using it can reengineering leave the "healthy cells," the people and processes, unharmed, and eliminate/ alter only the "unhealthy" ones. However, in "magic pill" mentality, many managers and executives seized on this as the panacea for all the ills that plagued their companies.

In *The Economist*'s Management Focus column (November 5, 1994), Michael Hammer tried valiantly (but in vain), to defend reengineering. He condemned those who put layoffs and downsizing under the mantle of reengineering. He denied Hamel's and Prahalad's accusation that it is purely a tactical initiative. Hammer claimed, "By significantly improving a firm's operating capabilities, the technique (reengineering) allows it to implement new strategies and, even more important, leads it to envision entirely new strategic options." His own choice of words betrays his claims. Using words such as "implement new strategies" and "envision entirely new strategic options," he admitted to these being cast in a supporting role to the strategy development. Then he wrote, "Reengineering offers an alternative perspective on formulating strategy, one based on operating processes rather than products and markets," except that is seldom how an effective strategy is developed. It is backward.

It is not that I disagree with everything about reengineering; many companies are full of antiquated processes that need reengineering desperately. Changing the shape of the business involves changing *processes*. The problem is that such efforts are not the total solution, and the way many companies undertake them (eliminating people while not changing work content), only worsens the problems.

Hammer stated the problem accurately and eloquently when he was quoted extensively in *FOCUS*, the publication of the National Center for Manufacturing Sciences. In the February 1994 cover article, he admitted, "Reengineering is disruptive, painful, and typically results in layoffs and downsizing. By some estimates, 70 percent of the companies which adopt it will fail to reap significant benefits." He went on to say, "Not surprisingly, collaboration and strong partnerships—between workers, between management and workers, and between customers and suppliers—are essential to successful reengineering efforts."

Hammer stressed, that "collaboration and partnerships are extremely important," exactly the basis of my first book, *The Power of Partnerships*. But a vitally important question must be posed here. Are managers and executives so desperate for solutions that they would gladly use one that fails more than two-thirds of the time? This is the case with reengineering.

Advice about Taking Advice

One of the problems with authors and consultants who have never practiced what they preach is that the breakdown of an approach usually occurs in application, not in theory. In engineering school, they used to simplify our problems by telling us to assume "frictionless pulleys and nonextensible ropes"; in other words, an idealized environment. The problem is, the real world has friction, and lots of it! Things are not just "nonideal," they are downright messy. People's lives and livelihoods are involved, and they get kind of sensitive about anyone or anything that threatens them.

Consider the results of a 1994 Pitney Bowes' Management Services poll, which showed that 83 percent of the largest industrial corporations have reengineered their workplaces, and 70 percent agree that it had brought greater productivity. The downside is that 75 percent fear their own job loss, 69 percent feel it's an excuse for layoffs, and 55 percent feel they are overburdened by work. No doubt, to compete in today's tough markets, everyone must do more with less. That is not the issue. The issue is how we achieve that goal makes all the difference in the world—for the long term. Fear is a great short-term motivator, but fails over the long term. People can live with a threat to their jobs if they believe that their leaders have a strategy and a plan that can succeed, and they know what they must do to implement that plan. Numerous follow-up studies have proven that the benefits from radical reengineering are short term, and that usually long-term declines followed.

Putting On the Brakes, Literally

Given the right conditions, people will work and innovate beyond a leader's wildest expectations. I recall a specific group of people in the Huffy bike plant who worked in the brake build-up area. They were responsible for assembling the right combination of control levers and cables-to-brake calipers before they went to the assembly lines for final assembly onto the bike. Obviously, brakes were always a big concern because of safety. One mistake could mean someone might be badly hurt, and at least result in a recall and major rework of products or product liability suit.

This particular group of people had been through much of our strategic learning training and had completely redesigned their work area for better throughput and improved inventory control (since a lot of the brake parts look very much alike). They had even written the capital appropriation request themselves (with a little help from their area coordinator) and were given $35,000 to erect shelving and buy new tools and fixtures. When a decision to raise the capacity of the plant by 25 percent was announced, they confronted their focused factory manager as a group. They knew that the current job layout would require more people (there were 12 of them, and the new output level would have required 15). This would open their work center to bids by more senior people (due to the change in staffing).

They made a proposal. They would "find a way" to increase their output by 25 percent, if management would provide them with a little support from the industrial and manufacturing engineering group. They did not want anyone on their team to lose their position in the team's work area, which they had designed so well. Management was skeptical, but had little to lose, so agreed to let them try. It was made clear that just "working harder," which would not be sustainable in the long term, was not a good solution. (The productivity of the group was already very high, as determined by MTM standards from the IE department.) If they proved there was no need for more people, their work center would not be opened to bids from other plant employees. After a few weeks, we were amazed to find them routinely able to produce 25 percent more, in yet another "reengineered" process layout. This is an example of how "reengineering" can work in the right environment.

When Reengineering Is Just Rhetoric

One of the most dramatic commentaries I have read on reengineering is by
Michael Mazzarese, a New Jersey consultant. In "Downsizing: Reengineering's
Bad Seed" published by *Executive Directions* in 1994, he wrote:

> *While the economy is growing, executive careers are disappear-*
> *ing...Downsizing burst onto the scene like a deus ex machina in*
> *the mid-1980s. Instead of saving the day, however, it has viciously*
> *turned on those who sought its help...The data are very clear about*
> *the results of their efforts: increased costs and decreased produc-*
> *tivity, exactly opposite of what they wanted."*

Citing the 1993 Harris "Labor 2000 Survey" issued by the New Jersey
Human Resource Group, he continued:

> *Corporations have begun to exhibit symptoms of organizational*
> *anorexia. The compulsion to look good at any price has cost organi-*
> *zations their most valuable resource: capable people. Not only does*
> *talent fly out the door, those left behind who escape this modern-day*
> *version of bloodletting, do not escape the feelings of violation, loss,*
> *and betrayal. Survivor syndrome sets in. Depression, denial, and*
> *distrust sap the energy, creativity, and spirit out of downsized orga-*
> *nizations. Management teams become risk-averse and less produc-*
> *tive. While people are taken out, workloads remain the same. More*
> *likely they increase dramatically. It is no wonder why these sur-*
> *vivors find that "nine to five" now feels like "five to life."*

Reengineering and short-term focused downsizing are destroying the
heart and soul of American companies (and perhaps of companies everywhere). More from Mazzarese:

> *A major paradigm shift has occurred. Managers are no longer*
> *viewed as assets. They are now considered disposable; throwaway*
> *employees. . . lost is the history that made the company great. Lost*
> *are the contacts that could be called on in an emergency. Lost is*
> *the memory of what was, what is, and what could be.*

He closed with dramatic emphasis:

> *Downsizing is not as neat and tidy a package as accountants and*
> *Wall Street analysts would have you believe. . . .Simplistic, quick-fix*
> *solutions,. . .have never worked. They usually result in disaster for*

everyone...except those tied to golden parachutes. As they jump into corporate oblivion, they leave behind organizations that become sick and somber places. . . . CEOs have chosen the tools of reengineering and downsizing to build 'Workforce 2000.' They are only beginning to see the fruits of their labor.

Manage the Numerator, Not Just the Denominator

Creating an environment in which people are motivated to do the right thing is a challenge; finding the right shape the organization needs to succeed is another. One of the most powerful ways of doing this is to use the "voice" of the customer as a means of aligning the organization's aspirations. This can be a rich source of organizational energy, and one that pays off in bottom line (and top line) results. Gary Hamel has often referred to "numerator versus denominator management." This bears some further explanation. One of the common management measurements is a ratio (or fraction) made up of a numerator—sales revenue (or operating profit in some cases) divided by a denominator—"headcount" (or cost of salaries, benefits, or people). Managing the results by changing one or both of the factors in this simple equation is the job of business leaders.

Growth as a strategic initiative has certainly taken hold in the past year or two. Unfortunately, for many, real growth is much harder to achieve than lowering headcount. Mergers and acquisition are not real growth; they are rearrangement of ownership. Real growth is a product of the best value supplied to a market with a carefully designed strategy and execution. Sound difficult? It is. But it is also very rewarding. The simpler and faster approach is to reduce the denominator. This part of the equation is almost totally within the management's control. There are no competitors, no market fluctuations, and few external uncertainties (other than which people get fired and which stay). Simply cut people and the denominator gets smaller. In the short term at least, the resultant measure (usually profitability) goes up. Along with this, executive bonuses, stock price, and esteem of the management team in the eyes of security analysts, go up—in the short term. Long-term results usually go in the opposite direction.

Some markets collapse suddenly, leaving major participants grossly overstaffed. Some companies just get fat or "bloated" with unproductive people. At times, the cost of operating in certain locations or with certain labor markets simply precludes anything but a major downsizing. At other times, technology eliminates whole classes of jobs, and there can be no suitable alternative but to downsize. In many cases, management fails to maintain a "lean" organization, gaining fat during good times, only to have to go on a "crash diet" to get back to fighting weight. A more positive scenario is offered in another *Fortune* article by Ronald Henkoff titled "Getting Beyond Downsizing" (January 10, 1994). It states, "Done wrong, it [downsizing] can pitch your company into a black hole. To get out, try to avoid layoffs, help survivors cope, and never forget the G-word: growth." The focus is a more balanced one, and recognizes that growth is the better alternative, unless things are so bad that cutting is necessary to assure survival.

One of my proudest claims as an operating executive is not that I never had to fire or lay off people; it is that I only did so when there was no other possible alternative, and that was not very often. Every manager or executive who operates a business for long will have to let go of some people sooner or later. There are always some misfits, deadwood, or otherwise mismatched people who have found their way into an organization and settled in for as long as they can get by. They need to be pruned just like dead or unhealthy growth on any living plant.

Clearly, it is harder to grow sales and revenue than to simply fire some people every now and then. But if cutting people is the first solution, you had better become good at it, because you will have to do it over and over again until no one is left (or you become the one who gets cut!). As Gary Hamel said: "This continuous downsizing—it's corporate anorexia. You can get thin but it's no way to get healthy."

Downsizing 101

Successful shape-shifting recognizes the unpleasant aspects of change and deals with them as humanely as possible. Sadly, downsizing announcements are remarkably insensitive. Business conditions are cited; uplifting slogans and new initiatives are touted as hope for the future; expected savings are calculated. Then the regrets are made, often as an afterthought. Such announcements are mercifully brief, and except for senior executives who are victims of the downsizing, names of the unfortunate are seldom mentioned. Let's consider the true impact of downsizing on people, because shape-shifting may and often does involve downsizing. The point is to show how much more desirable it is to shift the shape of the business or organization before denominator-based downsizing becomes the only or last-resort solution.

Ann Kapilovic, late, beloved friend of mine from Dayton, Ohio, was very sensitive to the pain companies inflict on people by poor management. Shortly before she died, she sent me an Ann Landers column that illustrates why even the survivors of downsizing are not likely to lead their companies to competitive victory. It is reproduced here.

St. Louis: I know all about downsizing. My husband is one of the few left in his division. The man never rests. He hasn't seen our kids with their eyes open on a weekday for ages. He has yet to take the vacation time he's earned. He checks his voice mail all weekend and lugs his laptop everywhere. His car phone is always busy. He can't attend his son's ball games, his daughter's dance recitals, school plays, or even a 6:30 family dinner at the kitchen table. He's not a workaholic—just a middle-aged guy with a mortgage and family.

Binghamton, NY: My husband and I both work for a huge conglomerate. We are carrying workloads that used to be handled by three or four employees. We come home exhausted after putting in 12-hour days, drag ourselves behind lawn mowers and vacuum cleaners at 9:00 at night, miss our children's soccer games and school plays, and barely see each other. As for our sex life, there is neither the time nor the energy. Nobody dares quit a job these days. It's too risky. Please Ann, tell corporate America that the stress is killing us.

There has to be a better way to achieve success than the "indentured servitude" of the professional working class. There are some alternatives. Some are organizational; some of them are simply human. If employee loyalty continues to decline and the belief that job security is an oxymoron permeates more people minds, priorities will change. Employees will eventually rebel against unprincipled leadership and abusive work practices. Those who do not will quickly realize that the reward for doing twice as much work is to be given three times as much! Members of Generation X are already deciding that they would rather work for themselves than for mindless or heartless corporate entities. Only the corporations with cultures that recognize the dignity and worth of their people and behave accordingly will continue to attract or keep the best people. The others will slowly decay, be acquired, or cease to exist.

In the next chapter I will say more about how to do things differently, and how to do different things to find a more effective, more satisfactory, and more successful way to stay competitive *and* employed.

9.

The Conditions of Shape-Shifting

Doctors can test people's reflexes by tapping their knees with a small
rubber mallet. But how do you test a company's reflexes?"
—from an EDS advertisement

ON THE ROAD TO SHAPE-SHIFTING

As itemized in Chapter 7, there are three steps to take when shape-shifting to produce change. To recap them briefly, the first is hearing and understanding the need for change; the second is helping people to internalize the need to change; and the third is acting to bring about that change. The next step is to realize that although changing the shape of the business is necessary, it is not easy.

Three conditions must be in place before the three steps for shape-shifting can be taken successfully. The first condition is a high level of competence in communications and information technology. You've heard the saying "information is power." Well, that is true only if it is the right information, obtained on a timely basis and shared (communicated) rapidly and widely. Reams of unsorted data, slow or late information, or that which is hoarded to preserve the power of a few managers will surely doom the entire organization.

The second condition is the proper culture, one that does not resist change but that embraces and capitalizes on change as the great opportunity it represents. This means an environment in which anyone who recognizes information (even "bad news") can fearlessly speak up. All levels of the organization must be encouraged and rewarded for such behavior and participation. This type of open culture, when properly encouraged and cultivated, will also be far more customer-sensitive.

The third condition presence of strong leadership. Notice I did not say "management." Certainly, sound management is important to success in any business, but strong leadership is more than important; it is essential.

Many managers and leaders are deeply committed to what worked for them in the past—what got them to their current position. Unfortunately, what worked in the past probably will not work in the future. I was president of Huffy Bicycles for almost 10 years—too long. During such a lengthy period of time, many situations seem to repeat themselves, and there is the risk of applying the same solution to them and not variations of new solutions. In fact, all situations are subtly different, but "autobiographical listening" filters out the differences and leads to the implementation of time-proven and familiar solutions. As companies have downsized experienced people out of their organizations, their corporate memory has been erased; what did or did not work and why is lost. Consequently, the natural instinct to do what was done before based on experience. They do not recognize the subtle differences that may be the difference between success and failure.

Unlearning the Past to Learn for the Future

Seasoned leaders and managers must learn to find those subtle differences, and to fight the urge to listen autobiographically or to practice denial. Newer members of the management team should be listened to very carefully, since more seasoned members will often reach the same, incorrect (autobiographical) conclusions based on old solutions. The autobiographical listener-executive often forces everything heard to fit a model she or he is familiar with. In doing so, the real, new solutions become lost in the historical interpretation of what worked in the past.

More important than this discovery process, in shedding the old dominant logic, is the need to devise new solutions that are better than the old ones, because competitors have certainly learned those old solutions as well! Peter Senge, in *The Fifth Discipline* (Doubleday-Currency, 1990) explored this process of learning. *Adaptive learning*, sometimes called *single-loop learning,* was also explored in the "Double-Loop Learning in Organizations" (*Harvard Business Review*, Sept-Oct 1977, pp. 115–125) by Chris Argyris. It occurs within a set of recognized and unrecognized constraints called the learning boundaries. Within these learning boundaries, organizational competitive progress may be made, but if competitors are developing their thinking and learning outside the boundaries, this progress will not be sufficient for market success.

Generative learning, on the other hand, yields a more powerful type of solution. Argyris describes this as "double-loop thinking," whereby the organization is willing to question long-held assumptions about its mission, customers, competencies, and strategies. It is in questioning these assumptions that the true power of shape-shifting can be utilized.

While I was president of Huffy Bicycles, we enlisted the help of Jim Barber, a consultant and former professor at Antioch College in Ohio. Barber introduced double-loop thinking to the hourly organization. He had worked and studied with Argyris, and his application of the learning process enabled an organization of 2,000 Steel Worker Union members to employ this double-loop or generative learning process in their expanded jobs. The result was a very powerful competitive advantage—an involved, empowered, and thinking, learning workforce of high productivity and incredible flexibility. Barber described this process in his article "From the Working Class to the Learning Class," *National Productivity Review* (Autumn, 1994). However, it was only through constant reinforcement of the importance of strategic learning that we were able to keep the momentum going. We learned through trial and error that it is important to use this new-found form of learning and thinking as soon as possible in relevant work situations to speed the process of change, and reduce resistance.

Learning Organizations Respond Faster

It has been widely recognized that highly developed, "flatter," better managed organizations are able to respond to change more quickly and efficiently. Such companies have fewer layers of people and less filters that information about the nature of the change must penetrate. If you have effectively flattened your organization's structure, you are better positioned to shape-shift. But too many organizations have been flattened without the proper advance work, leaving a less effective and unresponsive flat structure. Simply removing layers, without putting into place the training, communication skills, and culture, leads to disaster. If you can create (or have created) an organizational culture that treats change as an opportunity, not a threat, you are halfway there. If open, honest, frequent, and free communications at all levels of the organization are the rule, there is hope.

Organizations made up of informed and empowered people adapt better. Those that have attempted to become learning organizations are even better prepared to adapt to the new realities of the market. If TQM has been truly implemented to streamline processes and create a participative atmosphere of continuous improvement, then shape-shifting can evolve as an enhanced form of that initiative.

CHANGING THE SHAPE OF THE BUSINESS

Most of this long preamble about learning and culture has been a buildup to the essence of this chapter: The only way to effectively change the shape of value is to change the shape of the business that creates and delivers that value.

Chapter 2 illustrated the dimensions of the shape of a business. It is reproduced here in Figure 9-1. When a desired shape of value that is closely congruent with that of the customers or market has been defined, the next step is to shift to provide that shape of value. Again I warn against the temptation to do this quickly by "throwing resources" (i.e., people and money) at the problem. Doing so can at best achieve a temporary shift; it will not assure the long-term competitive position required to withstand the rigors of the competitive marketplace. Only by truly shifting the shape of the business can the shape of value change be implemented and sustained.

A few simple examples will clearly illustrate this concept. Consider a company whose target customers require a very fast delivery cycle. This could be accommodated in the short term by spending money on additional inventory, capacity, and people. Over the long term, however, this kind of imperfect solution will prove too costly, ineffective, and noncompetitive. What must change are the processes within the company, to be more responsive and

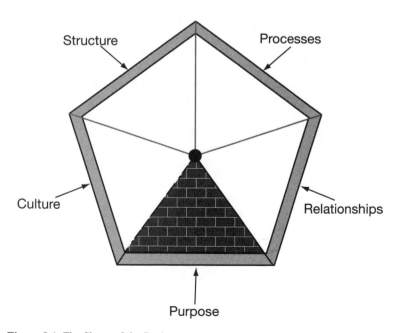

Figure 9-1 The Shape of the Business

more flexible. It is possible that only one dimension of the shape needs to be changed, but usually, several will require alteration.

To begin an assessment of how to shape-shift, draw a separate shape of value diagram for *each dimension*, depicting how the structure, process, culture, and relationships contribute to the various attributes (based on consumer desires and competitors' strengths and weaknesses). The shapes that result from these evaluations should match the shapes of the customers' or market profiles as closely as possible for best-value alignment. And remember, different customers within similar markets still may have different profiles.

Processes:
- Quality
- Throughput, speed, output
- Effectiveness, results-oriented
- Clear, simple, logical, flexible
- Documented, information-rich

Structure:
- Organizational levels
- Centralized versus decentralized
- Spans of reporting and information Flow
- Functional or cellular
- Global and/or local

Culture (Internal):
- Leadership
- Participation
- Empowerment
- Motivation and communication
- Openness and information

Relationships (External):
- Suppliers
- Customers
- Professional or special
- Trustworthy, honest, open, information-sharing
- Mutually beneficial and rewarding

Purpose:
- Legacy
- Guiding principles
- Vision and mission
- Core competencies
- Strategic intent

Figure 9-2 The Dimensions of Shape

Faking It Isn't Making It

Figure 9-2 adds some descriptive terms to help you define the dimensions of shape. Choose which of them would contribute to producing the respective attributes of value. To produce those attributes in any other way is artificial, temporary and unsustainable. Those who "fake it" often fail in painful and costly ways.

Imagine the company whose product quality is not very good, but whose customers demand high quality. True, a detailed inspection could sort out the good items, but at a very high and intolerable cost. In such a case, the processes and probably the culture of the company would have to change to that of a high-quality producer.

If customers require innovative solutions, one approach is to develop far more new products than needed in the hope that there are winners somewhere in the sheer numbers of new items, products, or services. Unfortunately, this is a resource-intensive approach that leaves many damaged companies in its wake. Truly innovative companies require a structure, culture, and processes that support innovation, not just the people and money to "try" a lot of things and hope.

Business in its basic form is not all that complex. What makes it complex is the infinite variations of people and interacting systems that must be dealt with. Actions have a time-delayed response. Good work, or bad, usually takes from six months to two years to have an effect in the competitive marketplace. Sure, some actions result in immediate response, but most major strategic or tactical maneuvers take longer—which is why action is needed *now*. When an individual or a company is successful, its success generates the risk, a risk of complacency, overconfidence, arrogance, or most of all, protecting the status quo, while competition makes progress on a new, more powerful shape. Now is the time to plot the shape of the future—future customers, markets, products, and plans. Actions you take now will pay off in the next 6 to 24 months. But what should you do?

Your strategy or tactics must be based on your experience and situational contexts. They must result from thought and reflection based on knowledge and insights into the shape of your current situation—competition, customer value, market/industry, core competencies, and capabilities. Beware anyone who prescribes for your situation or context based on *their* experience; they may give excellent advice, but if it is born of a different context it might do more harm than good.

The concept of shape-shifting is dependent on the cornerstone partnerships. Shape-shifting builds on all prior intellectual investments, making it the ideal form of integration. It uses not only prior improvements but leverages them to your benefit.

How many companies have this necessary hunger for innovative thought to use in their forward strategy? Outdated core competencies and capabilities too often are clung to like the remnants of a once-glorious ship that carried many companies and executives to success. On the other hand, some core competencies and capabilities are hard to duplicate and must be treasured, especially if they are based in the culture, learning skills, or purpose of the companies. Recognizing the difference is critical. When the pressures for short-term earnings cause reactionary management to jettison the critical competency people along with the dead wood, deterioration is usually evident a year or two later.

Checks and Balances

Consider the Deluxe Corporation. A decade ago, it was the leader in the market for printed checks. Deluxe's automated factories were the ultimate in technology and their high-quality, low-cost, excellent service and speedy delivery gave them the perfect shape to match their customer wants and needs. Banks want check-reordering to be simple and hassle-free; consumers want their checks accurate, inexpensive, fast, and delivered to their home. Deluxe did it all better than any other firm and held over 50 percent share of the market.

Then the market shifted out from under them. Check usage began to drop. Use of debit cards and electronic transfers became more widespread. Bank mergers forced down check prices. Niche competitors entered the market with unique products. Innovative startups like CheckFree and Quicken software offered new, better solutions. Joint ventures such as Microsoft and First Data promise to make bill paying via the Internet a reality in the near future.

Although Deluxe properly used its core competencies of printing and distribution to enter other markets, including greeting cards and stationery, it could not shift its shape fast enough to support the burden of the plants and automated production equipment that once was its competitive advantage. In time, its new diversified businesses were also eroded by the personal computer and new technology.

Deluxe is now shifting to a strategy that uses its transaction-processing capabilities more, but it reacted late and is paying dearly for it.

In the *IndustryWeek* article "Reinventing the Future" (April 17, 1996, pp. 32–38) Mark Bregman, technical advisor to IBM's chairman, said, "Gone are the days when a company could maintain that monopolistic position simply by being the sole possessor of critical product knowledge." The world is a much smaller place due to the advances of communications and computing technologies. What used to suffice as a proprietary advantage is now merely a "speed bump" on the road of competition. Apple Computer's easy-to-use operating system was jeopardized when Apple was unable to shape-shift rapidly enough to upgrade it, and management failed to see the necessity of licensing it to other producers to build critical mass for software developers. Instead, Apple relinquished part of the graphic interface to Microsoft, which used it to grow the richest, most robust forest of products in the computer industry today. With help from Intel's Andy Grove, Microsoft not only evolved to a user-friendly interface with Windows and Windows 95, but it implemented the combined creative work of Apple and IBM, who created the PC, to exceed both companies in market penetration.

BUSINESS IN THE FAST LANE

The Manco Duck in *Duck Tales* (Manco, Inc., March/April 1995) said, "The speed of changes has created *discontinuities* in organizations. It's likely that many of the people involved haven't fully grasped these new realities. They may lack a basic knowledge of how their companies are being *shaped* and how quantum change might affect issues like employment security." (My emphasis.)

Consultant, author, and strategist Mike Kami cites case after case of resistance to change. He explores several reasons in his presentations. "Complacency is the biggest killer. . . .The downfall of magicians is when they start believing their own magic. . . .The worst mistakes are made in good times, not bad times." Change is both the biggest challenge of the past few decades and the most important management and leadership issue of the coming decades. If leaders choose not to shape-shift, they will not survive in any current recognizable form.

Quick Fixes Cannot Support Slow Reflexes

The U.S. Census Bureau survey (1994) of employers confirms that many firms have been slow to adopt new management concepts. According to the survey of nearly 3,000 plant and office locations, only 25 percent use benchmarking, only 37 percent have adopted TQM (and some of them, poorly), and only 13 percent of nonmanagement workers participate in self-directed teams. This clearly illustrates that the practices of these companies do not match the "talk" of their management. The survey summary cites, "Despite considerable attention given to new modes of work organization, the use of high-performance work systems remains the exception rather than the rule..."

Do companies have reflexes as human bodies do? Of course. Companies are like living organisms that react in distinct ways to certain stimuli. Most, however, are "micro" reactions, not "macro" reactions. One of the key parts of our reflex system is the central nervous system. The central nervous system of a company is made up of its information and telecommunications systems and flow. If those are weak or ineffective, the company's reflexes will be rendered slow and useless.

Consider the story of the frog and the pot of boiling water. If a frog is thrown into the boiling water, it will jump out as soon as it hits the hot water. But, if the frog is put in the water and the water is slowly brought to a boil, the change will be gradual enough that the frog will not jump out, it will be cooked. This is a great story to make the point even though *it is totally inaccurate in fact*. Tests have shown that a frog thrown in boiling water dies from the shock and temperature, and the frog who is in the pot of slowly heated water jumps out when the temperature gets too high. There is a message in the very fact that this widely used story is directly and exactly wrong in opposite ways.

The story describes what happens when incremental changes are accommodated by maintaining the status quo, while the external environment is changing from where the internal strategy was effective. IBM is one of the best illustrations of this. They even had to go to a third party, SAP, for the software to run their own business. In one context, this creeping incremental change is also happening to many other companies and institutions (it may even be worse at universities and other large, bureaucratic institutions because they react to change even more slowly than most companies to begin with). In another context, the scene depicted by the frog story is happening in "fast-forward," providing even less time to realize that some terrible (or wonderful?) change is overcoming our defenses, and that we must do something, and fast! Shape-shifting is what must be done.

"Once Upon a Time" Is Gone

The foundations upon which many of our beliefs and behaviors are based are among the most rapidly evolving. Consider the ubiquitous telephone. Certainly, it has changed, from the old dial instrument with a bell-type ringer to the modern push button, tone-generating one with memory, cellular networks, and cordless options. But it is still a telephone. A *BusinessWeek* special report entitled "Phone Frenzy" (February 20, 1995, pp. 92–97) asked: "Is there anyone who doesn't want to be a telecom player?" How far have we come from Ma Bell's monopoly of less than two decades ago? The article describes a cafe in New York City that has a phone on each table. With a $5 order of food, the patron receives tokens to make a three-minute call to anywhere in the United States. A restaurant in the phone business? Why not?

Among the entities considered to be potential players in the deregulated communications business are such unlikely companies as gas pipeline companies (good cable routes for fiber optics), thruway authorities (another potential cable route), utility companies (they have poles too, why not string phone wires on them?), cable TV companies (they are already wired into a lot of homes), wireless and cellular companies (who says you need wires?). The cellular phone, once considered an expensive novelty at prices above $1,000, is now commonly priced at $10 or less (with a service contract), and everyone has one. Calls via the Internet now are not only possible but economical.

Such revolutionary changes prove we must shape-shift our companies and our organizations to new forms if we are to compete successfully in the future. As I've stated several times, we must shift from the core competencies and capabilities that got us where we are to a new set that will create value in the present and future. To do so, recognition comes first; then swift action must follow.

First, we must recognize and accept the need to change our shape. Leaders must create a clear understanding of and healthy dissatisfaction with the current reality. (This includes defining the current shape of the target markets/customers, and of the company itself.) Next we must decide how to change the shape, which of our core competencies and capabilities need to change, or be replaced, with what, and how. The weighted shape analysis described in an earlier chapter is a very useful tool to help arrive at this conclusion.

Organizations must become adaptive, learning organisms, which can then continuously shift shape as easily as the chameleon changes colors to fit the environment. Only learning organizations can do this. Senior management must become enlightened leaders who help create a shared vision of the future reality. Then it must be shared via constant communication and reinforced with behaviors and rewards/recognition.

Finally, we must creatively destroy what was, to replace it with what must be. If we do not, competition will do it to and/or for us. And, we must do all of this before our competition beats us to the solution—or we will become irrelevant.

PARTNERSHIPS ARE THE BEGINNING

Developing relationships into partnerships is the first and most essential foundation of shape-shifting. Shape-shifting encompasses the whole company, and it is this shape of the business that must be changed. In the next few chapters, I will deal with each of these concepts in depth. This book is not only a call to action (why, what) but guide to the types of actions needed (how) to get started toward a successful outcome.

In my previous book, *The Power of Partnerships*, I touched on shape-shifting near the end of the book, where I called it "partnership-based reconfiguration." Partnerships are necessary because their absence renders us unable to respond even if we recognize what to do to deliver the value needed for the future. If customer partnerships are not in place, feedback from the outside market will be poor or incomplete. If supplier partnerships are not sound, our ability to respond will be hampered at best, and precluded at worst, by the inability or unwillingness of our suppliers to support our changes. If we have not formed partnerships with our associates and employees, there is no way we will be able to respond properly to the needs of the marketplace. But it is the absence of culture-based partnerships with employees and associates that is perhaps the most overwhelming obstacle of all. In short, weak or nonexistent partnerships will hamper the process of shape-shifting.

CUSTOMER VALUE MUST CREATE ECONOMIC VALUE

Before we move on, let's review the concept of EVA (Economic Value Added) and the related concept of stakeholder value. These should be a constant benchmark against which to measure our shape-shifting. It will do us little good to create and deliver the best value if we do not earn a return in excess of our cost of capital. Profit in itself cannot be an actionable goal, but it is an imperative for continued viability. Ultimately, the customer value discussed thus far must be translated into another kind of value for business success—EVA. A positive EVA means, in simple terms, that the company is able to earn a higher return than its cost of capital.

Certainly, it is possible that companies could incur costs by offering value in excess of the desire of the customers to pay for it. If the cost of adding this "excess value" is not recoverable in price (or market position/volume to yield lower costs eventually) the company could become a consumer success but an economic failure. There are numerous examples, notably in the telephone industry, where the companies with the highest customer satisfaction do not deliver the highest EVA! Customer service is one area in which this risk is great. It is a powerful value influence, although it is less tangible and cost can add up rapidly, the returns can be even greater, if there is awareness of the economics of service. Excellent service also generates customer loyalty better than many other attributes, and reduces the impact of price over a longer term. Understanding these trade-offs can influence significantly the shape of the value targeted.

Another risk is providing "specification" attributes (sometimes called quality) in the product that are not perceived as worth more money, but add more cost.

If we consider the creation of stakeholder value and stakeholder management, a series of useful steps emerge. They are simplified here to itemize how to direct people toward the creation of a new shape. By using stakeholder management principles we never forget that the customer must "buy" whatever is created, resulting in four benefits:

1. Improved alignment to "pull in the same direction."
2. Better focus on all stakeholders and long versus short term.
3. Continuity of purpose in the face of constant change.
4. Flexibility to adapt in the way that strong partnerships provide such adaptive flexibility.

Remember, above all, the business must maintain its economic viability, and that means earning a return on assets greater than its cost of capital—thus creating a positive EVA.

With these final cautions in mind, the time has come to discuss how to begin the shape-shifting process in earnest.

10.

Assessing Shape of Value for Customers

The customer is interested in one thing only; results, the value we deliver to him or her.
—Michael Hammer, "Behind Reengineering,"
Executive Excellence, August, 1996
It's amazing how much you can learn if you simply ask other people rather than drive your own agenda.
—Lawrence Milligan, Senior VP
Procter & Gamble

FINDING THE SHAPE OF VALUE

The first and most important shape to profile is the market or customer. Dr. Carl Steidtmann is head of Management Horizons, an organization that studies the behavior of retailers and consumers. His findings reinforce why we must find a way to understand the customer's shape of value, and then match it with our own value creation and delivery efforts. According to Steidtmann, "It will get harder to make and keep a customer. Expectations are getting higher. Different strokes will satisfy different folks." How are we to understand those different "strokes?" The answer, of course is by developing their shape of value.

The answer, as I've said many times is, listen to your sources of information and knowledge, and listen carefully. This chapter illustrates the many different views on understanding how to provide value to customers. If you listen well to the customers, the insights you gain about which shape will provide them the value they desire will prove invaluable.

Whom to Ask

Determining whom to ask the pertinent questions about value is always an interesting challenge. To say "the decision maker" is not sufficient because that person or group of people is not always obvious. In a consumer setting, the answer may be more clear-cut; usually it is the purchaser and any associated "economic" gatekeepers such as spouses, parents, and so on. If the sale is to an industrial purchaser, the buyer seems obvious, but remember, often the people who define the specifications are more influential in the decision than the actual purchaser. A carefully written set of specs can include or exclude large groups of potential suppliers, and dramatically alter the purchase decision. The simple inclusion of a performance criterion based on a proprietary technology can limit the value decision to even a single source. In the retailer's/customer's case, the buyer may actually make the decision; or he or she may be limited by a senior buyer, merchandise manager, or even a committee if the product is part of a major category or a promotional plan. Favorable feedback by operations or field service personnel can include or exclude a supplier in certain cases. So, whom to ask is more complex than it would seem initially.

The answer then is that the question-and-answer process must cover at least three levels of value decision evaluators: the immediate buyer (who signs or places the order), higher manager/gatekeeper (who selects or approves the source to buy from), and a field/technical/operational person(s) (who may influence the purchase decision in many different ways). Note that I said "at least," because this exercise might reveal that the three should become five—or more! Since the goal is to define value clearly in order to develop an accurate shape of value diagnostic profile and diagram, those questioned and how frank and honest they are in answering is critically important.

What to Ask

Understanding value involves asking questions and carefully analyzing the answers, but it also involves observation and analysis of what the customer is buying now and the probable reasons why. Depending on how long and in how structured an environment these questions asked, there are some proven skills that can be employed. If the interview is not "formal," then it is most important to be prepared, to know what you want to learn before the meeting with the customer. Unless you have prepared by writing down the questions to which you would like answers, the conversation or discussion may veer away from your topics, and the questions may never get asked or answered.

This sounds obvious, I know, but in my experience, salespeople and executives often do not prepare well for this kind of situation. Then after the meeting, and much to their chagrin, they find they have not even posed the most important questions. I recommend you follow these few simple guidelines to help formulate questions:

- Always stick to the point of the question. Don't digress or give the person you are asking an easy way to evade the question or to give a vague answer.
- Keep questions short and simple. Simple questions get simple answers that are often more direct and useful.
- Each question should be only one question and get one answer. Multiple questions combined as one lead to indefinite or confusing answers.
- Avoid asking leading questions or influencing the response by the order of questions. You are trying to find out what the customer thinks and feels, not what you want to hear.
- Try to get a comparative response (to competitors, other products, etc.).
- Decide whether to ask an open-ended or closed-ended question on a topic, depending on whether you want the respondent to clarify, expand, (open-ended), or give specific, definite answers (closed-ended).
- Consider hiring an independent third party to formulate a series of the questions and provide an objective assessment, and complete diagnostic profile and shape of value diagram. (A third party will often get answers that are both different and more to the point that you could.)

How to Ask

Have a list of the descriptors of the value attributes handy to help frame your questions. I have repeated the list in Figure 10-1 for convenience, followed by some suggested questions to ask. Obviously, these questions should be tailored for your business.

When to Ask

Initially, you ask as often as possible without creating a conditioned or mechanical response. The goal is to get fresh, honest answers, but to be continuously aware of how things are going.

Quality:
- **Specification (Robustness, Refinement):** What is the intended or designed performance level or feature richness? *What is it you want? What must it do?*
- **Conformance (Information):** Does the product conform to the intended specification? How well? *Does it meet your needs?*
- **Consistency (Variability):** Is there a high level of consistency to the product or a low level of variability? *How consistent must it be?*
- **Reliability:** Does the product keep doing what it is intended to do, the same way, over and over for a long time? *How reliable must it be?*
- **Durability:** Does the product "hold up" or last a long time and through hard use or even modest misuse? *How long must it last?*

Service:
- **Courtesy (Intimacy):** Is the service courteous, pleasant, and friendly? *How are we to deal with?*
- **Ease (Simplicity):** Is the service easy to get or use? *Do we make it easy for you?*
- **Information:** Is it easy to find out the status of the product or service at any time? *Can we tell you what you need to know—fast?*
- **Flexibility:** Can the service be accessed and used many different ways? *Are we flexible enough?*
- **Adaptability (Responsiveness):** Can the service be tailored to specific needs of the customer, and be readily altered as situations change? *Are we responsive enough?*

Speed:
- **Convenience (Effortlessness):** Is it easy to obtain the product? *How hard do we make it?*
- **Timeliness:** Is the product available on a timely basis? *Do we get it to you on time?*
- **Flexibility:** Does the product arrive where, when, and how it is wanted? *Is it there where, when, and how you want it?*
- **Throughput:** Is the time from beginning to end of the cycle (of order/production/delivery) short and efficient? *Can we get it through the plant fast enough?*
- **Information:** Is accurate information available quickly? *Do we know where things stand?*

Cost (Low):
- **First Cost:** Is the first cost low enough to be competitive? *Are we competitive?*
- **Handling and Packaging:** Is there little waste in non-value-added costs in getting the product where/when it must be? *Where do we waste money?*
- **Throughput and Delivery (Information):** Is there an ability to know where the product is in its throughput cycle at little or no extra cost? *Do we know where things are?*
- **Penalties:** Do requested changes or nonstandard needs incur extra costs and charges? *Are we flexible enough?*
- **Premiums:** Is it possible to gain speed, flexibility, or other customized changes by paying a modest fee or no premium? *Do we expect too much?*

Innovation:
- **Uniqueness (Proprietary or Exclusive):** Can the product be unique, proprietary, exclusive, or customized? *Is it special?*
- **Cachet and Status:** Does the product convey additional importance or exclusivity on its owner for some reason? *What is special about it?*
- **Technology:** Is there a breakthrough technology involved with the product or some aspect of it? *Is it a breakthrough?*
- **Entertainment (Information):** Does some aspect of the product provide unusual entertainment or informational benefits? *What's really "neat or fun" about it?*
- **Style (Trend or Fad):** Is the product particularly ideal with respect to some current style, trend, or fad that makes it desirable? *Is it "hot?"*

Figure 10-1 Descriptors for Value Attributes

- Whenever a closely related topic is being discussed it is a good time to ask about the value being provided in whichever attribute is relevant.
- Before making any changes based on internal needs or assumptions is an important time to ask about the value perception of the customer.
- If there is a known problem, it is better to ask about it and ascertain its severity than to let it fester and provide a competitor with an opportunity.

Asking about a problem can be difficult but it must be done because it provides two good opportunities: to look for a root cause to avoid recurrence and to explain what remedial actions are being taken, and see if they are well received.

Ideally, there will be periods when a lengthy session will enable asking about the full range of value attributes, to encourage the customer's help in completing a shape of value diagnostic profile and diagram.

DIAGRAM THE ANSWERS

As these question-and-answer sessions occur, draw a quick diagram to record your impressions and/or the customer's answers (see Figure 10-2). Use the diagram as a discussion tool after the customer becomes familiar with it. Weighting is done best in dialogue with the customer. Seize the opportunity. Carry blank copies of the diagram shown in Figure 10-2 with you. Plot on the diagram right in front of the customer. You want to make them curious and involve them in setting the values.

Locate and mark the points on the 10-point (or 100-point) scale that most accurately represents the emphasis on each attribute by the customer (or market). Use the 0 to 10 (or 100) rating scale to locate these points. If you wish to use weighting for importance of the various attributes, take time to weight the five attributes relative to each other. Either divide the outcome by 10, as in the example of weighting, or change the gradations on the lines of the value pentastar to a scale of 0 to 100. If any of the factors multiplied by the weighting exceeds this, limiting the shape is acceptable, since the diagram will already be very skewed, representing a shape of value highly biased by one or two attributes.

Customers in very similar businesses may have very similar shapes of value. This is normal. Just be sure to be sensitive to the nuances that differentiate one from the other, and consider using weighting for those to better reflect the differences. Pursue a better understanding of these nuances in your questioning process. Try using the diagram with several different but similar customers. Remember, the absolute value of the evaluations is less important than the consistency, dialogue, and understanding that goes into them.

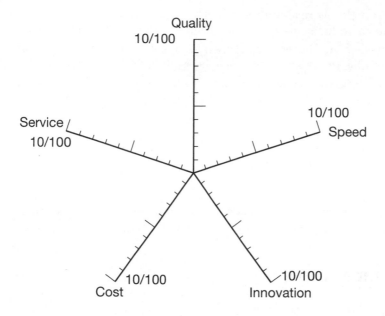

Figure 10-2 The Value Pentastar Diagram

Also remember that there is a minimum acceptable level for each of the value attributes, below which you will be barred from competition. It is important that you determine where that minimum level is and identify it on the shape of value diagram. An example of this in recent years is the necessity of using bar coding and other EDI (Electronic Data Interchange) protocols as a requirement of doing business with certain companies. Another example is that consumers have raised their minimum value level for quality in automobiles as a result of the dramatic progress made by the Japanese auto producers.

Once you have tried this exercise internally, find some friendly customers and ask them to complete the diagnostic profile and shape of value diagram with you. This is when you will realize the real power of such an approach. When the customer evaluates a value attribute much differently from you, a really important piece of information has made itself known. Again, do not "lead" customers. Let them select numbers on the profile and draw them onto diagram. Then discuss why and how they arrived at those evaluations. Adapt the definitions and descriptors to the dialogue, and tailor them to your own industry and situation; add to the list, change terms to fit, and meet your needs. It is only a tool! The goal is understanding the shape of value that matches the desire of the customer!

"WISHING OUT LOUD"

Next start a process I call "wishing out loud." Engage the customer to "wish" that the shape could be different—or just better (larger). In doing so, you will begin to find out what he or she might value more, or "next" even though the customer does not know or realize it yet. The benefit of this "wishing out loud" process is that it removes the restrictions normally present about asking for things that are perceived to be impossible. Nevertheless, exert caution. The customer may wish for "everything," and in doing so not prioritize any of the wishes. This is where the weighting process can help. Ask the customer to allocate 25 points among the things he or she wished for in proportion to their importance or desirability. Weighting the wishes can be very effective when combined with some of the question-and-answer processes that follow. True creative synergy can result, leading to revolutionary ideas for the business to develop and build upon.

Thinking about what might be desired in the future is often difficult, but very important. Making time to do this in a quiet, contemplative setting free from the distractions of the day-to-day business is critical. Getting to the future ahead of competitors is the point of this introspective, reflective communications process.

Question-and-Answer Techniques That Work

It is beyond the scope of this book to catalog the infinite number of techniques you can use to "get close to the customers" to understand value from their perspective. I will list a few that have proven useful in different settings. These techniques should provide a reasonable starting point. I included a few words of caution with each approach.

- *Hold key customer councils* made up of small groups of decision makers from your most important clientele. These can be held in conjunction with social or recreational events to create a more relaxed atmosphere. (These will not, however, tell very much about what the customers you do not sell think about you!)
- *Form customer advisory boards.* These can be useful for gaining insights into the shape of value desired, being delivered, or compared to competitors. Done properly, these boards can also help determine the shape of the business needed to enable the value creation and delivery. Industrial companies do particularly well with this approach. The boards should be made up of 5 to 15 members, who receive no cash compensation (to avoid any

appearance of impropriety), and meet two to four times per year (or on special critical decision-making occasions like potential acquisitions and/or plant expansions). The information shared with such of boards can be "near-proprietary," but it must be carefully screened to assure that confidential information is treated as such.

- *Conduct customer and/or (end-user) consumer panels* to reveal information filtered out by the intermediate customer. But take care; on these panels, there is always danger of the "loudest voice" dominating, or causing a "jump on the bandwagon effect" which distorts the true opinions of the members. Using professional interviewers may improve the validity of the responses.

- *Do complaint analysis.* Complainers can provide useful input about problems; but many customers do not complain, they just buy elsewhere. Futhermore, those who do complain tend to be of a more homogenous type, and probably do not represent the customer base accurately. Do not extrapolate general conclusions from this group. Call complainers back and ask for more information, then ask if their problem has been taken care of—and if not, take care of it. A "service recovery" situation is, ironically, a powerful time to build customer satisfaction.

- *Go on customer visits and sales calls.* These are most beneficial when someone other than the regular sales representative is the visitor who asks many of the questions. Upper management and nonsales staff should participate in these. Remember, there is always a degree of negotiation going on, so balance the emphasis given to specific issues carefully against that fact.

- *Conduct surveys.* These may be done in several forms, written or verbal and for several factors: on customer satisfaction with the total experience, on the effectiveness of the transaction process, on the product or service sold, or on more subjective factors such as cooperation, communication, and so on. Surveys can also be done with the intermediate customer and/or the end user or both. Each reveals different aspects of value and satisfaction. Surveys should be designed and administered by professionals who understand and assure the validity, the nonbias of the results, and more. Quick, simple surveys done by company sales, marketing, or customer service staffs usually reveal little that is not already known—although they do convey a "we care about you" message. They also infer that something will be done about those aspects whose ratings are poor. Don't forget to take action on findings.

- *Conduct intercepts and interviews.* This is a common form of consumer research being done in the shopping environment, which, if structured carefully and properly, can yield useful qualitative and some quantitative results. (Be careful if surveying buying intentions and prices. The only really accurate purchase intention survey I have ever seen is when the votes are cast with metal or paper containing pictures of dead presidents [in the United States of America] or leaders of state—i.e., with money!)

- *Encourage internal feedback or surveys.* This is useful in two ways. Senior executives can gain useful insights by holding sessions with front-line associates to learn "what really goes on." Since employees of a company are also consumers, surveys among those who are more removed from the product or service can also be quite informative. The past master of this was Sears, who conducted numerous "hallway" surveys of its salaried, clerical, and warehouse staff on new products. While far from conclusive, this technique is a quick way to learn how "ordinary consumers" feel about products.

- *Form customer satisfaction councils.* These consist of a group of representatives from different functions, divisions, organizational units, and so forth, who come together regularly to provide perspectives on this critical issue of customer satisfaction. As in any group session, watch for opinion dominators/influencers.

- *Hold focus groups.* This market research tool is useful for obtaining qualitative information, but is too small and limited to yield useful quantitative information. Focus groups can be very effective for exploring qualitative value aspects of a product or service. Make sure they are moderated by an unbiased professional. And videotape them to help capture the nuances of the discussion.

- *Employ quality function deployment.* This is a rather complex analytical tool used to prioritize the importance of the various aspects of quality, which can be extended broadly. Since it is a specialized process, I will not attempt to describe it in detail. A good introductory article entitled "The House of Quality," by John R. Hauser and Don Clausing (*Harvard Business Review*, May–June, 1988, pp. 63–73) describes the approach simply and completely. Consulting specialists can assist in such efforts, and this approach can yield substantial benefits in analyzing the importance of features and performance that are part of the quality or innovative content of products or services.

Finally, there is one other, informal approach I have found quite useful. It consists of making a phone call to a peer-level customer manager or executive and asking, "How are things going?" "How are you doing with us, and how are we doing with you?" Such questions will often expose important issues. At the very least they open a dialogue that is helpful in building relationships that lead to partnerships. In partnerships, many of the question-and-answer processes described happen naturally during partner meetings.

Timely Information Is Essential

Traditionally, a snapshot of the customer's interpretation of value could be taken every few months or once a year. But today, the rate of change and the intensity of the competitive environment requires that we know what our customers value and why in real time—right now! If we do not, and a competitor does, we risk losing business. As discussed earlier, value is situational and constantly shifting. If our product stops selling (in a retail setting) or is obsoleted by newer, higher-value technology, we had better know that immediately. How? That is the question each of us must answer for his or her own situation. Monitor any available point-of-sale data; ask often and make it easy for the customers to respond, using cards, fax numbers, 800 lines, e-mail or Internet sites, or whatever works for you.

Is the Customer Always Right? Justin Martin wrote an article in *Fortune* (May 1, 1995; pp. 121–126) titled "Ignore Your Customer." In it he talks about the minority of instances where the customers don't know what they value. (Recall the University of Tennessee research that revealed this fact as well.) His point, and mine, is that there can be too much preoccupation with giving the customer exactly what he or she thinks he or she wants. But most companies have the opposite problem. They come up with what they think is right and attempt to sell it to the customer, instead of listening and being responsive to the customer. Consider GM, IBM, and Sears. IBM kept pushing mainframes and software while customers wanted PCs and client-server software. According to Michael Bozic (then president of Sears), "We have been guilty of buying. . . and selling what Sears wanted to sell instead of what Sears customers wanted to buy." GM, too, was guilty of this when they continued to produce large gas-guzzlers even as the Japanese were methodically taking away their market share with small, gas-efficient well-equipped, high-quality cars.

When this kind of managerial flaw can be detected as a "malformed shape" then remedial action is possible before it's too late. In their book, *Customer Responsive Management* (Blackwell, 1996), Frank Davis and Karl Manrodt bring this topic into clear focus. Their premise, to be responsive to the customer instead of developing average, aggregate solutions that satisfy no one in particular, is becoming more feasible as the capability of the information infrastructure increases.

Although there are times when it makes sense to "ignore your customers" in new product planning, these are relatively few. If a strong partnership exists, customers will exhort suppliers to "ignore" their preferences in the interest of seeing innovative new products or service ideas. How crazy was Fred Smith to consider hauling packages on airplanes all the way back to Memphis, Tennessee, every night to sort and reship them throughout the country? Few customers would have supported the idea that spawned FedEx.

Martin closes his article on ignoring the customer with these words: "But if a company truly understands its customers' needs, it can in good conscience disregard what they claim to want. This will save you lots of time, not to mention aggravation and some potentially embarrassing moves." The point is, beware of ignoring the customer without a *very good reason*!

In *The Power of Partnerships* I wrote at length about the importance of strong relationships between customers and suppliers. Important shape of value considerations are built into these relationships. Keeping a customer satisfied is more important than ever as competition for new customers intensifies.

THINK FORWARD AND BACKWARD

In his article "Coping with Faster Change" (*Nation's Business*, March 1995, pp. 27–29) noted speaker Joel Barker cautioned entrepreneurs to think in terms of the next 5 to 10 years. How? It's incredibly difficult. Pick some event in your life or business of the past 10 years, and reflect for a moment on how much has changed in that decade. Nevertheless, Barker's premise is valid in some respects. Those who think forward and backward about the amount and nature of change are and will continue to be more successful than those who do not. Since you are reading this book, you fit in that category.

Now focus on some things that are "predictable." Demographics (barring war or plague) can predict with some accuracy how many people there will be of specific age groups since most of them are already born. Another thing is certain. All businesses will have suppliers, customers, employees (or the equivalent), and some kind of outside supporting partners. That is why it is so important to get these relationships in place and know how to maintain them.

Communication and transportation technology will also continue to advance, so the Earth will continue to shrink, adding to competition from distant places. Technology will also continue to improve productivity, requiring fewer people. This means the supply of people will be "in excess." Whenever this happens, some creative soul finds a way to put them to work doing something for which other people will pay; and somehow, an equilibrium is found. That doesn't mean the work or pay will be better, just that it will be there, but different.

Huffy Bicycles: The Anatomy of a Failed Shift (pun intended)

While I was at Huffy, some of our most disappointing failures came from mis-reading consumer research. Two, in particular, are worthy of mention to close this chapter. They occurred exactly 10 years apart, and both on bicy-cles whose names contained the word "wind." The first was the Aerowind. Its development was a case of getting too far ahead of the consumers' desires, and being so blinded by our own opinion that we did not pay atten-tion to our research. Part of our research was to independently test (in mall intercepts with members of the target market for the product) by compari-son with alternatives of the same type and/or price range.

The first step was to test "pieces" of the product—grips, seats, paint col-ors, frame styles, and so on. The next step was to test complete products, with graphics, names, and so forth. The test always included "benchmarks" in the form of current products (ours or our competitors) with proven sales performance. When the research for the Aerowind's new aerodynamically designed components was done, the various elements all scored poorly indi-vidually. The consumer failed to "see" the value. Still, we continued devel-oping the bike. It was a champagne-gold color, which had scored very poorly in research, but looked great in the high-intensity spotlights of our display room. Unfortunately, none of our mass retail store customers used anything but fluorescent lighting, which made the product look dull, and almost dis-appear into the background of the display, a fact we only realized later, because at that time, placing the product in a retail store setting was not part of our testing! While introducing the product amidst much fanfare at the International Toy Fair, we realized another error. Our new advertising agency had studied the bike market and concluded that lightweight, adult-sized bikes sold as well during the Christmas season as in the spring, and urged us to make this a Christmas feature product.

What the ad agency failed to do, and we failed to realize, was understand that the large bikes that did sell at Christmas were styled to appeal to larger *children*, not adults! Now we had an adult-styled bike, composed of low-scoring individual components and features, which showed poorly in the retail display environment, being promoted at a time of year when the target market was not active. Needless to say, it was a dismal failure.

Nevertheless, our retail customers trusted our track record, and stocked the bike. Of course, it did not sell. After redating receivables, providing markdown allowances, and canceling many reorders, we had to run a major (unplanned) advertising campaign with another (additional) rebate in the spring to pull products through at retail. The point is, we fell in love with our own creation, and did not listen to the value perceptions of the cus-tomer. We suffered a great economic loss and damage to our credibility as product marketers.

The next major error did not occur for 10 years, when a slightly different, but equally damaging new-product launch reminded us to make sure we understood the customer's perception of value. This time the product was the Crosswind bicycle, which was also a "leading-edge" product of the new hybrid or "cross" bike category. Mountain bikes had been huge successes, and had only one drawback: The large tires and frame, which made them suitable for off-road and dirt trail use, made them harder to pedal and ride on paved surfaces. Enthusiasts had already figured out that most riders stay on paved surfaces, and had begun substituting thinner tires with less aggressive tread on a slightly lighter frame.

In addition, our industry leader status and partnerships with suppliers had given us proprietary rights for the mass retail market to a new shifting system, Grip Shift, that was all the rage in the enthusiast market. Once again, we were entranced by our own creation. The combination of a cross bike with exclusive Grip Shift was, we believed, a "home run" in the highly competitive bike market. With the encouragement of our corporate executives, we priced it as high as we thought the market would bear, since no competitor could have the same features. Alas, our new, bright, aggressive marketing team overlooked one minor stage of the normal market research: The product was tested only among "cross bikes," where it scored very well; it was the most preferred of its class. But no one tested it in the environment at retail—among mountain bikes of all types and features, many selling at bargain prices (since that category was more mature, and price competition had intensified). When displayed among these beefy, feature-laden products, the Crosswind looked anemic and underequipped. The sophisticated Grip Shift was unfamiliar to mass retail consumers, and its unassuming presence, neatly integrated into the handlebar and grip combination (a major attraction to enthusiasts) made it even harder to recognize. Customers couldn't "see" the value.

In spite of "hang tags" proclaiming this new innovative feature, sales were dismal. Competing products looked like more value in the eyes of the target consumers, and it did not sell. For the second time, we had forgotten that value is defined by the consumer, and not by our impression of why a product seems valuable. These were both multimillion-dollar, painful lessons. Perhaps a lesson in humility is in order every now and then, lest we forget who defines value and how important the situation and context of that definition are.

11.

Comparing Shape of Value to Competitors

An outfit in denial may be vastly successful, planning hard for the future, busy, confident—and doomed. What kind of company is likely to fall into this trap? A vastly successful one.
—Walter Kiechel III, "Facing Up to Denial," *Fortune*, October 18, 1993, p. 163.

EVALUATE BY COMPARING TO COMPETITORS

It is very useful to draw value pentastars for your competitors, and then compare their shapes to your own. It is even better if the customer will help draw these for competitors. This will expose competitive strengths to build on or weaknesses that need attention. In completing competitive diagrams, always start by comparing yourself against your toughest competitors, keeping in mind that matching the customers' shape is the goal. There is often a tendency to either overestimate or underestimate the capabilities of the competitors. If you overestimate, you beat them by more; if you underestimate, you get clobbered. Which sounds better?

To do Value Pentastars for competitors most effectively, you will need good competitive intelligence. This means going far beyond what the sales force hears from the buyers, conventional wisdom, or trade gossip. Thanks to the Internet, there is now a huge amount of data on competitors readily available to those who will seek it out and spend the time to assimilate it.

Asking the right questions and developing sources from trade relationships fine tunes this knowledge. Critical observation only adds to the knowledge.

Surprisingly, few companies have any concerted or organized effort to collect information about competitors. Many that collect it do little with it. Sometimes what is not being said reveals more than what is. Few people brag about (or even mention) things they are *not* good at! One old saw says "a problem well defined is half solved." I say "a competitor well understood is half beaten!" Now there is a means to not only share and digest this customer intelligence data but also put it into a format that relates it to the ultimate decision factor—the shape of value provided to customers.

That is why this process is so important. This competitor shape of value diagram can be done initially in either of two ways: Select the one best competitor in the chosen market and do a shape of value comparison; or, if the market can be broken into niche competition, select a composite best competitor made up of "the best of the best," and compare to that. Although the latter is a much more stringent test to conduct, it can expose vulnerability to those competitors controlling segments of a market, which will lead to erosion later. The composite best competitor is an imaginary figure created by diagramming the best of each of the five value attributes of various competitors. The measure of composite best competitor is important for industry leaders, because it illustrates where they are vulnerable to attack. This concept comes from an approach used by AT&T for competitive evaluation. It is a very tough standard, but one against which any company aspiring to or enjoying industry leadership must measure. As AT&T market research manager Bill France points out, "a dominant industry leader is subject to erosion of their position from many competitors . . . . Because no one of them is a significant threat does not mean that the composite of them cannot erode a significant piece of market position." Because of this, a composite best competitor that embodies the best features of the toughest competitor in the criteria measured must be considered.

A composite diagram of an industry with three major competitors is shown in Figure 11-2. This illustration assumes that your company is one of the competitors, and that there are two others, a large one and a small one.

When you overlay the two competitors' diagrams and add your own, it becomes evident where your strengths and weaknesses lie. This will help illustrate how you perform in the eyes of your customers compared to competitors. Look for the differences or "value gaps." Carefully consider which attributes are advantages and which are disadvantages.

A. The larger competitor has an edge in innovation.
B. Both competitors are lower-cost producers.
C. You have an edge in quality

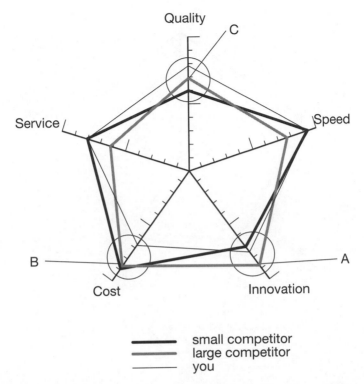

Figure 11-1 The Value Pentastar for Two Competitors for a Given Customer Market

If the example illustrated in the diagram in Figure 11-1 is accurate, the decision may be decided by whether innovation, low cost, or quality is more important. If a diagram of the shape of value is closely clustered, it may be necessary to use weighting to determine the probable outcome in a competition this close. Doing such a diagram in color, on transparencies, or on a computer screen allows overlaying the customer's "desired" shape on the same diagram. In this way, many competitive dynamics can be displayed and observed at one time; gaps can be discussed and diagnosed, and advantages can be built upon and used tactically or strategically.

When partnerships with customers are in place (or underway), you can ask the customer to help you draw this kind of diagram. (A very revealing comparison is to do one internally and have one done by the customer—for both you and your major competitors—then compare the differences.) Remember, such tools are good overall value profile indicators, but they are not sufficient to define the actions to take, since they are "averages of averages." To take action, it is necessary to break down the overall evaluation into detail. If two or more competitors are a threat, several separate value pentastars should be done, one for each competitor.

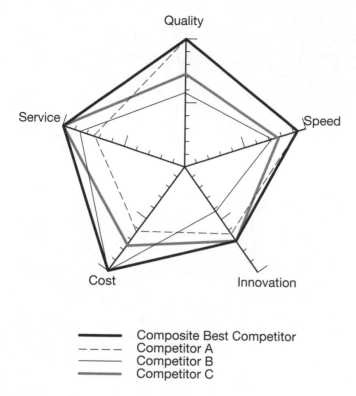

Figure 11-2 The Value Pentastar for Three Competitors

Figure 11-2 shows a diagram of three competitors and a composite best competitor. To keep this diagram from becoming impossibly "busy," I have not overlaid "you." As is evident by the examples I have chosen, measuring up against the best composite competitor is a daunting task. This is exactly what dominant industry leaders face. If a competitor is better enough on a couple of major attributes of value, that firm can undermine the leader's position. If several competitors all do this, the leader faces serious market erosion. In long-distance telecommunications, for example, at one time or another Sprint has won business from AT&T because of the transmission quality of its network (hence its "sound of a pin dropping" ad campaign). MCI won business thanks to its low-cost Friends and Family program. Neither jeopardized AT&T's leadership position alone, but together they became a serious threat. Add the plethora of smaller, specialized service discounters, and AT&T had to fight on many fronts, dealing with several value attributes at once—a composite best competitor.

DENIAL INHIBITS CHANGE

"An outfit in denial may be vastly successful, planning hard for the future, busy, confident—and doomed," wrote Walter Kiechel III in "Facing Up to Denial," (*Fortune*, October 18, 1993, p. 163). Misleading others is often easy, but misleading ourselves is easier still—because we want to believe our own views of reality. One of the most critical roles of a leader is to create a clear understanding of the current reality and a healthy dissatisfaction with it. "What kind of company is likely to fall into this trap? A vastly successful one" Kiechel concludes. Diagnostic profiles and shape of value diagrams such as I am proposing are only as good as the honest analysis that goes into them.

There are a few questions posed by W. Chan Kim and Renee Mauborgne, in "Value Innovation: The Strategic Logic of High Growth" (Harvard Business Review: Jan–Feb 1997, pp. 103–112), that we can use here to help break out of denial or conventional thinking. If we use our full awareness of the industry situation, competition, and our own competencies, then we can ask (emphasis added):

1. Which of the aspects we *take for granted* about our industry should be *removed or rethought*?
2. Which value and performance levels should we attempt to *raise* to whole new levels?
3. Which value and performance levels should we attempt to *lower* to whole new levels?
4. What conditions, factors, or situations might be *created* that no one has considered or offered to enable *whole new levels of value* to be delivered?

These are the principles Gary Hamel refers to when he describes "rule breakers." Once such questions have been asked and answered, we are ready to begin applying the shape of value graphical approach.

At first I was reluctant to include these simple graphical techniques in the book since they can lead to manipulation and self-deception (denial), both of which are very dangerous. But I decided to include them because the process of diagramming and evaluating each value attribute stimulates thought and dialogue about the reality of the current situation. The resultant shapes help reinforce and communicate the need to shift the shape of the business in a very tangible, meaningful, and visual way.

In my experience, the more you use this value pentastar to create a visual shape of value, the more ways you will find to use it. Add your own insights to make the most of this simple, yet powerful visual tool. You may find descriptions of attributes that differ from the ones I have defined, but as long as the number does not exceed five, the definitions are internally consistent, and the attributes cover all the important aspects of value, other attributes can be substituted. The five value attributes chosen have stood the test of time and expert thought, so replace them only with caution. It is better to do supporting shape of value diagrams relating to dimensions of shape, rather than to simply omit or change the attributes. (Diagrams used in the dimensions of shape will be covered in Chapter 15.)

The Competition Is Improving, Too

Even if your ratings are positive, never forget, your competitors are working on improvement and shape-shifting, too. The yardstick for best value is always getting longer, the barriers always higher.

Indiana University basketball coach Bobby Knight tells an apocryphal story about competition that is relevant here, and that I will paraphrase. A group was on a safari in Africa. One of the members was a big, strong, but out-of-shape "macho man." He volunteered to bring up the rear, while carrying the largest pack, a difficult job, second only to the lead person who must break the trail and set the pace. The day was hot and humid, and he was falling off the pace. The gap between him and the next person, an African bearer was lengthening steadily. As the group rounded a sharp turn in the dense jungle, the rest of the group disappeared from his view. Just as the man decided to pick up his pace and catch up, he saw a huge lion crouching on a rock ahead with a menacing look in his eye. The man struggled to untangle his rifle strap from the large pack. The lion snarled once and leaped just as the man disentangled his gun.

But the lion overshot his prey and went over the man's head, only scratching the man's temple. The man fired his gun into the air and the lion ran off into the jungle. At the sound of a gunshot, the rest of the group came running back. The man was embarrassed by getting separated from the group and being unable to free his gun, so he decided not to tell the truth about what happened. He told his party that he had been scratched by a tree limb and fallen, at which point his gun went off. When the safari set up camp that evening, the man sneaked off into the woods to practice disentangling his gun and firing it at an imaginary lion. As he was repeatedly seizing his gun, raising it into positions, and pretending to ward off the lion, he noticed the lion perched on a distant rock. He watched intently as the lion, over and over, practiced shorter leaps.

The moral of this little story is obvious. As Huffy Bicycles was building a dominant position in mass-market bikes in the late 1980s and early 1990s, competition was working to improve faster. One of its domestic competitors,

Roadmaster, used lower labor and benefit costs to equal or surpass Huffy as the lowest-cost U. S. bicycle producer. This was a devastating blow that seriously damaged Huffy's competitive position and profitability.

Similarly, even as Rubbermaid was building a dominant retail position in the 1980s and early 1990s, competitors were searching for its weak spots, to find an approach to shift their shape and improve faster. In the early 1990s, it was evident that these competitors were becoming increasingly dangerous to Rubbermaid's overall profitability by driving down prices in selected customer or product segments.

And as Sears was struggling to improve its position in retailing for much of the 1980s, its competition was improving faster. Only in the past year or two has it gained on the competition. Thus, it is not enough just to improve. Improvement must have direction (dimensions) and results (attributes). The accelerating rate of change in today's global marketplace makes that task even more challenging.

PART THREE

How?

"I THINK THE CHALLENGE FOR MANAGEMENT IN THE FUTURE IS TO SUBSTANTIALLY IMPROVE ITS ABILITY TO ANTICIPATE CHANGE. ...TO SPOT A PARADIGM SHIFT IN ITS EARLY FORMATION ...TO UNDERSTAND THE LONG-TERM IMPLICATIONS OF A NEW CHANGE WHEN YOU FIND IT. "
—Joel A. Barker, Futurist

12.

Shape-Shifting—New Partnerships

The ability of organizations to perform and continually improve their capabilities is the ultimate competitive advantage.
—Edward E. Lawler III, Director of Center for Effective Organizations, School of Business Administration, University of Southern California, quoted in *IndustryWeek*, August 21, 1995

DELIVERING THE BEST VALUE CONSISTENTLY

Up to this point, we have been analyzing what to do and why. It is far easier to describe what to do than how to do it. But now we must get to the hard part—*how* to provide the best value consistently. Discussing changes to core business systems is one thing; applying them to individual cases and companies is quite another, because no two situations are the same. Although most share common dimensions of structure, processes, culture, and relationships, each requires a unique solution, which is critical to value delivery. Remember from the University of Tennessee research team that the customers' interpretation of value is both situational and in a constant state of flux.

I developed this part of the book the way many of us manage. We know something has to be done, but we aren't completely sure how. We only know we must get started. So we start. Then we try to adjust as we encounter the unknowns or uncertainties.

167

About the time I reached this point in the book, I became intimately involved with the explosion of information technologies. I learned that even though the old ways still worked, industry consulting clients and university associates were finding new and better ways of operating, although usually by trial and error.

This reinforced my beliefs that company leaders have a responsibility to seek new shapes, to create a sense of urgency for change, even while the old ways are still successful. As I said earlier, the most important job of the leader is to bring about a clear understanding of and healthy dissatisfaction with the current situation. Then the leader must help the organization to build a compelling, shared vision of a more desirable future state. Finally, the leader must create an environment, design the path, and provide the resources to enable his organization to reach that future state. Once done, this must be repeated on an ongoing basis.

The harsh reality is that companies that fail to creatively destroy and then rebuild themselves to meet new challenges are usually overwhelmed by competitors that do just that. Author Jim Swartz refers to the phenomenon as *The Hunters and the Hunted* in his book by the same name (Portland, OR: Productivity Press, 1994). But beware: Do not destroy what you are until you have begun to build what it is you need to be, or you will be left with nothing! To begin to build what you need to become requires a clear understanding about how to shift your core competencies and capabilities, to create and deliver what is valued by your target customers. You must genuinely understand which of your core competencies and capabilities are the essence of your competitive position.

Let's examine the structure of a company—how it is organized and deployed to serve its customers and markets. Over the past few decades, various structural theories have become popular. There was centralization with vertical integration; then decentralization and local autonomy; most recently, outsourcing and what some call "hollowing" of corporations. All of these approaches have some merit. Each reflects the market knowledge of the time and the circumstances. As advances in information technology and communications brought to the fore entirely new possibilities in structure, companies scurried to implement them, often without fully understanding what value advantage these new structures could or would give them.

Suddenly, everybody had to work in "teams," even though many organizations lacked a team culture and hence became just groups of people going through the motions. Although Strategic Business Units (SBU) full functional "Divisions" formed to concentrate on specific strategic products or markets in the first wave of decentralization, made it easier to form tightly knit teams, later they trapped valuable people resources, denying them to other parts of the SBU's parent corporation. Vertical integration was a major advantage circa 1960 to 1970, but became a disadvantage in the early 1990s as technology and core capabilities shifted faster than the capital-intensive infrastructure could adapt. Restructuring was the thing to do, and everyone did it—not once, but several times.

The strongest companies "stayed the course," and though they may have been cycled through some of these shifts, they emerged stronger because of their constancy of purpose. In *Built to Last: Successful Habits of Visionary Companies* (Harper Business, 1994), Jim Collins and Jerry Porras described the importance of identifying core values and a sense of purpose. Their study of successful companies led them to conclude: "They [successful companies] have a basic set of core values and a sense of enduring purpose—a reason for existence—that changes seldom, if ever. These values and sense of purpose—which go far beyond just making money—are different from company to company, but within a given company, the core ideology remains tightly fixed."

But as we all know, the luxury of exhaustive study, *after the fact* is not possible for the business executive or manager. Thus such profound conclusions, while informative and useful, tell us only what worked in the past. They do not tell where to go now, how to get there, or what specific changes to make (or to avoid) in the future. We are left to "muddle on" as best we can. But keep these thoughts in mind as we embark on this somewhat perilous journey:

* The future is formed by evolution and revolution.
* You cannot extrapolate the past to predict the future.
* The best way to predict the future is to create it.
* You better do it fast, because competitors will be doing it too.

BRINGING ABOUT CHANGE SUCCESSFULLY

Change is difficult, and threatening. People like to maintain the status quo. Change processes fail more often than they succeed, despite the numerous books that have been written on the psychology of change. Leaders through the ages have approached it from different directions, with widely varying outcomes. Consultants earn millions of dollars facilitating change for companies whose leaders either are unwilling or unable to bring about change.

Nevertheless, change is not only necessary, it is essential to success. And the only reward for successful change is to be faced with the next one. Indeed, the only sustainable competitive advantage today is to have the ability to change, evolve, and adapt to continuous change better than the competition. Successful companies are proof of this.

There is only one constant factor in successful change processes—people. Books (this one included) and academics/consultants with their theories and practices have value only if they are used (adapted) properly and understood clearly by the people who must make the changes. A good place to start is to delineate a process for change. The following 10-step process is not complex, but it requires action and involvement at all levels of an organization. Senior management must take the lead, for the process will only be as successful as their leadership. Front-line supervision and middle management must believe in the change, too, and be involved in the preparation for it. There are many specific tools and techniques that will help you as you proceed through these steps, but the steps themselves are the keys to making successful change happen.

1. Develop a vision, mission, strategy, and operating plan as a guide for the organization or business. Involve all levels of the organization in the process. Then communicate the result in varying detail to all levels. Allow people a chance to question, dispute, interact, and gain equity in the plan before it is final.

2. Set high expectations with specific goals and objectives, but do not be unrealistic. Communicate those expectations, goals, and objectives along with the rationale behind them. Do not apologize if they are difficult. Just be honest. Embrace those who resist and consider their points carefully in planning what to do.

3. Build trust. Easy to say, not so easy to do. Start by being honest, fair above reproach (even when it is painful), and trustworthy. Go more than halfway anytime there is doubt. Regularly assess how things are going with people who are not a part of the "inner circle." Use anonymous surveys and other reliable response methods to find out if trust is truly building. Without it, nothing else will work.

4. Define each person's and group's role and responsibilities and job content. Enlist their participation in doing this. Keep it simple: list what they are expected to do (day-to-day roles) and what they are expected to get done (results and outcomes for which they are responsible). Ask for their help, and remember to say "please." Write the job descriptions, and revise them whenever they change—with people's involvement. Empower employees to have influence over as much as possible in their areas of responsibility.

5. Agree on measures that the people can use to track and how they and the organization/business are doing. Make these measures open and prominent and refer to them frequently. Revise them if they need to change. Identify boundaries and limitations. Relate the measures to external benefits, and to the strategic and operating plans. Provide the appropriate technology to make success possible.

6. Give frequent, balanced feedback, and lots of information about external conditions and "how things are going." Relate this feedback to the plans, and frame them against the external environment and internally set goals and objectives. Provide ideas to help and opportunities for others to help in those areas not working as hoped/planned. Use collaborative problem solving. Verify that the resources available are suitable to the job at hand.

7. Continuously update the people on the external situation—customers, market status, competition, other factors such as legislation/regulation. Involve them in gathering and sharing this information among themselves and their peers. Provide an easily accessible place for this process. Repeat the vision, mission, and plan over and over. Make it clear that successful results are expected.

8. Recognize and praise success and progress. Identify and critique failure and lack of progress. Enlist the people's help in building on success and identifying/remedying the root causes of failures. Encourage action—discourage inaction. Criticize results and methods, not people. If there are those not willing and/or able to perform at the levels required, make them aware of this and give them help with their problems. Then either help them improve or remove them from the organization. (There will be a small minority of people who just will not or cannot make it—get them out lest they infect the rest of the organization.)

9. Reward success and the desired behavior, both psychologically and financially—in multiple ways. Try to find a means of providing "ownership" in the successes, and share the wealth created by good financial results. Tie the rewards as closely as possible to activities over which the people have direct control, and that contain as few aspects as possible over which they have no control. As in building trust, fairness and going more than halfway is important. Don't forget to say "please" and "thank you."

10. Celebrate successes together, and share/grieve over setbacks together. Then resolve to do better, differently, and succeed the next time. Maintain an environment of enthusiasm, a positive attitude, cooperation, collaboration, and sharing. Meet often one-to-one and in small and large groups. Generate easy, informal interactions and discussion. Knock down the walls of bureaucracy. Emphasize getting the job done, taking care of the customer, beating the competition—together.

The preceding 10 steps have a heavy people focus. Obviously, there are a number of technology-related aspects to making continuous change happen successfully, but in my experience, these are easier to deal with than the people aspects of change. It is risky to focus too heavily on technology, structure, and so on, because it may give the illusion of success. Only when people have learned the new ways and unlearned the old will the change succeed.

The Rear View

Earlier, I discussed various question techniques to use to help define and quantify how and what to change in value and its attributes. Certain aspects of such techniques that involve customer satisfaction surveys are not unlike driving by looking in the rear view mirror. They tell us little about what lies ahead, only what is behind us. Success results from the confluence of market value "wants" and your ability to have the shape of value that can satisfy those wants (or better yet, something that creates and satisfies new wants).

Remember, the *right* shape will fill the customer's "bill of rights"—the right thing at the right time and the right place at the right price with the right features. To do this requires looking ahead, not just back, to become aware as early as possible of the need to shape-shift.

The Forward View

I've said it many times, but it bears repeating: Success often breeds complacency. Only those who regard success as a temporary victory in a much longer "battle" will continue to strive for more. As Jack Kahl, CEO of Manco, puts it, "The road to success is always under construction." You must decide, guess, and/or influence what comes next. Certainly, by looking in the rear view mirror, you gain some information about the general terrain, and this is useful, but far from sufficient. Looking ahead may yield a vision that is unclear, but that is better than no vision at all. Trying to stop, start, and shift to react to every competitive change is like trying to win a race from behind the leader by watching and copying his or her moves—it's almost impossible. You must invest a substantial amount of time thinking intently about the future—and few organizations do!

Enthusiastic, childlike curiosity is a good mind-set to take as part of this process of serious thought gets under way.

- Consider every bit of information you know or can know.
- Review your goals and future vision carefully.
- Survey the market and competitive conditions realistically.
- "Wish out loud" for what would be ideal.
- Conceive solutions far beyond what might be considered reasonable or prudent.
- Imagine entirely new possibilities. Refine some of these radical new ideas. Improve on them, consolidate them, combine them synergistically.
- Consider what their shape of value would look like to a customer.
- Think about how the shape of the business would have to change to create and deliver such wonderful new ideas, products, or services.

Then decide how to proceed. Once you have decided, put in the effort and the resources to get it done first. As one associate of mine used to say, "Success is a combination of inspiration and perspiration." Have a vision, and then set about making it a reality. Get started.

13.

Compensating Shape-Shifting

It is 1995. There is no such thing as a meaningless cog. A corporation is nothing more than a collection of individuals. Each one has ideas. Each one has power. Each one has potential. Help it along.
—from a Microsoft advertisement

RECOGNIZING CORPORATE RITUALS

Rituals are sequences of behavior that fulfill a human need, but may not be consistent with the current reality. In a business environment, it is especially important to limit these. Taboos are prohibited acts. Often the false optimism reflected in business plans that indicate dramatic improvement for the future without basis in fact represent a taboo against projecting continued poor performance—even if it is the truth.

Business behavior of all kinds must be measured, recognized, and rewarded when appropriate. Doing so can have a significant impact on success. Human nature requires recognition and rewards. Positive behaviors must be observed and recognized on a timely basis and then rewarded.

A fisherman was in his boat, with a line in the water, when he felt a strong tug on the line. He carefully pulled his line from the water. On the hook was a snake with a frog in its mouth. In removing the hook, he first had to remove the frog from the snake's mouth and throw it back in the pond. The fisherman felt bad, both because he had hooked the snake, and he had denied the snake of the frog it had caught. The fisherman searched for some way to compensate the snake for its loss, so he reached for his flask of Jack

175

Daniels whisky and poured a shot into the snake's mouth, and
threw the snake back into the pond. He rechecked his lure and his
line and threw it in again. In a few minutes, there was another
strong tug on the line. As the fisherman reeled the line in, he saw
the snake again. This time it had two frogs in its mouth. The
behavior rewarded was the behavior repeated.

While this story may seem silly, it's message is not. People actually
respond to rewards very much like the snake did. The old cliché "what gets
measured gets done," is not exactly true. It should say "what gets measured
and rewarded gets done."

Defining the Right Reward System

Many companies have tried different forms of employee compensation over
the decades. Frederick Taylor's theories on segmentation of work, and
Douglas MacGregor's on motivation, led to some of these forms, including
direct incentives for production output (piecework). Early "gainsharing"
plans were developed by Joseph Scanlon in the steel industry, and were later
followed by Mitchell Fein's widely used and successful Improshare plans.
Corporate executives usually benefit greatly from incentive bonus and stock
option plans, while hourly workers may participate in profit-sharing plans.
Except for the direct incentive plan, most compensation systems are only
loosely linked with behaviors, and thus may not serve as motivators. The
measures upon which this compensation is based have a great deal to do
with the behaviors rewarded and repeated.

A culture that is conducive to shape-shifting is one in which there is a
high degree of trust and teamwork. This makes individual incentives less
desirable since they reward individual performance, not teamwork. A shape-
shifting culture also requires a high degree of flexibility and a commitment
to learning. It follows then that a reward system in such a culture would have
to be flexible. Since economic rewards are only one part of a total reward
system, albeit a critical one, other forms of recognition are also necessary
and valuable. On this topic, I recommend the book *1001 Ways To Reward
Employees* (Workman, 1994) by Bob Nelson. Considerable thought must be
given to behavioral measures and associated rewards, because the behaviors
will closely reflect what is rewarded.

Individuals must be held accountable for the outcome of the processes,
tasks, and the areas of responsibility within their control. When individuals
work in teams, those teams can help those individuals get things done.
Although the team is an enabler, it is an intangible entity. The individuals
do the work. Any compensation system must recognize and reward the
outcomes of this work. To do any less is not only unfair, but leads to future

failures. The problem that all managers face in team settings is how to reward disparate production by individuals in teams. No one has yet reached a satisfactory general solution for this dilemma, thus they usually reward the team uniformly even though there was a disproportionate contribution by the various team members.

Why Incentive Compensation Plans Fail

There are many reasons for the failure of compensation plans, but a few so prevalent, they bear repeating here, before I describe some hypothetical plans.

- The plan is poorly explained and misunderstood or not understood at all.

This problem can be partly alleviated by enlisting the involvement of members of the group of employees who will be in the plan, both in plan development and communication. The repeated communication in multiple formats is required.

- The plan is poorly designed, short-sighted, or greedy/unfair.

If plans attempt to get too much from employees in work effort for too little compensation or if it incites very short-term performance at the expense of longer term, more important objectives, not only will the plan fail, but likely the company will fail.

- The plans are changed without warning or with inadequate warning and poor or no explanation of the reasons behind the change.

There are two problems here. One is perceived or real unfairness of rapid changes. The other is the potential for errors and unknown flaws in hastily made changes. A "shake-down period" is a good idea. Explaining the real reasons behind a sudden shift in pay plans is a necessity.

- The plans are confusing, or unnecessarily complex.

Too many measures are as bad as none. Even in high-trust situations they cloud what the real objectives are. In low-trust situations they reek of unfairness and manipulations—and become "dis-incentives!"

With this simplified list of reasons for failure, let's move on to a few types of plans that fit different situations. Remember, these are simply examples to get started. No one can (or should) design compensation system without a deep understanding of what behavior and results it is designed to incite and reward.

Hypothetical Bonus Systems

In the area of economic rewards, there are three tiers of reward that are used most widely with success.

1. Management (includes senior executives to the organizational level just above front-line supervisors and professionals): Incentive bonus programs should be based both on short- (one-year) and longer-term (three-year) performance. The longer-term bonus should be tied to the stock increase in value of the company in combination with cash to cover the tax consequences of the reward. The short-term bonus plan should be based on return on investment or some closely related measure that includes both profitability and asset management. Measures should differ for "centralized and decentralized" workgroups, with the majority ($2/3$ plus or minus) of the measure based on the workgroup's direct business unit performance, and the minority based on the larger corporate entity's performance ($1/3$ percent plus or minus). Centralized support groups not directly tied to any profit center should be tied to corporate performance, tracked monthly, and paid annually. If there is no corporate profit, this plan would have no payout (except by some special action of the compensation committee of the board, or at the owner's discretion).

2. Hourly and salaried nonexempt employees who fall under wage and hour law provisions: An "improvement-gainsharing program" is based on year-to-year improvement in a measures of increased value that vary by the work unit involved. Hourly workers (quality, service, speed, cost, productivity, etc.) would participate in small-group measures such as the output divided by the input[*] of a department that consists of fewer than 100 employees, most of whom are within line of sight of each other, and have a recognized "community of interest." Office workgroups might also have an output/input measure but one based on "transactions processed" (if that is their job) rather than "production." These types of improvement-gainsharing payments should be tracked daily and weekly, and paid biweekly or monthly to allow for some accumulation of a significant payment. Basing the plan on improvement at the outset eliminates one of

---

[*] Output is ideally the dollar value of products or services in a given time frame. Input is the dollar value of time, wage-related benefits, and direct expense/supplies consumed in the given time period.

the most difficult issues in traditional gainsharing plans—the entitlement mentality. Only if the business performance improves each year does it have a good chance for long-term success and provide any meaningful job security for employees. Thus it is logical to tie rewards to this kind of measure (which also supports shape-shifting to better shapes).

The base wages upon which such reward systems are paid often are determined by the prevailing competitive wage environment (or a negotiation, in the case of union situations). To encourage learning, a *pay-for-applied-knowledge* premium is a valuable tool. This defines a series of experiences (different jobs) and skills (learned off the job) that earn such a premium, but only as long as they are being used in the current or most recent prior work assignment(s). (Otherwise, credential accumulation will occur, but with poor retention of the learning and little or no benefit to the business.) This plan would pay regardless of corporate profitability.

A viable variation on this plan is a group incentive based on engineered standards instead of a base time period. This variation is suitable when a stronger incentive, "pull" motivation is desired and/or when there is no suitable base period on which to base the improvement-gainsharing. Maintenance and administration of such a plan is higher, but productivity gains should more than pay for it. Eventually such standards-based plans will plateau, resulting in no further productivity gains and continued haggling over the validity of the standards. They must then be terminated and replaced by some form of improvement-gainsharing or profit-sharing plan.

3. Front-line supervision and professional/technical employees: This tier must support the efforts of both of the prior groups, therefore their reward system should include parts from both programs. They should participate in the incentive bonus plan (at perhaps one half the rate of the lowest-level managers), and the improvement gainsharing plan at the same rate as the hourly employees. In no case should their total bonus from the two plans exceed that of their next-level manager's maximum potential under the incentive plan. (But they *can* earn a bonus when the management bonus plan fails to pay off—from the improvement-gainsharing plan.)

The intent of this part of the book is not to be a treatise on compensation systems; it can provide some potentially useful solutions as starting points to enable the shape-shifting to begin.

Needless to say, none of the three compensation models is suitable for all situations. The key is the principles upon which they are based—measuring the desired outcomes and rewarding the behavior that lead to these outcomes.

ABB Industrial Systems Does It Right

Compensation cannot be discussed as if it existed in a vacuum. The most important element of any compensation system is the basis upon which it is built—usually some form of performance appraisal system. The culture of the company and the compensation system must be also closely aligned.

Tight cultures usually create tight control mentalities, and compensation is part of the "carrot and stick," or "KITA" (Kick In The Ass) system of motivation (of demotivation). A looser, more flexible culture is better, more responsive, and adaptive but also harder to establish and sustain. Such a culture must be based on trust, open communications and collaborations. It also requires that many other dimensions of the business' shape be changed and this is not easy.

One excellent example of such a development is the self directed, self managed team structure at ABB Industrial Systems in Columbus, Ohio. In this highly recognized, award-winning business unit, various team members lead the team at different times based on their respective expertise. There are no "supervisors," and no single "team leaders." Capability determines who leads a given situation. Cross-training is widespread and essential. Superb quality systems are evident and necessary. Various team members are selected to lead elements of the teams work, such as quality, process improvement, scheduling, and so on.

A key element supporting this kind of intense collaboration is their sophisticated 360 degree performance appraisal process. All team members are appraised by all others, using a computer network–based system with an easily completed checklist. Anonymity is protected, yet the appraisal is done by those most knowledgeable about the work performance of the person being appraised. The *process* is necessary to reinforce the behavior that is essential to the *culture*. The *structure* supports both. Not surprisingly, *relationships* with suppliers and customers are also strong, responsive and partnership based. When the entire shape of the business is in alignment, the compensation system is the reinforcement and reward, not the motivator.

Management

The higher levels of management should have a compensation plan based on a salary, which increases by merit increases or lump sums (when someone is at or near the high end of the range of pay for such a position), and include at least an incentive bonus based on the short- (one year) and longer-term (three year) performance of the company in generating a satisfactory return on the assets utilized. The short-term bonus program outlined is a useful form of one year compensation. If there is a desire to make this bonus a sort of "golden handcuffs," it can be paid out over a three-year period, 50 percent at the end of the year when it is earned and 25 percent in each of the two succeeding years. The three-year program ideally should be tied to either the performance of the stock (in a public company) or the average return on equity against a broad comparable measure of similar companies (Standard & Poor's 500, for example).

Individual Contributor

There also should be a dual salaried pay ladder: one for increasing supervisory/managerial responsibilities and another parallel to it, and of equal amount for individual, technical, or creative contributors. This pay scale is much discussed but is still absent or neglected in many businesses. These key technical or creative contributors are not served by being promoted into managerial roles where their individual expertise is poorly used and their lack of interpersonal or supervisory skills set them up to fail or perform poorly. Such people—creative artists, industrial designers, software designers or programmers, and so forth—often make up one of the core competencies of a business. Their personalities usually are not those of a supervisor or manager, but rather a "creator."

Front-Line Supervisors, Professionals, and Technical Specialists

Front-line supervisors have what may be the most difficult job in business. They must understand and identify with the issues and objectives of two very different groups: hourly workers and upper management. They are expected to meet the needs of the former and the goals of the latter. For this reason, they should be included in the incentive compensation plans of both those groups. While they should not expect to earn more than the next level in the organization in good times, they should be rewarded for exceptional performance of the workforce even in the "not so good times."

Professional and technical specialists are often equally important. These are the customer service staff, engineers, technicians, accountants, and the like who provide the support needed for the front-line to operate effectively.

These positions are often filled via promotion from the working level functional, entry-level technical and salaried nonexempt or hourly group leader positions. Their preparedness for supervision and the responsibility of leadership is often very limited. Unless they can succeed on technical know-how (not usually sufficient), natural leadership ability (risky), prior experience (sometimes off-the-job leadership roles), or on-the-job training, they suffer miserably when they first take on such a supervisory job. They go from being responsible for their own efforts and relationships as part of an organization to being responsible for the efforts of numerous others, as well as the coordination and direction of that group's efforts. In his book, *Skills for Managerial Excellence* (Simon & Schuster, 1995), Robert Bidwell covers the challenge of this situation in an entertaining and enlightening fashion. Actions must be taken in any shape-shift to deal with the issue of the preparedness of new, first-time supervisors, or their rate of failure will prove unacceptably high.

Hourly Employees

There is little doubt that individual incentive compensation (often called piecework) is the most directly productive in increasing output and efficiency because pay is tied directly to that output. There are circumstances when this form of compensation is still appropriate. Examples are individual jobs in a field service environment or factory where the work output is entirely within the employees' control (such as garment sewing in a nonassembly line process). Some service jobs also might be paid on an incentive basis, such as "cottage industry" jobs often outsourced to small contractors. Pay must be only for good-quality work—which is often an issue when detection of poor quality occurs after a substantial time lag—but this principle is inviolate.

When team performance is involved, direct incentives usually do not support teamwork, and often work against it. The individual is motivated to take care of his or her own work and earnings to the exclusion of all others. Small-group incentives or some form of improvement-gainsharing is better for team situations.

The problem with both of these forms of hourly compensation is the maintenance and accuracy of the standards required for measurement, although there are rigorous scientific ways to do this. The MTM Institute has excellent measuring systems and can arrange for training of both supervisory/technical and hourly employees in the application of direct incentive standards. Another problem is the maintenance of standards in the face of rapid change, and in the evaluation of the "nonstandard" conditions encountered in a dynamic work environment. Because of these factors, such direct incentive compensation plans for hourly workers suitable are not for shape-shifting situations. They are better suited for stabilizing or sustaining the current direction.

Labor-based gainsharing programs became very popular because they rewarded both the company and the employee for the behavior desired; that is, greater productivity. However, these programs have two problems in application. The first is that if the program pays out for a lengthy period of time (which it will if it is successful), a sense of entitlement develops; the bonus is expected, rather than earned. The second problem, and the one more relevant to shape-shifting, is that of selecting and maintaining a base period upon which to calculate the improvement. The tremendous change in the nature, mix, and assortment of jobs, products, or services provided often can render large segments of the base calculation period obsolete in a very short time (one year or less). When this happens, not only is a lot of administrative work required to create or adjust the base period, but a trust issue arises if the resulting calculation reduces the bonus payment—which it almost always does, (not for reasons of manipulation but for reasons of being lower on the learning curve of productivity).

Consequently, I recommend that all improvement-gainsharing plans: a) include a medium-sized group with some agreed-upon community of interest, product family, department, or other to avoid groups trying to maximize their gain at the expense of another group, or shift; and, b) be based on an improvement over some comparable prior period, such as the entire previous year or the same month or quarter of the previous year if the business is seasonal.

CONCLUSION

The principle of compensation is simple: It must be fair and reward the desired results. Fairness includes being competitive to the prevailing rates of compensation in the market and comparable to what people with similar experience, education, and skills are receiving for similar efforts. Somehow, translating these simple principles into practice is far from simple—but it is critical. Alignment of measures and pay with important strategic, tactical, and operational goals is especially critical to reinforce the behavior and results desired. The best companies usually find ways to attract the best people and earn the best profits. They also pay above average, and many include an unusually high component of performance-based variable pay (bonuses) for exceptional performance. These are the companies that will most successfully become the best shape-shifters.

14.

The Power of Partnerships

All value chains will be seen as an interconnected network of businesses that at one time compete, at other times collaborate, but at all times adapt to the changing demands of consumers.
—Dr. Carl E. Steidtmann, in a speech at the
1996 International Housewares Show

CORNERSTONE PARTNERSHIPS

To enable shape-shifting to occur, the four cornerstone partnerships—with suppliers, customers, associates, and "special partners"—must be in place. Although these relationships are just one dimension of the shape of the business, they are critical to success.

Partnerships, as I defined them in my first book, are "interdependent relationships between companies and people who share common goals, strive to achieve them together, and do it in a spirit of cooperation, collaboration, and fairness." There need not be shared ownership to have a partnership; many alliances are "nonequity" in the ownership sense, and many are based on mutual dependence. But can these really be considered partnerships? Maybe, depending on how the parties behave and view their relationship. Too many are only "marriages of convenience" or necessity. Business partnerships should be expected to progress in the same way as successful marriages, through the stages of euphoria, monotony, adjustments (sometimes) difficulties, acceptance, followed by fulfillment. They are both relationships that, if done well, create a total that is greater than the sum of the parts. Both are often tried. Some fail. Some succeed. Over time, the partners grow together or they grow further apart. The process, the give and take, the hopes for success, and the determination to make "it" work are all necessary parts of getting there.

Defining the Four Cornerstone Partnerships

The four cornerstone partnerships (see Figure 14-1) have six common characteristics on which they are founded. The first four are basic principles of human interaction, and last two are fundamental business perspectives.

1. Character, integrity, honesty
2. Trust
3. Open communications
4. Fairness
5. Self-interest of both partners
6. Balanced rewards versus risks

Supplier Partnerships

A law of physics states, "Matter can neither be created nor destroyed." Or, more simply, "You can't make something from nothing!" This expresses the importance of a supplier partner in its most basic form. Suppliers are usually people and companies who provide materials or parts; they also might provide services or information. Have you ever thought what it would be like to try to conduct your business, without someone to provide you the raw materials or information to which you add your special value before selling to a customer? Not a pretty thought. One of the common characteristics of many of the finest companies in business today is that they use the finest materials and develop the best supplier relationships. Is it a coincidence? I doubt it. Supplier partners are a very valuable resource, and can be a competitive advantage.

Employee and Associate Partnerships

Whether you are the owner of a business or an executive, manager, professional, or "just an employee", you've probably already discovered the importance of partnerships. One of the most rewarding partnerships you can form is with your coworkers, or "associates" as many of the forward-thinking companies call them. The importance of everyone's role in a business is much easier to identify when they are thought of as associates or partners. If forced to choose only one word to describe the ideal characteristic of this partnership I would say *fairness*. I once asked in an employee forum: "What is the definition of a "fair deal?" Probably the best answer was, "A deal you'd take either side of." The second word I would use to describe successful employer-employee partnerships is *consistency*. Few things are more difficult to dealt with than inconsistent "bosses" or employees. Partnering with employees/associates is important to success—there is no other viable option (except to outsource everything).

Customer Partnerships

An often displayed sign in offices reads: "Nothing happens until a sale is made." Marketing authority and Harvard professor Theodore Levitt puts it another way in his book, *The Marketing Imagination* (The Free Press, 1983), "The purpose of a business is to create and keep a customer." I can't think of a simpler, more direct way to say it. Without someone to buy what it is we have to sell, there wouldn't be much point in the existence of our business enterprise.

Another sign I like on this issue states the two most important rules regarding customers. Rule number 1: The customer is always right; Rule number 2: When the customer is wrong, refer to rule number 1. Another way to say this is that sometimes it's hard to live with them, but it's impossible to live without them. And the best way to live with them is as partners. Customer-partners are the essential link to the end user, and are the ultimate definers of value.

Special Partnerships

There are two kinds of special partnerships: one I call professional partnerships and the other I call personal partnerships. There are many different kinds of partnerships that fall under this category. Competitors even partner with each other to succeed over other more fearsome competitors (or to protect their industry from an external threat).

Long-term advisors; local, state, or federal governments: universities; consultants; sales representatives—all can become special partners. Usually, however, there are more influential partners that are the most important in this sense. It could be a spouse, a trusted friend, or a business partner. It could also be a valued consultant, a mentor, a "boss," or someone

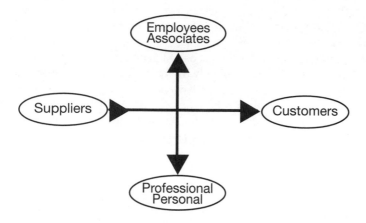

Figure 14-1 The Four Cornerstone Partnerships

in your community, club, or church. Every successful person I have ever met has one or more of these special partnerships, which they value highly and which was instrumental to their success.

The Synergy of Partnerships

Human beings do not like conflict, anxiety or uncertainty. Relatively few of them are loners in comparison to the joiners or participants. There's something about cooperation in work, competition, and success that makes the victory sweeter and the loss more bearable. Partnerships enable the potential for synergy—that widely used but poorly understood word. Synergies are possible both within a single partnership and among several partnerships. Many names are used to describe business partnerships— alliances, joint ventures, mergers, and more—but whatever the name, a partnership is only as good as the intentions of the people involved to make it a strong, fair, and lasting relationship. In the absence of these factors, a partnership is doomed, whether it was sealed with a handshake or by sig- natures on a contract.

When powerful partnerships have been built with suppliers, associates/ employees, and customers, you are ideally prepared to shape-shift to meet the needs of your target market. And if the customer partnership is solidly entrenched, you will have advance warning about the direction in which to shape-shift. If your suppliers share your goals and vision, and have equity in your business' success, they too will be poised and alert to the signals to shift formation. If your associate/employee partners have been led (not driven) to understand the opportunity provided by rapid change, and to embrace and capitalize on that opportunity, then your chances for survival, and success are greatly enhanced. Prosperity might even become a part of your vocabulary—albeit spoken softly, because the ability to create wealth and prosperity attracts competition, fast.

The concept of partnerships is so broad and powerful, and its role in the ability to shape-shift the enterprise is so pivotal, that it can be considered the critical enabling factor. If one stage of the enterprise reconfigures itself in a new market direction or paradigm and others do not, the change leaders will be forced to absorb all the discontinuity while adapting to the changes themselves—an impossible task. If a single partner, be it supplier, manufacturer, or customer, tries to go it alone, that partner will fail. Only when partners make the changes in concert can they succeed.

From Individuals to Groups to Teams

One of the things that makes America a great competitive society is the individuality and originality of her people. Sometimes, however, that "rugged individualist" mentality gets in the way of partnerships. Case in point: When I arrived at the Celina, Ohio, plant of Huffy Bicycles, in 1983, most of the workers described what they did by naming the machine they ran or the type of process they operated. "I'm a press operator, or a welder; or, I work in the wheel room," were common responses. It took a concerted effort to break these people out of their "I don't want to depend on anybody but myself for my earnings" mentality.

Some simply refused, but the majority yielded to participating in small production cell groups. This "weaning" process was accompanied by the introduction of Improshare, Mitchell Fein's gainsharing system (on top of the direct incentive system), and later by a plantwide "base rate" which replaced the direct incentive (piecework) system. The plant was really too big (2,000 employees) for the ideal culture and interaction, thus the decision to break it up into smaller "focused" factories.

Within a few years, if asked the question "what do you do?" most would answer differently, saying, "I am a bike builder," or "I am part of a Rim Line Team," or "I am part of the painted frame and fork factory." Ultimately, all but a few (and a few individual contributors are necessary) became part of the new team-based partnership culture. In his book, *The New Partnerships* (Omneo, 1994), Tom Melohn describes the power of dealing with his employees as partners very graphically, "[I]f you take a couple drops of human dignity and respect—just a couple drops—and put them on employees, and if they believe you, they'll swell up just like a sponge."

This entire process at Huffy was accompanied by an innovative new training process that went way beyond the TQM or employee involvement training we had done earlier in the 1980s. We called it "strategic learning training," for factory people. With the help of consultant, James Barber, we undertook to greatly enhance the involvement and flexibility of our hourly workforce (and management too) using 12 one-hour sessions to create a learning organization in a factory setting. The results, after some rocky early sessions, were amazing. Involvement and participation led to real learning and double-loop thinking. Teams began taking unheard-of initiatives. Hourly people traveled to supplier partners to resolve difficult problems (such as chronic rust problems on steel tubing) by interacting with the supplier's hourly people. Hourly employees conducted plant tours for customers and prepared requests for budgets or capital appropriations. This partnership between the company and its union employees led it to a decade of unparalleled success during a very difficult competitive era.

The Power of Partnerships

Partnerships have proven to be infinitely more powerful than individual effort. Quoted in *Fortune*, Peter Senge said, "People working together with integrity and authenticity and collective intelligence are profoundly more effective as a business than people living together based on politics, game playing, and narrow self-interest." True partnerships are based on strong principles, which in the words of Stephen Covey, author of *Seven Habits of Highly Successful People* (Simon and Shuster, 1989), ". . . are deep, fundamental truths...." He refers to them as the "true north on a compass," not negotiable or changeable. These principles are fundamental to institutions, associations, and organizations, not just to businesses.

And the concept of partnerships leads inevitably back to that very important topic: Customer Value. Customer value is the ultimate "scorecard" on which is determined who wins and who loses in business. Because value is defined in the eyes and minds of "outside" customers, partnerships can be an invaluable way to discover and understand it (an "outside-in" process). I have already listed and described at length the attributes that combine to comprise value in the shape of value, but there are other ways of determining what customers really value.

In the book *Know Your Customer* (Blackwell, 1996), Sarah Gardial and Robert Woodruff cover the topic based on years of real-world research conducted with leading consumer products companies including Gatorade, SeaRay boats, Saturn, Eastman Chemical, and others. One of many important points they make is that popular customer satisfaction measures only describe how customers feel about value at that time. What is needed is a way to assess what they want now and in the future, when they (the customers) often don't even know themselves. How better to take the first step toward achieving this than by forming a close-knit partnership with the customers, and building that bridge to the end users.

BUILDING ON THE PAST

Over the past several decades many excellent approaches have been developed to help achieve the goal of most businesses, to create a sustainable competitive advantage that can be converted into superior economic returns for their owners/stakeholders. Many of these were re-creations of old American approaches that were used against U.S. industries by the Japanese (and renamed in Japanese words). Others were renamed reapplications of basic techniques, used in the United States, and then forgotten in the demand-driven 1960s. Some, however, were genuinely based on a new and improved understanding of how to succeed in a different, and more rapidly changing competitive environment. I have already touched on the most well known among modern managers and executives—quality circles, JIT, CIM, employee involvement, participative management, TQM, QFD, Kaizen, the theory of constraints, competing-in-time, lean production, activity-based costing/measurement, strategic alliances, category management, EDI, VMR, QR, agile manufacturing, reengineering, and many more.

These approaches all focused on a single- or partial aspect of the entire enterprise. Some were useful primarily in operations, others in quality, engineering, accounting, or sales. Some applied to business processes or activities across several disciplines. What none of them did was to generate a complete integrative basis for the overall business strategy and its execution in the current total business context. Perhaps this was because until recently, few management strategists understood or accepted manufacturing or operations as a key point of strategic advantage. Or, perhaps it was simply because it is usually easier to fix a part of something than the whole thing. With this shortcoming, let us consider one new type of partnership.

The New Partnership

In my first book, I omitted one new kind of partnership. Because the book was written from a people-oriented standpoint, I did not delve into technology's role in business, and the subsequent partnerships that forms between people and technology. This new information and communication technology–based partnership can enable entirely new forms of organizations. It can also make possible faster and more informed response to changes in markets or competitions than ever before. I will discuss the "networked" organization of the future in detail later on.

Get Lean (But Not Mean)

The field of logistics and the concept of lean production has perhaps come the closest to connecting with the importance of partnerships. First, lean production implementation sets a goal of reducing manufacturing through-put times and improving product quality by creating flow manufacturing processes. The second action extends the capabilities of flow manufacturing up and down the value (supply) chain to the point at which the greatest opportunities exist—from the customer all the way back to the raw materials suppliers.

This is a good beginning, but only when the entire network of partners is integrated will the business be able to develop a competitive strategy for delivering the maximum customer value. Many of the previous piecemeal approaches yielded specific advantages for their users when competitors had not yet successfully improved that portion of their business. The ability to create sustainable competitive advantage is no longer dependent on any single type of "improvement," since the conditions in the environment are not static. What creates the competitive advantage today may be rendered ineffective next week, or next month, because the environment, technology, market, or competition has changed.

Shape-shifting builds on the power of partnerships to adjust continuously. In fact, the linkages between partners enable the shape-shifting of the business, to best utilize the core competencies and capabilities of the organization and adapt them to the external competitive environment, in whatever form it takes.

15.

Changing the
Shape of the Business

Companies have to learn how to leverage their resources and change the
structure of their organizations so they can succeed....
—C. K. Prahalad, *Competing For the Future*,
Harvard Business School Press, 1994

The old truth is still the best truth: a company has to know the kind of value
it intends to provide and to whom. Only then can it link its knowledge
resources in ways that make a difference...
—Brook Manville and Nathaniel Foote, "Strategy
as if Knowledge Mattered," in *Fast Company*,
April–May 1996

FLEXIBLE LEARNING ORGANIZATIONS

During my presidency at Huffy Bicycles, we realized that our competitors could readily buy the same technology that we could. Consequently, trying to create any sort of sustainable advantage based on customer value had to be done in some way the competition could not emulate easily or quickly. Since bicycle manufacturers are not very integrated as manufacturers, and depend on the same component suppliers for much of their content, this offered little help. We might be able to buy better because of our size, but this was too tenuous an advantage to depend on. Since we also demanded the highest quality and service expectations, we were not so sure we bought at the lowest "first cost," just that we bought the best total value.

To find a source of competitive advantage we turned to our people and processes, because we knew we had one asset our competitors did not, a workforce with many years of experience and know-how in building bikes. If we could transform this workforce into a flexible learning organization, then perhaps they could adapt their skills to whatever kind of bikes, components and customer demands came along.

Creating a Learning Organization

As we undertook this daunting task of creating a learning organization from a United Steel Worker union workforce we knew it would take a couple of years and thousands of hours of "classroom" time, but it worked. Barber documented much of this evolution in his *National Productivity Review* article, "From the Working Class to the Learning Class" (Autumn 1994).

A learning organization is a very powerful tool. It is like a living organism. Just as the parable of the trees in the introduction illustrated strong parallels between natural ecosystems and business systems, there is a similar parallel of a learning organization with a learning organism. Co-dependent natural systems like a beehive or a flock of birds, and a human learning organization share many of the same capabilities and characteristics. Its ability to adapt and change is greatly improved as learning occurs. One aspect of performance, maintaining "coordination," becomes increasingly important as the speed of change increases. The body does this by way of the central nervous system, sending messages back and forth to the brain, carefully sequencing the timing of bodily motions and functions. The brain also gathers external information and processes it to allow the body to know what external conditions it is encountering. The combination of these external and internal information systems and the instantaneous, interactive communication within the body is what enables human reaction to be so swift and adaptive on an almost unconscious basis. The faster change occurs, the faster the organism must respond, in order to maintain good coordination among it many parts.

The Role of Information and Communications Technologies

It is in the coordination effort that the breakthroughs in information and communication technology come to the aid of business. E-mail, groupware, shared networks, the Internet, the World Wide Web, and related information technologies have made possible a much more rapid and coordinated "central nervous system" for the large organization. Geographical dispersion no

longer inhibits the flow of information since it can be digitized and trans-
ferred around the world at the speed of light. Organizations must learn to
use these instantaneous, simultaneous, asynchronous global communications tools to help them shape-shift more effectively and with greater precision than the competition.

The Value of Timely Information

Wal-Mart realized the importance of the new communications technologies
before most competitors, and parlayed it into a tremendous competitive
advantage. This enabled the discount retailer to build a superior information
and distribution system at lower cost than their competitors—a tremendous
competitive advantage!

Wal-Mart's point-of-sale system gathers extensive data about what its
customers are purchasing. Its Retail-Link system provides up-to-date, real-
time information on what is selling, where, for how much, and at what rate.
Wal-Mart suppliers can access this system at any time for the items they provide to Wal-Mart. This results in a powerful customer-supplier partnership,
which extends to the consumer.

Communicate to Collaborate

But what about the factory or large corporate or government organization?
How might they use the new people-technology partnership? Until now, the
emphasis has been on the formation of teams. Teams are a wonderful, powerful force—when they work properly, but in my experience, this is a minority of the cases. The social dynamics of teamwork are challenging, and the
constant turnover represents one of the most daunting aspects of that challenge. Behavioral scientists describe team behavior as a progression of
"forming, storming, norming, and performing." This phenomena is a very real
obstacle to team performance in most dynamic environments. Another
obstacle is the reality of human nature, which despite management's best
efforts, means people sometimes simply do not or will not work together har-
moniously or effectively.

In his book *No More Teams! Mastering the Dynamics of Creative
Collaboration* (Currency Doubleday, 1995), Michael Shrage contends that
teams are often a sham. "As surely as the clock imposed a new concept of
time and the telephone breached the barriers of conversational distance,
new technologies are emerging that will radically transform the way people
share their thoughts." The more important point he makes is that the real

goal is true collaboration, which is often not the case in teams. "Collaboration takes communication back to its roots." *Communicare*, the Latin verb on which the word *communication* is based, means "to share." Our definition of communication has evolved to mean the exchange of information, but this is not always the same as "sharing." It is at this point that the concept of the new partnership takes on real meaning.

Organizations can and must learn. It is through learning that they develop their ability to continuously adapt to changing circumstances. Organizations must also learn to share; information and communications technologies alone can not guarantee that sharing occurs. People still must relate to people, and once that is achieved, information and communications technologies become powerful forces. Shrage says, "Organizations that attempt to substitute increased communication for increased collaboration will learn the hard way that there is a tremendous difference."

Organizations that attempt to collaborate without a free exchange of communication and information also will fail. They will also become frustrated in the process. Their motives may be noble, their aspirations high and their desire great, but if they do not first make the personal connection while sharing information, they will achieve disappointing results. Organizations also often fall short in their efforts to coordinate their actions due to inadequate, untimely, or incomplete information. At best, it may expose too late what would have been the right action or decision. Many "team meetings" that struggle on endlessly are mired in this quagmire of knowing the right thing at the wrong time, all because of poor timing or coordination of information and action. This leads to frustration and failure.

Busy schedules preclude that *all* the members of teams be in all the meetings. But, modern groupware, work-sharing, intranets, and video communications systems can form the necessary linkage—become the virtual, perpetual meeting. This technology can help generate the coordination, cooperation, and collaboration needed among team members—if only we learn to use it properly.

Making Peace with the Future

A fine example of a large organization that shape-shifted is Lockheed Martin Tactical Aircraft Systems (LMTAS) in Fort Worth, Texas. Founded during World War II, in April 1942, to produce the B-24 bomber, more than 7,000 military aircraft have been produced here. Five unions represent the workforce, and its prime customer is the government. At first glance you would think this was not exactly the ideal environment for a shape-shift. Yet this highly unlikely candidate for a shape-shift could see the handwriting on the wall as the Cold War ended and the USSR split apart. The fall of global Communism signaled the need for massive change.

Working with the International Association of Machinists (IAM), LMTAS forged a new team-based relationship in the area of safety and health issues management. At the beginning of 1996, LMTAS President Dain Hancock began the implementation of the first stage called the "organization evolution," which reorganized the plant into focused, integrated product teams—interdisciplinary, interdependent teams with responsibilities for tasks, scheduling, and budgets associated with a given product. Customer focus was always a strong point with this company due to the mission-critical nature of its product. Such a combination of product-focused teams and customer-focused core organization made for a highly developed customer/product shape-sensitive business.

This huge, old facility and culture still has a long way to go before it has successfully completed its shape-shift. The important fact is that it has started on the journey and is already seeing successes, and successes will fuel the shape-shift in the future. Supplier partnerships are now an integral part of supplier relations. Purchased costs have gone down, and quality of material received has gone up dramatically. The entire organization is beginning to learn of the potential of this new shape.

Striking Oil

Another good example of a successful shape-shifting process is the Oil Field Pumping and Service Equipment plant of the Halliburton Company. This 32-year-old operation is located in the heart of the "oil patch" in Duncan, Oklahoma. It is one of six that make up Halliburton's Equipment and Products Operation, and provides both products and services for the oil field. The plant opened in 1964 and was recognized as one of the top 10 plants in the company from its inception. However, the plant's success was jeopardized by the oil crisis of the early 1980s when demand went from very high to very low in a few short years. As price and delivery became driving forces in the late 1980s, the plant struggled through a number of refinements, but its problems escalated.

In 1990, with the market and industry stabilized at a much lower demand level, it became apparent that traditional manufacturing approaches would not be sufficient. By 1992, Halliburton began to make major changes. A change in the shape of the business led the way. Structure was changed first. Product-based factories were formed to flatten management levels while enhancing responsiveness. The culture change was next. The command and control management style was revamped. A self-directed team structure with a skill-based pay structure was initiated. But the old ways died hard. Rules that had been enforced in the past to "control" behavior were replaced with 11 leadership principles. These principles did not just materialize from thin air; they were the product of a series of workshops involving key individuals and plant leaders, many of whom thought the process of developing the principles was at least as important as the principles themselves.

A further structural reorganization followed. It integrated key functions including procurement, sustaining engineering, and logistics. Buyers and planners were united in a single integrated function. Quality became the responsibility of production, not a separate organization. Scorecards were developed to track results.

No sooner had this major shift taken place than a major process change was initiated, an example of shape-shifting at its best. The focus factories were converted to continuous flow manufacturing. Computer models were used in combination with fundamental approaches such as Kanban. The results were dramatic: Inventory levels fell, as did cycle times; on-time delivery improved significantly as did productivity, quality, and, not surprisingly, financial results.

Was this enough? No! More recent efforts have moved the product-focused factories to business units. The heads of the focused factories have been replaced with business unit heads; and cross-functional teams address all the priority areas.

This plant been through at least *three* shape-shifts; but more important, it is now prepared to continue shifting to match the evolution of customer needs, market conditions, and competitive threats. A statement that symbolizes Halliburton's commitment and understanding of the power of its new direction reads: "The Duncan EPO Center leadership believes that the people closest to a problem will develop the best process solution, so employees are empowered to make decisions and implement changes that affect the overall process." This is an excellent example of continuous change for competitive advantage.

BACK TO THE FUTURE

Let's review: To shift the shape of value, we must first alter the shape of the business. Each of the dimensions of the shape of the business has a profound effect on one or more (usually most or all) of the value attributes. (For convenience, I am again including the Shape of the Business diagram and the Dimensions of Shape definitions in Figures 15-2 and 15-3.) The only dimension of the shape of the business that should not change is purpose. The purpose is the anchor, the compass that keeps the business steadily on course through the market storms it must endure.

Because the previous chapter dealt entirely with partnerships, I will only make minor references to them in this chapter. The three other dimensions of the shape of the business will be the major topics of discussion here: structure, culture, and processes.

Over the past several decades, numerous businesses have restructured, eliminating layers, and either centralizing or decentralizing, or both. As I've said, flattening organizations can be useful to enhance the flow of information; but it can also be devastating as, in many cases, it eliminates numerous people and jobs that previously were instrumental in getting the work of the business done. Too often, changes are made without the proper preparations and foundations in place. That is why I covered partnerships first; they often represent strong foundations. If the behaviors and values essential to forming partnerships are not present, the subsequent structural and cultural are changes also likely to fail. The Halliburton case study illustrated how to do it correctly.

Quality changes can spring only from a culture that is serious about starting with good design and specifications to achieve the desired degree of quality. Processes that are well organized, effective, controlled, and documented are also necessary to reduce variability, which is the essential factor in improving conformance quality, once the degree of desired quality has been defined. In the 1970s and early 1980s many companies tried such shortcuts as increased inspection and whatever the quality program "du jour" was, and in the process wasted huge amounts of money to gain only minimal or temporary improvements in quality. Then, thanks to the persistent and irascible preaching of octogenarians W. Edwards Deming and Joseph Juran, companies began to get the message.

Processes began to change, driven by cultural change. Structures were not obstacles as much as diversions. Many companies altered the reporting point for the quality function, but that was mostly superficial. Once a collaborative culture led to improved designs and then orderly processes, quality began to improve rapidly. Nowhere is this more evident than in the U.S. automobile industry.

Service and speed came next. The creation of delivery services including Federal Express and UPS enabled next-day delivery of packages on a consistent basis. Fax machines made it possible to send documents around the world in minutes. Industries whose lead time was formerly weeks had to respond in days, then in hours. (See Figure 15-1.) Many believe these new services and technologies fueled a new behavior of waiting until the last minute, thus creating unnecessary urgency. Whatever the reason, speed is now an essential attribute. In an interview in *Fortune* (January 1997, pp. 135–137), AlliedSignal CEO Larry Bossidy raised these questions faced by companies at the verge of the twenty-first century: "Are we ever going to be able to satisfy an ever more demanding customer? [In] the food business,

Aerospace Components	30 days to 1 day
Mail-Order Products	5–7 days to overnight
Industrial Supplies	2–3 days to same day or overnight
Office Products	2–3 days to same day or overnight
Dry Cleaning	1–2 days to 1 hour
Photo Processing	2–3 days to 1 hour
Messaging Technologies	2 days to 2 minutes; (fax) to 2 seconds

Figure 15-1 Examples of Delivery Time Compression

they deliver in 10-minute windows. In the aerospace industry you used to deliver in 30-day windows; now it's overnight. Do we have the processes—the robust processes—to deliver in 10-minute windows?"

Structure has a profound effect on many companies' ability to respond to change. Large, bureaucratic companies still operating with the command-and-control mentality require days or weeks to make critical decisions. Sign-offs alone can delay a result by days. The advent of widespread use of groupware and intranets now make it possible to dramatically shorten the response time and enhance speed—except where the power structure prohibits it. Even where the processes have been refined, and the working level-culture (usually in remote divisions) grows more open and collaborative, structure gets in the way. Innovation is one of the most frequent casualties of an unwieldy structure

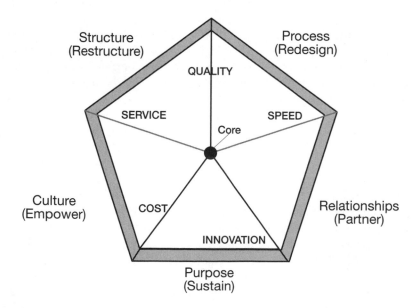

Figure 15-2 The Shape of the Business

Processes
- Quality
- Throughput, speed, output
- Effectiveness, Results-oriented
- Clear, simple, logical, flexible
- Documented, information-rich

Structure
- Organizational levels
- Centralized versus decentralized
- Spans of reporting and information flow
- Functional or cellular
- Global and/or local

Culture (Internal)
- Leadership
- Participation
- Empowerment
- Motivation and communication
- Openness and information

Relationships (External)
- Suppliers
- Customers
- Professional or special
- Trustworthy, honest, open, information sharing
- Mutually beneficial and rewarding

Purpose
- Legacy
- Guiding principles
- Vision and mission
- Core competencies
- Strategic intent

Figure 15-3 The Dimensions of Shape

that requires multiple approvals for new products and capital expenditures. Only when faced with a competitive coup do many large companies set aside their cherished committee approvals and expedite the capital needed.

The Personal shape-shift

For all kinds of companies, shifting the shape of the business is the only way to shift the shape of value. Those companies with more than four or five divisions and $3 to $5 billion or more in sales are the ones that must heed these words. These are the "big trees" that will be surpassed by the younger, rapidly growing new trees if they do not respond. Most of these are inhabited by a cadre of executives who reached their positions by doing things in ways that are totally obsolete in today's hyperspeed world. Many executives age 50 and up may have seen their rate of learning slowed or stopped; many are nearly computer-illiterate compared to their younger counterparts. And because they usually congregate with their peers, they may not even realize how far behind they are. But it is never too late to start. Most of my own modest computer literacy was developed after age 50. Bureaucratic behavior with a command-and-control mindset simply cannot respond rapidly or creatively enough to compete in today's cyber-competition. Benchmark to most nimble practices and begin today to learn how to survive and succeed tomorrow. Personal shape-shifting can become the launchpad for a companywide shape-shift.

USING THE EXPANDED DIAGNOSTIC PROFILE

Based on the preceding discussion, we can now use the diagnostic profile as another type of tool, to help determine where and how our shape of the business is not consistent with, nor supportive of the required shape of value. The example profile shown in Figure 15-4 has been completed for a hypothetical company, Company X. Its value pentastar is diagrammed in Figure 15-5.

It is evident from the value pentastar that Company X has a relationship problem first and foremost. Note the small relationship pentagon. This indicates a disaster in the making if the company cannot bring its external relationships into closer correlation to its internal culture, shown in the largest pentagon. At this point, the speed and service that have obviously been derived from primarily internal cultural influences are in jeopardy if the external relationships fail to support the needs of this company's customers.

It is also clear that this is an innovative company. But note that the lag between the evaluations of the processes and the culture indicate problems. The structure is closer to the culture, but not quite "there" yet. In this kind of diagram, these shapes should be similar in size and congruent in shape, pointing at the primary value attribute advantages (and weaknesses) of the business.

On the positive side, if the culture evaluation is accurate, this is an excellent environment for implementing a shape-shift. Senior management can alter the structure and support the organization in redesigning the processes.

Quality:
Very poor 1   2   3   4   5   **x**   6   7   8   9   10 Best in class
6 Structure   7 Culture   5 Processes   4 Relationships
22/4 = 5.5 Total Quality Rating

Service:
Very poor 1   2   3   4   5   6   **(7)**   8   9   10 Best in class
8 Structure   8 Culture   7 Processes   5 Relationships
28/4 = 7 Total Quality Rating

Cost:
Very poor 1   2   3   4   5   **x**   6   7   8   9   10 Best in class
4 Structure   7 Culture   6 Processes   5 Relationships
22/4 = 5.5 Total Quality Rating

Speed/Timeliness:
Very poor 1   2   3   4   5   6   **(7)**   8   9   10 Best in class
6 Structure   9 Culture   7 Processes   6 Relationships
28/4= 7 Total Quality Rating

Innovation:
Very poor 1   2   3   4   5   6   7   8   **x**   9   10 Best in class
9 Structure   10 Culture   9 Processes   7 Relationships
35/4 = 8.75 Total Quality Rating

Figure 15-4 Expanded Diagnostic Profiles for Company X Shape-Shift

The structure is evidently at the root of the cost competitiveness issue this company may be facing. Breaking down the shape of value diagram this way helps expose issues that are concealed by the composite diagram shown in Figure 15-6. The composite diagram reveals only that this is a company that depends on its innovation capabilities, and is vulnerable to attack by low-cost or high-quality competition. The weighting technique used in an earlier chapter may reveal even more about the seriousness of the threat by skewing the resultant profile.

Exploring the use of the various graphical techniques can be invaluable while shape-shifting. But remember, they will reveal only as much information as the honest appraisal and realistic understanding upon which they are based. If a company is in denial, no analytical device will work. Only the marketplace, the relentless truth-teller, will define the outcome. But this kind of diagram and evaluation process, if done properly, will often expose weaknesses that no one has been willing or able to discuss in the past.

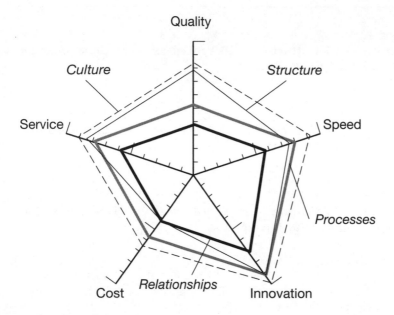

Figure 15-5 The Value Pentastar for Company X

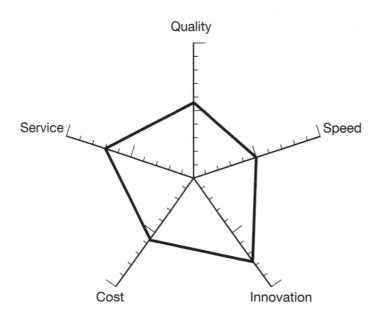

Figure 15-6 The Value Pentastar for Company X Averaged

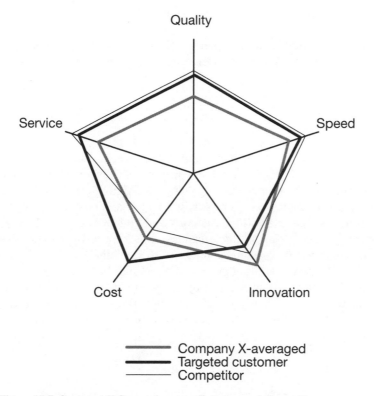

Figure 15-7 Company X Comparisons to Customer and Competitor

Customer and Competitor Comparisons

Now let's assume that we have plotted the shape of value for a targeted customer and a major competitor, as shown in Figure 15-7. We can superimpose these on the diagram to expose the areas of risk and competitive weakness in the value we offer to our targeted customer.

By analyzing this diagram, we can conclude several key points. The competitor offers the quality, service, and speed the customer wants more effectively than Company X. If the customer assigns a higher relative importance to the value attribute of low cost than to innovation, and the competitor makes only a minor improvement in cost (or our assessment is only slightly wrong), Company X may be in danger of losing this customer to the competitor.

As noted previously Company X is an innovation-driven company. Note the way the shape points toward the innovation attribute; the relative resource cost of that attribute "pulls down" the attributes on the other axes of the diagram. Consequently, Company X would be well advised to make sure that its target markets and customers assign a similarly high value to innovation, or it will undoubtedly become vulnerable on several other value attributes.

This simplified example can be expanded to encompass several competitors, several customers, or used with weighting to represent as much detail as desired to guide action.

CONCLUSION

In the interest of space, I only included one example of each type of shape comparison (Figures 15-5–15-7). The real-world use of these diagrams would result in many more such comparisons. By using transparent overlays or computer graphics, these shapes can be rapidly generated and easily compared.

If such diagrams are done with consistency and honesty they quickly and graphically reveal the areas of the business that represent competitive strengths and weaknesses. Reaching consensus on such analyses is an excellent platform for the shape-shifting process which must be undertaken. The diagrams are also effective communication tools with which to involve the entire organization in the shape-shift. Only when the organization understands and accepts the need to change can it bring about the changes needed rapidly and successfully.

16.

Organizing to Shape-Shift

Organizations must change radically; we are at the beginning of a
revolutionary time in business. Many companies that have enjoyed fabulous
success will find themselves out of business in the next five years if they
don't make revolutionary changes.

—Mort Myerson, Chairman of EDS

Make dust or eat dust!

—Anonymous

FUNCTIONAL ALIGNMENT

In the business world, occasionally it is possible to wipe the slate clean
and start over, but usually that is not the case; and starting over presents
unique problems of its own (like not realizing you forgot to reinstall what
was imperative to serving the customer). When companies are formed, each
functional responsibility is often associated with only one person. This
results in the cross-functional team we seek to recreate today. As companies
grow, more people are required to do these jobs; and because they come
from similar backgrounds and perform similar work, they are grouped into
like departments. This parallels the way factories were organized and thus
made sense. In some respects, this also paralleled the way nature first grows
groups of the same species concentrated in one area or locale—until disease,
predators, or other natural forces cause the homogenous group to be dis-
rupted or destroyed.

As the functional departments expanded, they began to serve "masters"
other than the customer. Often these masters were part of the corporate hier-

archy, just as was often the case in many classic large organizational models such as the military and the Catholic Church. (These two organizations provided the model for many of the evolving hierarchical organizations in commerce over the past centuries.) As serving the organizational masters becomes more prevalent, serving customers and creating true value becomes less so. This is tolerable only as long as competitors performed the same way. Value understanding was often distorted by interpretation as it is passed up the hierarchy (or bureaucracy).

My hopes are that the concept I will describe will fit many companies, and the exact form may fit a few. The concept of cross-functional organizational structures has been widely embraced as a good way to get the important things done in companies. Vertical organizations often described as silos are usually effective at administration and control and provide a modicum of structure, but seldom do they accomplish the really vital things like creating and delivering value for customers. Because of this, let us craft one possible solution that retains the best of each of what we have, and add the best of what has been missing. We will also use the advances in communications and information technology to best advantage in doing so.

Value-Creating Units and Super-Silos

It is now time to reestablish the purpose of two specific types of organizational structures referred to in this chapter: The first is the *value creating unit* (VCU) and the second is the *super-silo* (SS). Each has a distinct purpose, whether in a conventionally structured company or in one attempting to use the repertory company approach, described later.

The VCU deserves description first since it "creates and delivers value." It is a unit that encompasses all of the talents and cross-functional know-how needed to create and deliver value by being close to the customer, understanding value, creating and delivering products services that provide the shape of value desired by the customer. A typical VCU is led and managed by a person whose organizational status is equivalent to any current functional senior officer (vice president or general manager). The VCU team is cross-functional and contains all or part of the following functional skills and positions among its members: marketing, sales, new product development, operations (such as purchasing, manufacturing, and planning), financial analysis, and technology (supporting products and/or processes). Additional skills may be necessary, and can be added or deleted as required by the industry, market, or scope and type of the value to be created and delivered.

The functional (vertical) silos so often referred to when describing departments of a conventional organization came into being for a reason: specialization and efficiency. The elements of the previous functional organization that do not belong in the VCU include those jobs that can be done essentially independently of the product or market focus. These belong in highly efficient service organizations I call super-silos and include accounting/finance, human resources administration, information technology and systems, and resource/assets and technology.

- *Accounting/Finance*, especially payroll, accounts receivable and payable, cash application, posting general ledger entries, and supporting functions such as tax, audit, capital expenditure analysis, and so forth. (There must be good linkages to the VCU counterparts in accounts receivable to customer service or sales and accounts payable to sourcing or supplier relations).
- *Human Resources Administration*, including wage and salary administration, benefits management, regulatory compliance, and contract administration.
- *Information Technology and Systems*. This is a new form of the function, which is a generalist group that selects, develops, and supports the architecture and hardware/software of the systems needed to support the strategic and operational decision making of the company.
- *Resources/Assets and Technology*. A combination of physical/people, resource allocation, coordination in market positioning/brand image, and research and development or technical support staff, which can be used by the VCUs for specific help, coordination, guidance, assets, special skills, and knowledge. People must move freely in and out of this super-silo to and from VCUs as their needs and capacity fluctuate. This is the one super-silo that is most variable from company to company and among different kinds of businesses. It is also the one most in danger of growing too large and powerful; thus its size, power, and functions must be carefully monitored for opportunities to decentralize functions into the VCUs.

Each of these super-silos is headed by a traditionally titled person such as chief financial officer (CFO), chief people officer (CPO), chief information officer (CIO), or chief resource/technology officer (CR/TO). Careful application of such titles is imperative to avoid "title inflation." More than four or five such titles (or the extra titles of senior or executive vice president) are a symptom that these super-silos contain functions that probably should be decentralized into VCUs. These people are equal in rank to the heads of the VCUs but are in supporting functions. Without the VCUs creating and delivering customer value, there is no reason for them to exist.

SUPER-SILOS SUPPORT

A good way to imagine these four silos is to think of the legs of an platform or table. (see Figure 16-1) These functions may or may not be vertically integrated within the regular employee base of the organization; they are, however, essential to the success of the VCUs. The top of the platform would be made up of the VCUs oriented as "value pipelines," taking goods and services from supplier partners, adding value in the transformation process, and delivering value in goods and/or services to customer partners. Their number or type may grow and shrink as markets and products change. The process of shape-shifting will usually alter the number, type and make up of VCUs more than it does that of the super-silos.

Repertory Company Concept

It is in the VCUs that the repertory company concept works best, although it is also applicable to the super-silos. A repertory company is a term obviously borrowed from the theatrical field to describe a troupe of performers each possessing differing talents—dancers, singers, actors, a director, stage manager, and so on. Each member's contribution varies with the needs of the show/work being performed, In a musical, the singers and dancers may take the leading roles, and the dramatic actors take a secondary role. In a drama,

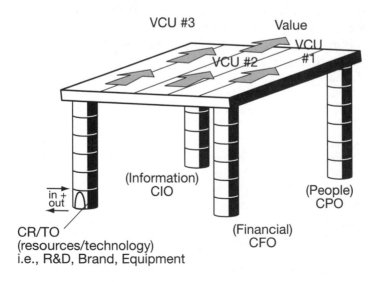

Figure 16-1 Super-Silos Support Value-Creating Units (VCUs)

the reverse might be true. The point is, again, none of the members of their troupe feel (or are) particularly inferior or superior (although there are always some "star" performers acknowledged by the entire troupe). Their roles vary as the needs vary. Their composite knowledge forms a much greater sum than the total of the parts. Thomas Koulopoulos, in his book *Smart Companies, Smart Tools* (Van Nostrand Reinhold, 1997), said there is almost an "instinct" that develops in such teams or troupes. This is a useful model for the organization of value-creating units, and that instinct is one companies must develop.

The flexibility of roles and responsibilities is an important part of shape-shifting. The ability to gain personal satisfaction, recognition, and contribute in an important manner is key. Typical organization charts with boxes and lines hierarchically arranged are far too limiting and often counterproductive, as are many other models using concentric circles, circles around a core, and other geometric constructions. All fall short, simply because they all put people into rigidly or narrowly defined roles, and that is too limiting. As industries merge, and the boundaries between them blur and dissolve, so must the talents of the people in organizational units. Thus the repertory company model of a dynamic, constantly shifting organization.

Outsourcing Model

In several of the super-silos, where most of the work is or can be disassociated from the core product or service of the business, an outsourcing model may be more effective. The resources/technology silo contains specifically relevant know-how, and is designed to permit people to come and go as needed by the VCUs. This silo may at times contain some of the most important and valuable resources of the company, yet people can move between the VCUs and silo, provided plans and provisions are made for this. This is how the organization can flex without losing vital core competencies and capabilities or trapping talent in certain VCUs too long. Some people will move more readily between VCUs; others may move in and out of the employ of the company as "free agents."

Is this a radical concept? Hardly. It is a natural adaptation in the logical evolution of teams working on projects. The recognition of the value-creating unit replaces the older strategic business unit (SBU) model, which had a tendency to overburden itself with noncritical supporting skills (better placed in the super-silos) and tended to become an organizational structure that rivaled the old bureaucratic hierarchies and trapped (people) resources in them. Will this model require some new thinking? Of course. Recall the warning about generalized solutions. They do not work unless they are adapted to the specific situation and culture. Watch for those in super-silos who attempt to become "power brokers," and remind them they are intended to be support structures.

If adapted intelligently, this model is a means to facilitate and make shape-shifting a continuing process—as it must be. The alignment of the VCUs with customers and markets is the best way to assure that the people in those units maintain a clear understanding of the value perceptions of customers. The alignment of the super-silos to perform largely administrative tasks superbly enables the effectiveness and scale economies needed to keep costs low. The movement of people between the VCUs and super-silos and in and out of the repertory company can maximize the use of talent to create and deliver value better than any current organizational approach.

Mobile Management

The organization that comes closest to this model is Oticon Holdings, the Danish hearing aid company. Lars Kolind, in a presentation at *Industry-Week*'s Global Leadership Conference in 1996 commented, "We have one job class of employees at Oticon: adults."

Kolind uses the phrase "Free the power of the people" to describe what he is trying to do at Oticon. There are no titles, no published work rules, no offices, only mobile workstations on wheels. The company operates in a paperless environment. Employees scan all paper-based information into the networked computer system for easy access by all. All employees have cellular phones, thus freeing them from any wire ties to a specific location. Even Kolind must come in each day to find an appropriate place to temporarily park his workstation, in proximity to whichever workgroup he wishes to interact with that day, that hour.

There is a form of performance feedback system. Each employee has a mentor, and performance feedback is done by a group of peers who have worked with the employee and his or her mentor.

The beautiful Danish wood furniture that once furnished the headquarters was sold at bargain prices to employees. And every employee who wants one is supplied with a computer by the company to use at home. They are encouraged to take advantage of this, and most do. This extra productivity is well worth the hardware investment, says Kolind.

Does this "structure" work? When Kolind took over in the late 1980s, the market capitalization of the firm was only about $50 million, and today it is over $500 million. Oticon shifted its shape from that of a hearing aid producer focused primarily on low cost and small size (like everyone else in the market) to a company that redefined its objective to build miniature personal computers that fit in the ear, to assist people in hearing better. Kolind is the true model of a shape-shifter. He is always contemplating how next to shape-shift to reach the next level of achievement. (Do not attempt to emulate the model they have implemented without considerable thought and preparation. It is at the very extreme leading edge of flexibility and responsiveness, but also a very difficult one to copy.)

Locating the Silos

As Oticon proves, the vertical silos that represent central support functions can be retained and recentralized (or outsourced) to take advantage of information technology and core competencies (even if it is someone else's). Accounting, finance, human resource administration, legal, compliance, customer service/telemarketing information system support, and sometimes sales representation, ideally are done in one or a few large sites. Networked computers can easily feed information to those sites and report back to the decentralized value creating units. This large administrative (super-silo) support center function does not even have to be located in a single place or even owned by the company or organization it supports, although sometimes there are strategic or business reasons it should be. In other cases, this can be outsourced partially or totally, depending on the competencies that are core to the strategy of the business or organization.

Care must be taken to explain this organizational model to the senior executives of these functions such that they clearly understand how their roles support the creation and delivery of customer value in the VCUs. Otherwise, they can become too powerful and dominate the business (to its ultimate demise). These super-silos are the "scorekeepers," the "ruleswriters," and the "protectors" of the corporate records and resources. A common structural mistake is to locate the office of the top corporate executives (COO, CEO, business unit heads, and so forth) in the same building with these super-silo functions. That is often a mistake. These top executive leaders should spend most of their time with the VCUs, where customer value is being created and delivered, or with customers, suppliers, and other partners on the "outside." The problem this presents is that VCU sites are often geographically distributed, and no one site is ideally suited for the CEO/COO. Perhaps, as at Oticon, these people should have no single primary office, but rather a series of "flexible" offices at the VCU sites, and a separate "strategic headquarters," which is essentially a gathering place for the leaders to think, debate, interact, and make strategies and plans. This strategic headquarters can then be located almost anywhere.

The Balance of Power

By 1996, the Newell Company had successfully grown to a $2.5 billion consumer products company with a return on beginning equity of 20 percent

over the past decade. Newell had achieved most of its growth through acquisitions (over 50 in the past 25 years) and by a process it calls "Newellization."
Newell sells basic, staple products to the public through the mass retailing
channel. It sells from 2 to 12 different product classes to major discount,
home center, office superstore, warehouse club, drug, hardware, department,
and (occasionally) food/convenience stores. More than 30 brands, such as
Anchor-Hocking glassware, Pyrex cookware, Levelor blinds, Sanford writing
instruments, and others, make up Newell's four major product groups.

Within its housewares, home furnishings, office products, and hardware
and tools groups, individual business units, what I call value creating units
are formed to take care of its customers and products. The "Newellization"
process features a focused business strategy, improved customer service,
and partnerships with customers. Newell's goals are to eliminate corporate
overhead through centralization of administrative functions, trim excess
costs, tighten financial controls, improve manufacturing efficiency, prune
nonproductive product lines, reduce inventories, increase trade-receivable
turnover, and improve sales-mix profitability through the application of program merchandising techniques.

To accomplish these goals, Newell balances the way functional responsibilities are divided between the corporate level and the divisions. Centralized
at corporate level are the key administrative functions such as finance and
employee benefits; those related to manufacturing and marketing are the
responsibility of the divisions. Newell's divisions concentrate on designing,
manufacturing, selling, and servicing its products under the direct supervision and leadership of a division president. Each of these presidents is also
the chief marketing officer for his or her division, and meets regularly with
customers to remain attentive to their needs. This organizational structure
streamlines the product introduction process and aids close communications
between all of the value-creating units. The most senior executives are
located in a small strategic headquarters—not with the super-silos or any of
the VCUs. It is at this "retreat" that the key managers can meet to plan for
the future with corporate leaders. The proof of the approach is in continued
success both in the marketplace and financial terms.

HOW THE REPERTORY COMPANY CONCEPT WORKS FOR VCUs

The picture I would like to create here is one of a series of repertory companies each situated close to its markets and customers. Each would have
regular members whose core competencies and capabilities are aligned with
the needs and desires of the customers in those markets, and supported with
intellectual information tools, which Koulopoulos calls "smart tools." Each

would have a general manager or director, responsible for the results of the repertory company.

When the repertory company (VCU) requires more resources of a certain kind to meet the needs of a particular customer's shape of value, then that company may do one of three things. First, it may borrow or buy resources from another VCU within the parent organization (or even from the super-silo site, if the requisite skills reside there). Second, it may draw on a pool of skills that reside in a super-silo location, such as a technology or R&D center, assuming that the needs are sufficient to support such a center. When the members of that corporate support center are not being drafted/leased by the VCUs they work on a priority list of customer-valued projects funded by income from the VCUs, and "owned" or sponsored by one or more VCUs. Third, it may find contract, temporary, or migrant help ("free agent" or "bit players") to support its needs. This last option is becoming an increasingly viable source of flexible help, since the massive downsizing of corporate organizations has resulted in a great deal of talent in this job pool. A key element of Newell's success, for example, is that virtually all of its division presidents are veterans of other Newell divisions, having been moved as the performance of the company required it. The same is true of key managerial talent at lower levels.

Another key element of this type of structure is that the core teams working in the customer value creation and delivery units are multifunctional and multitalented. Just as in the repertory company theatrical model, these are the "on-stage," front-line performers. It is upon their skills that the success of the performance depends. Thus, these should be the most highly compensated positions in the business. It is entirely appropriate that their compensation be tied tightly to the performance of the company. When the company does well, they should do very well, too, and vice versa. Longer-term incentives such as stock ownership in the parent organization must also be a part of their compensation, to align them with both the performance of their unit and the entire parent organization, as discussed in the chapter on compensation.

An essential part of this process, structure, and culture is collaboration. Whether the word *teams* is used is purely a semantic issue. Perhaps a better word to describe this concept for some companies is *community*, or *network*.

The ideal repertory company develops a strong sense of community among its members. The community has an internal and external network through which it exchanges information and builds stronger relationships. Since the organization is essentially a living organism, perhaps it is appropriate to borrow the term *DNA* from the scientific world to describe its patterns of behavior. The organization and the community, which is formed by the repertory company, if left intact for a reasonable time frame will develop

an "organizational DNA," which governs its behavior and reactions to external threats and its own needs. This organic model is how the most powerful,
effective organizations function. It is also why merging two or more of them
is difficult.

If two organizations decide to "get married," they may be able to merge
their DNAs and eventually produce offspring organizations that carry traits
of both parents. This model is easy to describe, very complex and difficult to
produce, yet incredibly powerful when it works.

For such a business to work properly, it must have a good, functioning
"central nervous system," that is, the information and communication system and the network it works through, both human and electronic. Few dispute the power of a human network to get things done. The information
network is the electronic parallel to this. This system must be the most effective combination of *proven* technology available, and must be supportive of
the social and operational needs of the organization.

CREATING THE REPERTORY COMPANY

A few examples will help clarify the repertory company model. Consider a
hypothetical consumer durable products company whose market is primarily North America and secondarily the rest of the world where similar products are or might be used. The products are part of an existing line, but new
in function and configuration. The repertory company is formed by naming
a "conductor" or "director," who is the VCU leader (business team manager,
or the equivalent in traditional terms). This is often a general manager in his
or her first P&L position promoted from a highly successful tenure in some
other functional or team discipline. Often, marketing positions create this
type of leaders, but they might come from multifunctional disciplines such
as logistics if the company is one in which information and involvement is
widely spread. Marketing roles currently called product managers or brand
managers are among the first additions to the repertory company. These are
the members who translate "what the customer will buy or might want" into
terms the rest of the company can understand. Market research may be part
of the unit or may be on loan from the resource/technology super-silo (R/T
SS) or from an outsourced supplier-partner.

The next members of the team came from product development, R&D,
or engineering. These are the people who develop and commercialize ideas,
from concepts to drawings to hardware that works. Specialized technology
requirements, however, can often be met by someone loaned from the R/T
SS. An industrial designer, graphic designer, or stylist might be part of the
team or also might come from the R/T SS. Operations talent is the next to be
added, including tooling/equipment or process engineering, manufacturing,

purchasing, or some other combination of the skills that acquire and/or make products A financial and/or cost analyst is important to help assure that the products, when complete, will meet financial objectives of both the customer and creating positive economic value.

Sales input to and support for the company depends on the structure of the VCUs. If sales can be decentralized to the VCU without sacrificing the customer's desires for representation or the economics of the industry, input and support is most easily provided. In some cases, the customer's needs and wishes will dictate this decision. Recently, packaged goods giant Procter & Gamble eliminated what were frequently called "the Seven Dwarfs," multiple sales representatives historically calling on the same retailers, and selling the products from their seven major business units. Procter & Gamble replaced them with a multifunctional "customer business development team," representing products from all of the business units and product/brand categories. This customer sales and service model is a development that has only recently emerged to address the consolidation of customers, which is occurring not only in retailing, but in most major industries as the large get larger and the small are either acquired or disappear.

If some form of common salesforce serving multiple product, service market, or geographical VCUs is used, then the marketing members of the team must draw sales input from periodic participants who come from that sales VCU. Other members of the repertory company may come from the fulfillment or delivery functions, or these, like sales, may be part of a separate VCU, whose mission is to take and fill orders. (In many industries, this is being outsourced to telemarketing centers and/or tied into contract logistics companies.) The exact configuration is and must be fluid, so it defies a single model. Adapting to the needs and wishes of the customer in the value attributes of service and speed may enhance competitive position or merely protect it from erosion by a competitor that already has done so. Remember, there is no one-size-fits-all solution. Each organizational structure must be adapted to the needs of the customer—its shape of value.

Other talents needed in the repertory company depend on the specific nature of the product and market. The size of the company and project will also determine whether the repertory company must have one or more than one organizational level. Some companies try to restrict this, but the best solution is "whatever seems to work best." A large repertory company such as the Chrysler platform team that created the Plymouth Prowler may require three or more levels. But keep in mind, each level is a barrier to communication and collaboration. Two levels should suffice for all but the largest projects or products and companies. If more than two levels are required, the size and bureaucracy that can result may negate the flexible, collaborative nature of the repertory company approach. Broad flat structures interconnected with networked information should reduce the need for hierarchical levels.

STAYING ON TOP BY STAYING ON TOP OF VALUE

To this point, one assumption underlies all discussions—that the strategy and tactics of the organization are properly linked to the right customer value and the consistent delivery of that value. If this is not the case, return to the beginning and reread the preceding chapters. I cannot emphasize too strongly how important it is for an organization to be externally focused in its search for what is (and will be) valued by customers. Even though customers often do not know exactly what they value and why, the process of searching for it will help clarify this for the company. If done properly, this can also be a powerful positive reinforcement of your business as a value provider once the customer has realized what that means. Newell states its reasoning this way:

> *Newell's unique combination of centralization and decentralization creates an efficient corporate structure. It also creates a responsive entrepreneurial spirit and culture at the division level, resulting in better customer partnerships, superior performance, and higher profitability. This dual structure is a prime contributor to Newell's ability to meet its aggressive financial goals.*

In every case, the four critical partnerships described in my first book, *The Power of Partnerships,* will position a business to have the best possible access to the information needed to help understand best value and its delivery. In some cases, particular partnerships will not work well or at all. It is important to recognize when this occurs to avoid a "blind spot," which is vulnerable to competition. In other cases, the core competencies that "got you there" will no longer be valid, appropriate, or sufficient to "keep you there." When this happens, a very dangerous condition can exist. A business can be very successful right up until it crashes precipitously because of a fundamental shift in customer value perceptions or delivery systems. The absence of advance warning is a symptom of the absence of solid partnerships with customers, suppliers, employees, or outside partners. Protecting the self-interest of a small group of senior executives who attained their lofty positions through skills and competencies that are no longer competitive is a primary cause of the decline of businesses.

People Must Change or You Must Change the People

In writing on core competencies, Hamel and Prahalad stopped short of ascribing these solely to the people in an organization, but in my experience, core competencies are embedded more in the people than in the environment. Certainly, the combination of the two is essential, and if either the environment or the people change drastically, usually the core competency will also change. This can be good or bad. If a competitor "steals" key knowledge workers, the core competencies and capabilities may be lost. If new management changes the environment, equally damaging effects may result.

My specific concern here is not those two cases; I want to address those situations when competencies and capabilities become outdated or inappropriate (no longer valued by customers), because this is when really devastating failures occur.

Shift Core Competencies with People

It is imperative to migrate the core competencies and capabilities without destroying what your organization successful in the first place. Your core competencies must support the shift to the required shape of value, and take your core capabilities along with them. Nature mutates and evolves to adapt to changing environmental threats and changes. Herds and flock migrate to new environments. Companies must, too. These core competencies and capabilities are embedded in the organization which is usually resistant to change. There are "immune systems" in companies just like in the bodies of plants and animals (and humans). The immune system can either try to maintain the status quo (not possible—stability is death), or adapt and evolve to a new stronger condition. Since these are "embedded" in your people, *the people must change or you must change the people*. Some of the people, and in many cases a lot of them, will recognize the need for change. They will be afraid to change. Another important role of leaders is to lead people to places they would be afraid to go alone.

Change is risky, but not changing is riskier. How many people accept the need, and then actually change depends on how well the leaders encourage and communicate the need for the change and how well the organization understands why it must change. Note that both the communication and understanding are necessary. One does not necessarily result from the other. A lot also depends on what kind of culture and relationships are in place—and how they are operating. If suppliers, employees, and so on are not part of strong relationships, well connected to a good culture, they will not change (or at least not rapidly enough).

The ability of your organization to learn is also a critical element in the ability to make these essential changes. Nature demands a learning system—either learn (evolve and adapt) or die. The speed of adaptation depends on the speed of learning. The speed of change depends on the speed of learning.

Learning depends on the desire and the openness of the minds and hearts of the people. Stephen Covey has a phrase that comes to mind in this context: "I don't care how much you learn until I learn how much you care." Learning must be retained, and to achieve this, the reasons and need must be understood and then be reflected upon, before real learning happens. The willingness to learn and make changes depends on trust and leadership, which is fundamental to partnering—*relationships* and *culture* both. Thus the loop is closed.

As I have been moving through this chapter, I have carefully chosen certain words. These words are the dimensions of the Shape of Business described much earlier in this book. The dimensions are the keys to how a business creates and delivers the best value. Unless these dimensions change, the shape of value will not shift far, or for long. Keeping the shape of value shifted artificially without shifting the shape of the business requires a huge investment of resources, and is still only marginally effective.

Deluxe Corporation, cited earlier, is one such case. Likewise, large, mid-priced, mall-based department stores lost much of their business to strip-mall or freestanding discount stores that offered better value with greater convenience. The merchandise selection, presentation, promotion, and underlying economics all changed. Kmart and other early discounters took Sears' business. Then Wal-Mart took Kmart's by doing what it did better. Regional discount store chains continue to falter and fail—their shape of value simply does not measure up in today's environment. General Motors' ability to produce large, comfortable cars with many cosmetic features but poor reliability fell prey to spartan, economical, reliable small cars from Japan. Once the Japanese cars had captured the value perception of the customer, they began to add back the features and size to enhance profitability.

The point is, when core competencies become out of date or misaligned with customer value, it is imperative that companies recognize it early and act fast. Sometimes they can shift their competencies, by education, restructuring, process reengineering, and associated measures with largely the same people. Very often, however, many people will cling to what they did that got them where they are, which as I've said so often is exactly the wrong thing to do. When this happens, there is almost no alternative except to change some of the people. This was the case with Sears. It is also the case with Kmart and with General Motors.

Rick Maurer's work, *Beyond the Wall of Resistance* (Bard, 1996) goes into considerable detail on resistance to change. The learning organization concepts I defined earlier make up the only "environmental" way I have found to bring about large-scale change in a group of people who have been successful doing things one way for a long time. Even then it is slow and only partially successful. If attrition and retirement take a large enough toll, the number of people who must be replaced is reduced. Some people will simply not accept responsibility for their own future, by keeping themselves and their competencies competitive. Others will not adopt new ways of doing things or new behaviors. It is for these reasons that I prefer to think of and refer to people as partners. As partners, people are more likely to share in the responsibility to keep up their end of the partnership, to upgrade their work habits, competencies, and capabilities. If the rest of the partnerships are working properly, it will be evident which competencies and capabilities are still valued and why. This must guide strategy, organization development, and tactics. Communicating not only the "what" of strategy but the "why" can help in this transition. It is not easy. It is difficult. But the world is an increasingly competitive place where doing difficult things is the price of continued employment survival.

17.

The Future Shape of Work

What really matters is people. People with the right leadership are an unstoppable force.
—Pasquale Pistorio, CEO of SGS-Thomson Microelectronics

Security is mostly superstition—it does not exist in nature. Life is either a daring adventure or nothing at all.
—Helen Keller

THE POST-CAPITALIST SOCIETY AND ITS IMPACT ON VALUE

Noted business authority Peter Drucker coined the term "post-capitalist society" to describe what he believed to be a likely picture of the future for business and society. One major premise of this concept is that not as many people are making or moving things now as in the past, and the number is likely to continue to shrink. The traditional, capitalistic factors of land, labor, and capital are being superseded by the new economic resources. If Drucker is correct, the implications for managers, workers, and companies are significant. His hypothesis that "value is now created by improving productivity and innovating, two jobs that require applying knowledge to work" confirms that the downsizing of traditional organizations is likely to continue. Fewer people will be required to make and move things, and these jobs will disappear forever. True, many new jobs will be created, but they will require different skills and training. Even the so-called service sector which was to be the savior of the total employment picture, is now falling prey to technology. Computers and information technology are capable either of taking over or drastically simplifying the most numerous jobs in the service sector, people who "wait on" or help cus-

223

tomers, either in person or by phone. Anyone who has received a computer-generated call, used an automated teller machine, selected from a voice-mail menu, or inserted his or her own credit card at the gas pump has felt the impact of this technology.

Preparing for Knowledge Work

To prepare for knowledge work requires an entire generation (maybe two) to become much more familiar and comfortable with computers and related technology. A further implication of this trend is that "outsourcing" is no longer a dirty word. Companies cannot afford to be only moderately competent in anything that is not core to their strategy. The burden of fixed costs and staying competent is too great. This makes outsourcing a desirable of shape-shifting; that is, to distribute necessary work to those who can do it best. In some cases the word *delivering* means exactly that. Some of the nation's most competent delivery companies such as FedEx are taking over delivery of all kinds of products or services for other major companies. They call these new services *contract logistics*. By outsourcing a noncore area, resources can be focused on what is core, and often more of that can be "insourced," resulting in a stronger, more competitive core.

Implementing Cross-Functional Systems

Previous chapters discussed how to get things done. There is little doubt that cross-functionally is the operative process. That is how the VCU concept was born. Managers in the new environment, after having been trained for years to control and be responsible for results, must now learn to "let go."

One of the negative consequences of reengineering (beyond the mindless downsizing of jobs) is the stress placed on people expected to do the work previously done by two, three, or more of their associates. In many of the instances, the systems and processes have not been changed enough to permit this. The result is either much longer work hours and/or work poorly done. The irony is that many companies that expect such output from their reduced workforces are those hiring such organizations as the Covey Leadership Center to help employees get their life priorities straight. This conflicting message is doing untold harm. How can employees put "first things first" *and* do three to four times the work in the same amount of time, with limited process improvements?

Doing More with Less

In a series of columns and articles, former *IndustryWeek* writer Tom Brown touched several raw nerves on the "doing more with less" issue. There is little doubt that increased productivity is essential to continued survival. But is this requirement causing "corporate anorexia" from the continued reductions in staff without corresponding reductions in workload or improvement in processes and systems?

Brown asks whether lean and mean has to be inhumane as well. He cites the results of one company's unlimited cost-cutting initiatives:

- One person now works what used to be four to five jobs.
- Voice mailboxes are routinely stuffed to capacity, so there's no way to return calls quickly. (E-mail is also overloaded)
- Work hours are stretching ever later.
- The sense of job security has evaporated.

Brown then asks a crucial question: "Can morale ever be high when operating costs are so low?" Adversity need not breed low morale. Some of the highest morale I have ever seen was in a workforce straining to protect their jobs and future from foreign competition. There is more to this issue than *what* is done. *How* it is done matters, too.

While I was writing this, I spoke with an employee of a plant where I had once been the division president. She called out of desperation because the remaining 800 employees (out of 2,000) were fearful that the plant would be closed. During our discussion, I asked if the company had offered to keep the plant open in return for "givebacks" in pay, benefits, and work rules. She admitted that such talks had occurred more than a year earlier, but that "the employees could never give up so much after the way they had been treated!" Trust was just too low. When I asked her to elaborate, she said she suspected that if the situation had been explained in a more cooperative and respectful way by someone they trusted, they might have "worked something out." She referred to the adversarial way information was shared in times past as an example. People have a remarkable capacity to endure, understand, and accept "bad news," but whether they *do* accept it has a lot to do with the delivery and the history of the relationship.

NEW SOCIAL CONTRACT

The term *new social contract* describes the new working relationship between companies and employees. Another of Tom Brown's columns

defines a social contract as "a set of mutually held beliefs between two parties about their reciprocal expectations." He quotes Denis Sullivan and
Randy McDonald, a pair of GTE executives, who, with their team, generated
a very important list of considerations for this new social contract (my
emphasis added):

- A form of *partnership* is replacing paternalism in the emerging relationship.
- Instead of viewing employees as a cost, companies must now view them
  as *value-adding resources*.
- Employees are no longer "entitled" to benefits and security, but must
  earn them by *adding value.*
- Instead of trying to *control* what employees do, corporations need to
  unleash broad *involvement*, moving behavior from conformance and risk
  avoidance to high levels of challenge and risk-taking.
- Perhaps most important, both employer and employee need a *greater
  focus on customers' wants and needs*.

These statements tie the efforts of people working in teams, to build
partnerships to create and deliver value. Brown's closing sentence says it all:
"This is not just a new program. It's a new way of work life."

A New Work Life

Let's face it, "job security" is an oxymoron. Retirement is rapidly becoming a
thing of the past. In *We Are All Self-Employed: A New Social Contract
Affecting Every Worker* (Berrett Koehler, 1994), author Cliff Hakim expands
on this concept. He uses an assortment of terms in line with the concept of
shape-shifting; "Organizational structures are being reshaped." "The era of
'CEO as despot' is over." "[A]n environment where ongoing learning is encouraged." And perhaps most salient of all: ". . . winners work flexibly and diligently, matching their skills with customer needs."
   This conceptual "tough but fair" approach to self-responsibility is gaining
considerable momentum and empirical support. Even in cases of intense collaboration as cited earlier in Michael Shrage's work, the concept of being up
to date and independent enough to disagree is highly regarded.
Unfortunately there are still many organizations where such outspoken and
independent actions will speed one's move into "self-employment."
   Authors Gary Heil, Tom Parker, and Deborah Stevens present an excellent list of ten challenges for building an intrinsically motivating environment
in their book *One Size Fits One*:

1. Creating a cause worthy of commitment.
2. Building core values that guide performance.
3. Committing to the truth and sharing a sense of reality.
4. Ensuring that every person has a meaningful role.
5. Increasing accountability, but not more of the same.
6. Developing ability commensurate with responsibility.
7. Building cooperation instead of competition.
8. Abolishing the corporate caste system.
9. Developing an optimistic, caring, and supportive environment.
10. Building trust, one employee at a time.

This type of an environment is not only motivational, it also forms the basis for a new social contract between employer and employees.

What does all this social commentary have to do with shape-shifting to create and deliver the best value? Everything. Only when we listen in an open and unbiased manner, and then interact collaboratively can we reach consensus on what the best value might be. Andy Grove, CEO of Intel, is noted for his encouragement of conflict as a way of flushing out the "truth." Value is an elusive thing, and the camouflage of less than honest input, weak feedback, compliant participation or token collaboration renders it invisible. Value hides behind the conventional wisdom and the politically correct viewpoint better than the most adaptable chameleon blends into dense foliage.

In his "Managing Your Career" column in the *Wall Street Journal* (November 29, 1994, p. B1), Hal Lancaster wrote, "Don't assume that the organization will provide you with clearly defined career paths and carefully crafted developmental experiences." I will go further than that. Make sure you are contributing value in all the things you do. Then, your "job security" will be as an independent contractor who just happens to be employed by a given company at any point in time. Working with teams in a collaborative environment will enable you to attain what University of Tennessee professor Jim Reeve refers to as "reputation capital." This is the element of your professional worth that gets you selected when people are choosing teams, and provides a job security far beyond what any company can offer.

There are not many alternatives to this approach. "We're at a point of absolute, supreme discontinuity. Human beings were not built to process what we're going through now," proclaims futurist/market forecaster Watts Wacker in the pages of *Fast Company*. "Complaining that technology changes fast is like complaining that rocks are hard: it's true but useless," echoes writer Jim Taylor in the same issue.

What are business people to do? Dig a hole and hide? Freeze with paralysis in fear of failure? No! "Take control of your destiny" is my answer. Many people have begun to make the transition from viewing the job they are in as a permanent situation to just one of a series on a career continuum. This alters how people view their contribution to value and their loyalty to any company.

When there is this loose connection between work, job, career, and occupation, people's view of the value they create is altered permanently. If they do not create sufficient value, they will likely be removed from the job, and replaced by someone who creates more value. This is the dilemma of middle management everywhere. For many years a large percentage of them created value by being a conduit of information, plans, results, and alternative courses of action between hourly workers, foremen, and top management. Information technology and self-directed teams have shattered that job description, and rendered part of it nonvalue-additive. Thus, the large cuts in middle management ranks.

A secondary result of this change is that information, which middle managers previously "massaged and managed" often to support their position or worth before passing it up or down, is now passed on by networked computers. Not only is the value added by many of the middle managers reduced, but the power and influence they wielded is gone with it. Middle managers must and are finding new ways to create value; and if they are creating it in their current role, they must find a way to make that evident to senior management. There are still many important tasks to accomplish, related to planning and organizing work, leading and coaching teams, and so forth, and these will continue to be valued roles of the middle manager whose job survives.

Job Shift

IndustryWeek magazine interviewed Bill Bridges, author of *Job Shift* (Addison Wesley, 1995) about the direction of jobs. His comments were insightful and thought provoking.

We've forgotten that the job is a social artifact, and that before the year 1800 societies did just fine without jobs . . . . Self-directed work teams are another step on the path toward a jobless society. . . . Most jobs in today's workplace are done in specific places during specific times. Eliminate that structure, and there's still work that needs to be done, but is there a "job?". . . .[R]eengineering also threatens to consume jobs as we know them, because it tears apart organizations that were set up functionally, where jobs were very easy to describe, and reassembles them based on the work processes that weave through the organization.

It is interesting that the phrase "tears them apart" is used in conjunction with reengineering; the destructive connotation persists. One important point of all this job rhetoric is that continued shape-shifting, which is mandatory for continued success, disrupts traditional job structures and concepts. Jobs may not be eliminated totally, but their shape, content, location, and how they add to value is a constantly changing montage, not a still life. The Wainwright and Halliburton examples described earlier clearly illustrate the magnitude of change that must occur. The central issue is value. The subordinate issue is the structure and situation—the shape in which that value is delivered.

The concepts defined in prior chapters of horizontal and vertical organizations working in harmony are not radical. Companies all over the world are evolving to this model out of necessity, as this is being written. Just as *everything vertical* was wrong for delivering the best value, so is *everything horizontal*. The proper shape, the one that shifts as the customer/market need changes, is the key to delivering best value. Even with this admonition, some companies still focus on less than the ideal goal. The direction may be right, but as we discovered in earlier chapters, satisfaction and customer value are situational, and ever changing. Thus, our objective must be best value both now and in the future. If we understand and create best value, we will satisfy the customer at the right time and place. Just as a football team cannot directly influence the scoreboard except by scoring touchdowns or field goals, companies cannot influence satisfaction without providing value, as defined by customer, in that situation and at that time.

To complete this loop, the path to follow to deliver value, from an organizational perspective, is through participation and empowerment. Empowerment is a badly misused word and practice. Empowering people means giving them the power to control their own destiny in a task and output sense. But to do this without defining the boundaries of their participation providing the training and the resources needed and setting clearly defined expectations is not empowerment, it is abdication. That is what many companies have done, not necessarily out of malice, but out of ignorance. That these so-called empowered employees have no trust in management is no surprise. They are left wandering in the participative wilderness of their work, untrained and unsupported, feeling lost and disenfranchised in new-found responsibilities they cannot fulfill, while their management beats their chest about the great empowerment program.

Trust is built by saying and doing things consistently and fairly. Behaviors speak louder than words, and help build the trust that is essential to forging sound cultures and strong partnerships. The culture and the partnerships, as stated repeatedly, are the cornerstones upon which strategy and execution must depend. When this approach is followed to its logical completion, the creation and delivery of best value *can be* achieved. Notice I did not say *will be* achieved. There are many pitfalls along the way to creating and delivering best value. Most of them are of our own creation, but some come from competitors and outside influences (market fluctuations, regulatory or trade issues, etc.). How well we Shape-Shift our organization and business will determine how well we are prepared to create the shape of the business that will create and deliver best value. With this in mind, let us move on to the topic of vision, mission, strategy, and the longer view on how we might, in the words of Hamel and Prahalad, "get to the future first" and with the best value!

18.

Predict the Future by Creating the Future

Underlying the operations of every company—working like its spine or cerebral cortex—is its value delivery system. A company's performance is the direct result of how effectively the system is structured and managed.
—George Stalk and Thomas Hout,
Competing against Time

CREATING AND COMMUNICATING THE VISION OF BEST VALUE

If we accept the premise that the best value really does "win" a competitive advantage, how do we shift our shape to create and deliver this best value? Much of this book has been devoted to specific aspects of the answer. In this chapter I pull things together from the mission, vision, strategy, and tactics viewpoint.

Creating and consistently delivering best value depends first and foremost on understanding what value is all about. We have already covered this point thoroughly. Once there is a good understanding of value, then the essential element of creating and delivering it is the shape of the business. Since any business already has some "shape," its shape-shifting is the essence of best value creation and delivery. The diagram in Figure 18-1 integrates the entire shape-shifting concept.

Traditional solutions have proved to be too fragmented, dealing only with limited aspects of the shape. To create the best value and deliver it consistently, all of the parts must be in balance. Remember, the four partnerships are the cornerstones. Without them in place, any other efforts will fail or result in less than the best value. Once partnerships are formed (remember,

231

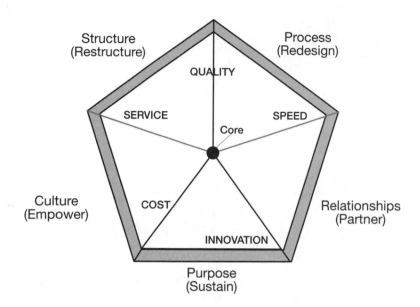

Figure 18-1 Integrative Model of Shape-Shifting

they can never be "complete" or "perfect"), then the other parts of the integrative model can become the focus of attention.

Choosing the Playing Fields

Hamel and Prahalad pleaded with business leaders to get to the future first and use industry foresight to do so. They urged us to pick playing fields on which we could win, and if possible, redefine the rules to give us an advantage. How?

First we must consider the *structure* of the business. What is its physical structure? What is the architecture of organization? How do the value creation and delivery processes work? More important, how *should* they be structured? What kind of *culture* is needed to support the processes? Does this culture exist, and are external partnerships being developed to support the culture? What combination of the value attributes do the targeted customers and markets value and why? By defining this thoroughly, we can more fully understand the type of *structure, process, culture* and *relationship* needed. Finally, is our *purpose* sound and clearly embedded?

I said before that the first step in shape-shifting is to determine the shape of value desired by the targeted customers, but there is actually one step prior to this, and that is to decide which kind of business you are going to be in, and how and why you have a chance to succeed in this business given current market and competitive conditions. The diagnostic profiles and shape of value diagrams shown earlier will help you answer those questions, but not without considerable thought. The list in Figure 18-2 repeats the descriptors for the value attributes and the questions to pose to arrive at this answer (also shown in Figures 5-2 and 10-12).

Aspects such as financial resources, employee talents, and so on are not covered in these tools; therefore, a diagnosis of what constitute the core

---

Quality:

- Specification (Robustness, Refinement): What is the intended or designed performance level or feature richness?
- Conformance (Information): Does the product conform to the intended specification? How well?
- Consistency (Variability): Is there a high level of consistency to the product or a low level of variability?
- Reliability: Does the product keep doing what it is intended to do, the same way, over and over for a long time?
- Durability: Does the product "hold up" through hard use or even modest misuse?

Service:

- Courtesy (Intimacy): Is the service courteous, pleasant, and friendly?
- Ease (Simplicity): Is the service easy to get or use?
- Information: Is it easy to find out the status of the product or service at any time?
- Flexibility: Can the service be accessed and used many different ways?
- Adaptability (Responsiveness): Can the service be tailored to specific needs of the customer, and be readily altered as situations change?

Speed:

- Convenience (Effortlessness): Is the product accessible with little effort?
- Timeliness: Is the product available on a timely basis?
- Flexibility: Does the product arrive where, when, and how it is wanted?
- Throughput: Is the time from beginning to end of the cycle (of order/ production/delivery) short?
- Information: Is accurate information available quickly?

Figure 18-2 Discriptors for Value Attributes

Cost (Low):
- First Cost: Is the first cost low enough to be competitive?
- Handling and Packaging: Is there little waste in nonvalue-added costs in getting the product where/when it must be?
- Throughput and Delivery (Information): Is there an ability to know where/when the product is in its throughput cycle at little or no extra cost?
- Penalties: Do requested changes or nonstandard needs result in extra costs and charges?
- Premiums: Is it possible to gain speed, flexibility, or other customized changes by paying a modest fee or at no premium?

Innovation:
- Uniqueness (Proprietary or Exclusive): Can the product be unique, proprietary, exclusive, or customized?
- Cachet and Status: Does the product convey additional importance or exclusivity on its owner for some reason?
- Technology: Is a breakthrough technology involved with the product or some aspect of it?
- Entertainment (Information): Does some aspect of the product provide unusual entertainment or informational benefits?
- Style (Trend or Fad): Is the product particularly ideal with respect to some current style, trend, or fad that makes it desirable?

Figure 18-2 Discriptors for Value Attributes *(continued)*

competencies of the corporation is imperative. (Hamel and Prahalad have provide the basis for this in their *Harvard Business Review* article.)

The second step in the process of shape-shifting is to assess how the shape of the business supports and enables the shape of value desired. This step requires thorough analysis since it involves every aspect of the business. Do not move through this step lightly or too quickly. A group evaluation and considerable dialogue involving multiple levels and functions of the business are imperative if you want to arrive at a complete and objective assessment.

Outside counsel and advice is also recommended to assist in this critical evaluation. Without the right ideas of how to shift the shape of the business, the resulting shape of value will not be viable, competitive, or sustainable.

DERIVING THE VALUE ATTRIBUTES

First, let us discuss the speed attribute, and then move on to the others.

Speed

Is speed one of the most important attributes? I think so. Economists claim the cost of living is falling due to the greater utility value of the things we buy for little or no higher prices. Others say the value of time itself is deflating. There is so much more to do, to learn, to absorb, and time is perishable. No amount of money can buy it back once it is spent. For that reason, speed is inflating in value. Raw speed may be the single most powerful deflator/inflator in business today. Faster computers and more powerful information/communication infrastructures are the driving force behind this dimensional shift.

For airline or package delivery companies, speed certainly is a critical value attribute. Fast food restaurants that are not "fast" will eventually lose customers. Office products dealers and wholesalers that cannot deliver in 12 to 24 hours will lose out to those who can and do. Mail-order companies must offer next-day delivery to be competitive. As banks, securities brokerage firms, and travel agencies go online, the time and effort required to complete transactions goes down dramatically. In fact, it is difficult to think of any business in which speed has not become a critical success factor.

Sometimes customers dictate the need for speed. At other times, if one company chooses to make speed the basis for differentiation, its competitors must match it in order to avoid being at a disadvantage. For example, custom-made suits have been available in 48 hours in Hong Kong and Taiwan for years, but this was enabled "artificially" by throwing people resources at the need—low-wage workers working around the clock. Now, a computer takes the measurements and feeds them to computerized cutting machines that make parts that seamstresses can join on computerized sewing machines. The result: custom-made suits in 48 to 72 hours, anywhere, anytime.

Structure

Whatever the reason, if speed and convenience or timeliness are required, the support structure must be able to provide it. This indicates the need for a highly efficient, yet decentralized customer contact structure with excellent central coordination. What kind of structure offers the best speed? One that has a very fast, effective information infrastructure combined with effective production and delivery structures and processes.

The Right Speed

A lot of companies try to use speed as an asset in the competitive arena. Usually, they do this by carrying inventory and "working faster." Such an approach is a great idea initially, but is prohibitively costly as a long-term approach. It is what I call "faking it." Dell Computer, however, is doing it right. Michael Dell, chairman and CEO, realized that "speed is everything in this business." Coupled with this priority was a determination not to sacrifice service (customization) and low cost (a necessity). Therefore, Dell set about shifting the shape of the business to create the speed it needed. By early 1997, a customer order placed by 9:00 A.M. on Monday could be on a delivery truck by 9:00 P.M. on Tuesday. And Dell's low inventory investment, rapid cash turnaround, and modest manufacturing costs enable it to underprice many rivals by 10 to 15 percent.

How? By major structure and process improvements. Dell requires that the majority of its components be warehoused within 15 minutes' transportation time to a Dell factory. Dell also uses "electronic commerce," especially via the Internet, to minimize the time from order to shipment. The company calls it "velocity," and it results in a sale being converted to cash within 24 hours or less via credit card payment on the Internet. Contrast this to the 30-plus days for rival Compaq, which sells through more traditional resellers with regular business payment terms.

Since Dell doesn't start manufacturing until an order is booked, there is little or no finished inventory in the pipeline. There are components at the suppliers' nearby warehouses. In an industry where component prices often fall weekly, this means that Dell also gets the benefit of downward price movement on parts, as soon as or before that movement hits end-product pricing. Other companies must work off older, higher-priced inventory. Thus, speed begets lower costs as well.

To build the rapid supplier network, Dell reduced the number of suppliers from 204 to 47, and built strong relationships with those that remained. Further reductions in costs came about as a result of Dell using its systems capability and supplier partners to merge shipments of computer monitors with finished computers at the customer's destination, thereby eliminating the cost of moving the monitors to Dell before being shipped to the end customer.

A culture change also was important to Dell's speed initiative. Telephone staff can steer purchasers to "recommended configurations," which also happen to be those most readily available. Emphasizing the financial results and their importance also helped bring about the culture change. CFO Tom Meredith said, "We spent 15 months educating people about return on invested capital, convincing them they could impact our future."

By selling more PCs over the World Wide Web, Dell further increases speed and lowers costs, because it takes only a handful of people to process Web orders versus the hundreds that staff the phone lines. As speed increases, the barriers for competitors similarly go up. Dell is shifting its shape to create competitive advantage that thrives on continuous change.

Cost

Cost is usually one of the most important criteria in any competitive business. Obviously, then a highly efficient, low-cost delivery system is critical. The Dell study shows how speed and cost go hand in hand. Similarly, the warehouse club method of retail distribution, practiced so well by Costco represents a low-cost delivery system that buys and sells low and fast, but in a limited assortment. Volume buying, low-cost facilities, high levels of mass handling, a small staff, self-service, and extensive information systems seem to be structural imperatives for such a low-cost model. Simplicity in assortment or variety or highly flexible production (like Dell's) are other primary determinants of a low-cost structure and process. Complexity costs extra—although computing power is discounting that cost rapidly—if organizations can only keep up.

For Members Only

There is a lesson to be learned from what occurred in the wholesale, or warehouse, club industry. This wholesale retail format was developed by innovator Sol Price after he sold the FedMart stores on the West Coast. Price felt that there was a distinct market for stores that were more like warehouses than traditional stores. If such a store-warehouse could be made a membership club and cater to wholesale purchases by small businesses, it would serve a niche that was largely being ignored or abused by distributors. His idea was to buy and stock the club merchandise only in the best-selling, high-volume SKUs (stock keeping units) used by these small business owners. In doing so, the club could turn its inventory very rapidly and effectively use the terms from the suppliers to finance the working capital needs of the business. Using warehouses located off heavily traveled thoroughfares further reduced the cost of operations. A no-frills, bag- or box-your-own environment completed the concept. Price calculated that the club could afford to sell at only 10 percent gross margin—less than half required by a normal discount store, and lower than most distributors could offer. (The distributors, like regular retailers, were compelled to carry a far wider assortment of inventory, thus reducing their inventory turns and raising the margins they must charge.)

Price Clubs were an immediate success, doing huge volume out of a single location. Over $100 million sales per year was not uncommon for a single Price Club location in southern California. Wholesale membership dues were low ($25/year) but afforded members lower prices than "retail" customers. The wholesale members also bought more per visit, and usually of a more profitable product mix.

As the club format expanded, others jumped in. Consolidation was rapid, and early entrants, which often opened in smaller metro markets or with less sophisticated discipline, fell by the wayside and were acquired including Price, either by its premier West Coast competitor Costco, or Wal-Mart's Sam's Club. Within less than 10 years, only a handful of large club chains remained—Costco, Sam's, B.J.'s.

It was then that the horizon darkened. During the consolidation, operating results became clouded by the closings, acquisition costs, and so on. After the dust settled, it became apparent that something was wrong. Few clubs were making money, but no one was sure why. A negative shift had occurred. Simply put, most of the management of these clubs were now retail-oriented; they had forgotten what made them unique—their wholesale member customers. The large volume of small businesses buying at wholesale gave way to huge numbers of consumers, raising costs, proliferating assortments, and buying less per visit. These were shifts away from the core format advantage over discounters. Many clubs even found themselves paying for prime retail locations for new "store" openings—another mistake.

The economics of discount "retailing" were counter to what had made the club format viable. Whether the shift was intentional or inadvertent, it moved the club operators into a shape of value that did not match their primary (profitable) customer. The survivors recognized this after a year or two of flat or negative earnings growth and low/no growth in sales, and began the attempt to shift back. Of course, the competitive landscape also had shifted, and it wasn't as simple as going back. Nevertheless, club operators are now slowly returning to the economic model and customer value shape that made them successful.

The lesson: Be careful not to shift too far, too fast, lest you lose sight of what made you successful in the first place—core competencies, matched to a particular type of business and customer.

Innovation

Is innovative content of utmost importance? If the innovation is one of style, then perhaps The Limited's concept of rapid style changes and using air freight from semicaptive suppliers is a good model. Information systems reveal what is currently selling, but innovative styling experiments, with rapid feedback and response would seem to be the right approach. Gap stores would support the premise. If the innovation takes the shape of a status enhancement, then a "cachet" must be included in the value creation and/or delivery process. Ralph Lauren's and Tommy Hilfiger's successes have proven this concept. Creative, often entrepreneurial people working in a low-structure environment will usually come up with the most innovative concepts and ideas. Most of Japan's leading-edge new car designs come not from Japan, but from their California creative design studios. If the cliché "less is more" has merit, it is in the amount of structure for an innovative function. There is, however, a downside to that low structure for innovative organizations—loss of control and financial disaster like Nets, Inc. Truly successful, visionary entrepreneurs who build innovative businesses seem to find a complementary type of manager to take care of the structure requirements of the shape of the business. They also invest that person with the authority to put appropriate resource limits on the innovative part of the organization, lest they overextend the company to its ultimate demise.

Blowing Hot Air

Twenty-some years ago, two college students, Chad Erickson and Dave Dornbush, had an idea that led to the Snackmaster line of food dehydrators. They bootstrapped their way from nothing to a reasonably successful business by designing ever better versions of their original idea. By the mid-1980s, their product was the standard against which others were measured. Both men were innovative thinkers. Erickson was an advertising major "on paper," but a mechanical tinkerer and inventor at heart; Dornbush was an expansive promoter and inventor who could see the potential in many ideas. Their original company, Alternative Pioneering Systems, was renamed American Harvest.

The concept of using hot air in small home appliances was expanding. Convection ovens had just appeared and were selling well, as were hot-air popcorn poppers. These two entrepreneurs decided to go the convection oven one better and design a different, better appliance. They named their invention the Jet Stream Oven. It worked by using very high-speed air movement. It could cook at microwave speed, but brown foods like a regular oven, and do it all in a transparent plastic housing appliance, so the user could watch the food cooking.

Concurrently, a new media tool—the infomercial—had just become popular, and it lent itself perfectly to explaining the use of this totally new cooking appliance to consumers. Sales skyrocketed. So did inventories, complexity of the business, accounts receivable, and working capital needs. Trouble began with increased distribution of the product; and then disaster struck. Wal-Mart decided to sell the item based on its "As Seen On TV" appeal, and placed large initial store orders to fill the pipeline.

As American Harvest expedited supplier shipments of components (the major piece, the powerhead, was made in Asia) and expanded production facilities, the pressure built. Just as purchasing management and the supplier decided to add an extra quantity of components to the production plans to "get caught up," retail sales data came in. It was not selling at retail! The structure of American Harvest had been built to accommodate sales demand and support rapid growth, so there were few checks on the buying plans, and fewer on the cash flow dilemmas just looming over the horizon.

Infomercial sales flattened, then began to decline; they no longer could support the heavy media expenditures. Inventory and purchase commitments soared, and the retail launch at Wal-Mart flopped. This wonderful new product baffled retail customers who, unlike infomercial customers, could not see it work. It just looked like another (rather expensive) countertop appliance of indeterminant value. Orders were canceled just as the extra inventory landed at the ports. Incoming orders and cash flow dried up just as the accounts payable became due. Cash flow problems mounted rapidly. The lack of structure damaged the innovative, entrepreneurial company badly.

Although later new-product successes gave the company a reprieve, it was unable to recover from this three-year old problem. It was forced to file for bankruptcy, and was later purchased by an erstwhile competitor. The entrepreneurial culture was so strong that it overwhelmed the need for structure.

Service

Is service of paramount importance? Perhaps the service companies, such as American Express or Marriott Hotels that are constantly searching for better ways to serve their customers, or mail order companies, such as L.L. Bean or Lands' End would be appropriate structure and process models. Here the balance of personal warmth and friendliness with sophisticated information systems provide a structure to emphasize the value attribute— service—most important to their customers. It has been proven over and over that employees will seldom treat customers any better than they are treated by their employer and peers. Good internal service begets good external service. Is the culture right for this to customer service mindset exist? Are relationships in place or being actively developed to support the service the customer needs? Are the structure and process geared to support service?

Quality

If quality or complex functionality is the premium value measure, perhaps the model would be the jewelry, camera, electronics, or bicycle dealer system, where many suppliers can offer items of apparently similar quality. Only with a distribution system organized and structured to explain the complex functionality or emphasize the quality and provide assurance that value is there does the consumer accept that there is a perceptible difference in the quality of the merchandise. In each case, the structure and culture is dictated by the relative priority the customer places on the specific mix of attributes that make up value. There is no doubt that Lexus and Mercedes-Benz and its dealers go to extremes to convince current and prospective buyers that there is a perceivable quality edge to a Mercedes or a Lexus over closely competing auto brands.

WHAT CUSTOMERS WANT AND EXPECT

What are the most important criteria in the market you have chosen? Do different customers rank these differently; and if so, which ones are in closest alignment with what you do best? Answering these questions sounds so simple, but too often they are not posed seriously, and are glossed over in the exuberant rush to compete. Remember: First define the problem, then solve the problem—not the other way around! Use the diagnostic profiles and shape of value diagrams extensively. Complete them with thoughtful answers, and hotly debated assessments for yourself, your customers and competitors. Then use the expanded diagnostic profile format to assess the shape of the business dimensions for you own company, and how they match the necessary shapes of value desired by customers and compared to competitors. What has to change; how, how much, and how fast?

Many industries develop rapidly and then consolidate down to a few (usually about three) major competitors, and an number of niche players. For a niche player, particularly, but even for the major players, reviewing the industry's shape of value diagrams is valuable. Figure 18-3 illustrates a hypothetical diagram in simplified form. The product is upright vacuum cleaners. Hoover has been the traditional leader. Royal (Dirt Devil) the innovator, and Eureka the low-price fast follower. (Remember this is an oversimplified example to illustrate the approach.)

Note the near parity on speed and service. All three use essentially similar distribution systems and service processes, so structure and process create little differentiation. If we were to survey consumers and weight this diagram, we could assess if there might be a basis for advantage created in these attributes. The clear differences are illustrated as Royal's innovation, Eureka's lower cost/price, and Hoover's perceived quality/brand leadership. For any other manufacturer to attack one (or all of these three) they would need to devise a way to create customer desired attributes that were better than the best competitor in the most critical value decision drivers, and nearly equal in the less important attributes.

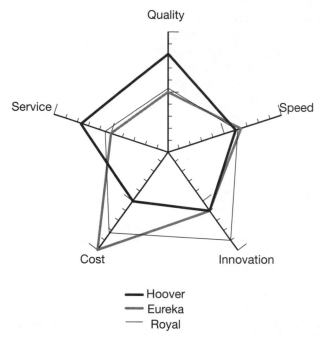

Figure 18-3 A Hypothetical Diagram of Vacuum Cleaner Manufacturers

Test the conclusions by using the weighting system to redo the profiles and diagrams for the top three to five customers and the most serious two to three competitors. This entire sequence might take several hours or several days, but isn't success worth that small amount of time? Often overlooked are the value, perceptions, and expectations created by brand names or reputations. A business associate told me the story about several lines of large appliances, all made the same way, the same production processes; but one brand had three times the customer complaint rate. Its quality was no worse; the customers' expectations were just much higher for that brand! Consider such nuances carefully.

A common ingredient in these examples is information. The systems to provide the information are derived from the processes required to consistently understand, identify, and deliver value. Do not simply automate antiquated processes. Redesign them into new, more value-oriented ones, eliminating the nonvalue-adding steps and emphasizing the aspects that are valued most. To do this, the shape of the process and structure elements must be *integrated*. Decentralized customer contact without excellent central coordination quickly becomes a false value. Low-cost purchasing with expensive distribution systems yield mediocre values for the end user/purchaser. Highly personalized service with no information is as frustrating as information-based service with no personal touch. This interaction of structure and process is why reengineering alone usually fails or provides less than the desired results.

Closing the Circle

One of the most common approaches to value is to "ask the customer." This was discussed in an earlier chapter, but is worthy of another mention here. Asking the customer is effective only if it is possible to find customers who can imagine things that do not exist and ask for them. Otherwise, the shape of the "new value" provided at the request of the customer will come just in time for the maturity part of the cycle, when price competition is most intense and profitability lowest for both supplier and customer. There are customers (you will figure out who they are) who do have the foresight to ask for the unimaginable, and these are valuable partnerships to cultivate.

Once the structure and process dimensions of shape-shifting are recognized, two others become obvious—or do they? The interaction of the people within the business culture is a critical determinant of the results of the best structures and processes. Reengineering's worst failures are those where the people are not properly involved, where the culture not only is top-down (which may be necessary), but precludes the involvement and participation of those who must deliver the actual results. In the 1970s and 1980s, General Motors spent huge sums on automation, but omitted one major ingredient—its workforce. Since relations between GM and the UAW were not good, adversarial approaches were taken. The employees who were there to operate the new automated equipment viewed it as a threat to their futures. With this perspective and culture, how could GM ever hope to make this new, expensive automation work to its full potential?

Many of the basic tenets of what has been widely described as TQM are essentially to make sure the people who must do the work are involved in designing and developing (or at least influencing) the tasks they must perform. The Toyota system so widely admired is one of continuous improvement "suggested" by the workers, and then evaluated and implemented by the very same workers.

Finally, we come full circle, to partnerships. External relationships are at least as essential as internal ones, and most of the same rules apply. Without cooperation and support from external partners—suppliers, customers, and special partners, nothing much of value can happen.

DEVELOPING VISIONS, STRATEGIES, TACTICS, AND PLANS

With this 360-degree vision of the integrative approach to shape-shifting in mind, let us move on to the implementation. Of primary importance in the area of open communications is that the entire organization have an accurate and realistic view of the current market situation. (This goes for both current and desired markets, competitors, and customers.) Although management can inform employees of this situation, it's better for the employees to become involved and participate in the assessment. By participating, employees not only learn this information first-hand, but they pass it on to their peers, thus reinforcing management.

Once the understanding of the current situation is solidly in place, it is necessary to create a vision of a desired future state for the business. This vision must be a shared vision, all the participants (internal and external), have their own piece of the vision. Peter Senge's chapter "Shared Vision" in *The Fifth Discipline* (Currency Doubleday, 1990) describes this well.

Creating a mental picture of the future is a daunting but essential task. Therefore, the leader must direct the effort. The vision must be grand enough to create the "tension" between the current situation and the future desired state—to incite extraordinary efforts, yet have enough substance so that all employees of the company can see their role in it. The specific values underlying the vision usually are less important than the consistency of expressing and sharing those values. The vision is an important part of the purpose dimension.

Once defined, the vision must be regularly restated in many forms; therefore, a brief, easy-to-remember vision statement is desirable, although this is not always easy. Furthermore, the vision must be reinforced by behaviors to drive home its importance.

The following are some guidelines for developing mission statements:

- Keep the statement short, simple, and direct.
- Do not make it so broad that it loses its meaning to your company.
- Do not use jargon or fancy language.
- Test it on teenagers and family members. If they do not understand it, simplify it.
- Make sure it can be understood instantly by your hourly workforce.

Next, to give the vision credibility, map out a path for achieving the goals set forth in the vision statement. The path must be laid out with sufficient detail to enable and cause people to become motivated to reach the future state. NOTE: You (no one) can "motivate people." People must become motivated themselves. You can only create the right environment for it.

Here are some examples of excellent vision and mission statements

---

Intel's mission is to be the preeminent building block supplier to the new computing industry worldwide.
—Intel Corporation

Our vision is to enable a seamless flow of information between paper and digital forms, from person to person and from device to device.
—Hewlett-Packard LaserJet Solutions Group

FAILING TO PLAN IS PLANNING TO FAIL

After the vision is clarified, a strategy must be developed that describes what must be done to achieve that vision. This process of strategic *thinking* is different from strategic *planning*. The former is "thought work"; the latter is the documentation to communicate, track, and measure progress. Many companies do the latter; few do the former.

The implementation of the vision is perhaps the most difficult undertaking. Hamel and Prahalad exhort managers and leaders to really consider the long-term view of the business. Finding time to "get away" to really think about the future is one of the toughest issues faced by managers and executives of today's organizations. Like the dreamer with his or her feet on the desk, gazing out the window, "getting away to think" can be perceived of as an excuse for daydreaming or "goofing off." To the contrary, carving out time to think is an important element in formulating a successful approach the future.

Sadly, few businesspeople find or set aside adequate time to engage and discuss, think, debate, and reach consensus about the future of an industry, business, or organization. Too often, the pressure of day-to-day business and the constant stream of interruptions and distractions comprise this endeavor. A day is certainly not enough time for this to occur. In my experience, two to three days is the minimum time people need to disengage from the turmoil and take part in constructive dialogue. Additional time must be set aside for "reflection," which is why the "getaway" should be to a peaceful (even isolated) setting—not a big-city hotel or a conference room at the office. A natural setting seems to enhance reflection. Perhaps there is more than a coincidence between the ability to see business issues more clearly in the presence of nature, and the similarities between business and natural ecosystems. (Remember the Parable of the Trees?) Clichés like "can't see the forest for the trees" have come about because they communicate the message in such a clear metaphor.

Once constructive dialogue, debate, reflective thought, and contemplation have taken place, it is time to begin the communication process.

Another difficult process is to reduce complex issues and topics to their essence, yet retain the important elements. I am a big believer in one-page summaries. I suggest that you take each of the critical value creation and delivery issues, and condense it to less than one page each of statements (preferably in bullet formats). Then rehash it relentlessly, with everyone in the organization from the vice presidents to the maintenance personnel. This step is often overlooked, resulting in organizations that lack unanimity of purpose and goals.

Mapping Concise Strategic Plans

It is amazing how many companies invest hundreds of hours of management time to fill binders with lofty strategic plans and statements, only to shelve them until next year. A strategic plan must be a living document, used every day and week, understood and owned by the whole organization, not just the elite group that drafted it and the clerical staff that did the typing. For this reason, I am a proponent of concise, focused, usable, and communicable plans of no more than six pages.

The first page should be devoted to the mission and vision. The second should contain the market assessment, current and future, including a description of the competitive environment. The third page should describe the basic strategies (the "whats"). The fourth should expand on these with implementation tactics or operational steps (the "hows") for executing the strategies. These strategies and tactics should deal with the value creation and delivery statements, and be tested against the value attributes and dimensions of the integrative approach to shape-shifting and be built upon your core competencies and capabilities. Determine what works the way things are currently shaped, then figure out which shapes must change. Do not compromise to make it easier; remember, lowest common denominator solutions are the path to mediocrity and failure. On page five, list the critical unresolved issues, the risk/reward assessments, and the critical assumptions underlying the plans.

Next, gain consensus on the contents of these five pages, which are your summary strategic plan. Get the "buy-in" of the top management at this stage, but realize there is a lot of validation needed at other managerial levels before this plan can be finalized.

Finally, on additional pages, draw a shape of value diagram realistically for the total corporation, and one for each VCU. These will be the representations of what the business and each VCU needs to do now, and provide the basis for comparison to customers', competitors', and future shape of value diagrams. In future planning sessions, additional diagrams should portray how and why the next shape-shift will change the diagram.

Let us consider a well-known situation to illustrate how using the shape of value diagram might have helped bring about a different outcome in the auto industry over the past few decades. First consider the customer's shape of value for an auto prior to the early 1970s oil crisis, and for the decades that followed (Figure 18-4).

Now consider the profiles of a midsized Chevrolet and a comparable Honda in these same time frames (Figure 18-5):

Chevrolet made progress in virtually every attribute of value. Their problem and market share loss was created by the fact that Honda made far greater progress. To make matters worse, the Honda shape of value more closely matches the 1990's consumer's desired shape of value. Winner: Honda. Loser: Chevrolet. I could have done this example with Toyota versus Ford, or even Chevrolet versus their domestic competition. The outcomes would have been more or less the same.

Tracking the shifting shape of value is something that must be done a lot more often than once a decade. In some product categories it must be done almost constantly, and certainly no less than each year. Simply tracking shifting value shape of the business is not the challenge. The challenge is altering the shape of the business to create and deliver the desired shape of value better, faster, and more insightfully than the competition.

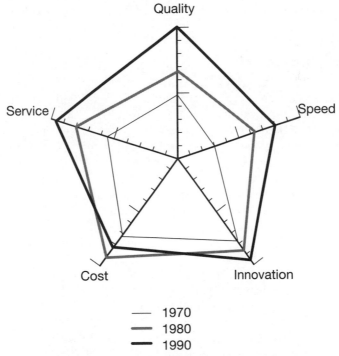

Figure 18-4 Value Desired by Customers of Autos in the U.S. Market

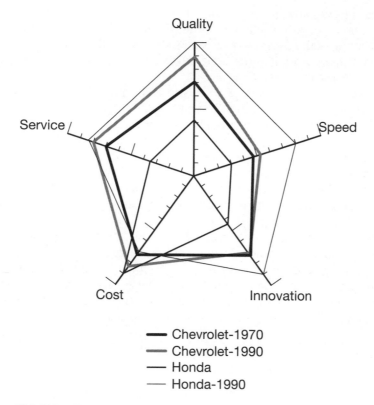

Figure 18-5 Value Desired by Customers of Autos in the U.S. Market

Test your plans from every angle. Plan attacks as if you were the competitors and knew every weakness in the plan or the company. Determine what would happen if such a competitive attack took place. Draw customer and competitor shape of value diagrams. Debate, argue, and discuss them. How would the plans be able to shift in order to blunt such a competitive threat or market shifts? What would you do to defeat yourself, if you were the competitor? What would you do if the competitor did that? Could the business shape-shift quickly enough to meet and defeat such an attack?

Share this summary strategic plan with the other members of the organization. Note that again I did not say just management. Much of the truth about the current situation and future potential lies in the minds and hearts of all levels of employees, associates, and outside partners who must make it happen. (Choose the external partners carefully since this will mean divulging your most confidential competitive plans for competing in the future.) Start with those inside partners and only the most trusted of outside partners to validate the plans, strategies, vision, and mission. Evaluate the probable outcome of these moves in advance.

BE A LEADER, NOT A FOLLOWER

Deciding on the value to create is a challenge. To begin, be original and imaginative. Too many companies plan strategy by watching competitors and reacting. That is the way to finish second or worse. The value delivery system is an essential element in identifying the value that wins. Jim Swartz touched on many aspects of this in his aforementioned book *The Hunters and the Hunted.* There is little doubt that the concept of systems crossing traditional functional organizations has emerged as the most effective way to deliver value. Swartz summarized this effectively:

> *Those who designed the best value delivery systems became the dominant military powers—the hunters. Starting in the eighteenth century, however, value delivery systems became more a means of generating wealth through the production of goods and materials than a means of producing coercive power. There are no ways to organize work that are universally good. No solution is permanent. To remain a hunter, the process of transformation must be a continuous one.*

This is a very powerful statement considering the number of managers and executives who attempt to simply read books or hire consultants to lead the way to success. If the reference they use or the consultants they hire prescribe a standard solution, the path to failure is imminent. At the very least, the path will not yield the best results because many others will have taken it too, some of them competitors. Is it any wonder that reengineering works less that one-third of the time and then provides no unique competitive advantage?

VCUs and Super-Silos Revisited

With the admonition in mind that there are "no universal solutions," let's construct the sample VCU, outlined earlier. To start, it would contain *marketing* people, to determine what is valued by customers (what will sell); *financial analysts*, to help evaluate economic feasibility; *product designers*, to develop products (to convert ideas to commercial reality); *sales* and *customer service*, to maintain the day-to-day contact with customers (to stay in touch with current views of value); *process designers*, to devise the processes to make the products or produce the services (how to make what will sell); *manufacturing, purchasing,* to buy materials and supervise the production; and *logistics/distribution*, to confirm the product or service is delivered when, where, and how it is desired.

The silos left standing (described earlier as super-silos) have important roles in a supporting sense. For example:

- To hire and train/retrain the necessary people (talent); ensure that they are paid, and that the other aspects of their employment are properly managed; to plan for future needs.
- To keep score financially, tracking the costs, expenses, and so on; to help the organization evaluate the probable outcome of its plans so adjustments can be made if needed.
- To collect the money and pay the bills; to maintain appropriate financing; to comply with all relevant laws, regulations, and so forth.
- To have all the information and communication systems in place that enable and enhance the VCU's and super-silos' performance.

A special type of of silo that contains the resources and assets necessary to do valuable work for the VCU pipelines, but is not dedicated to only one VCU (unless the company has only one). This consists of skills in technology, market research, advertising, brand management, production process analysis, physical resources, and a wide range of others vitally important to the business. This one serves several (VCU) masters in the process of delivering value to the customer. It is important to keep track of the people in this special silo because they often possess some of the core competencies and capabilities of the corporation. Using and sharing those core competencies and capabilities freely among the VCUs is essential to success. This is one of the key differences between VCUs and the traditional SBU (strategic business unit) structure, which was prone to trapping resources in a single SBU to the exclusion of the others.

RESOURCES THAT SUPPORT THE SHAPE

As I've stated repeatedly, "the best value wins." To "win," we must find the proper shape to create and consistently deliver the best value to our customers. We must also make our best effort to assess the probable outcome of our strategy before we plunge into the implementation. Is our shape right, and are we in "good shape?" Do we have the resources to effect the outcome we want? Is our talent, with its core competencies and capabilities, up to the task? Are these core competencies and capabilities embedded in the organization and culture? Are we competitive on those things that are "core?" Have we outsourced to partners who are competitive in non-core skills?

Do we accept that if the market shifts radically, there are only two alternatives: the people must change (learn different, related core competencies and capabilities) or we must change the people? To do anything else would be to invite obsolescence, mediocrity, or failure. Peter Drucker has spoken emphatically on the (mis)allocation of valuable (people) resources to problems instead of opportunities. Frequently, we tie up valuable resources working on projects that we should not be working on at all or that are not "core" and thus will have minimal impact on the success of the business.

GOALS, OBJECTIVES, AND MEASUREMENTS

If we do just as we planned, will we like the outcome (financially? competitively?). We know what kind of performance will keep the business viable financially, so why wouldn't we estimate or project forward the probable outcome of our plans and see if we would like the results? Is economic value created or added by our success? The future is unpredictable, so the projections may be wrong, but the thought processes that lead to them are valuable. Businesspeople frequently attempt to manage retrospectively. They make decisions and then wait until the results are in to see how they like them, then make adjustments. As I said before, this is like steering a car by looking in the rear view mirror.

If evaluations show that customers believe certain value attributes are disproportionately important, then measurements should be weighted to those. If the "normal" importance is assigned to various measures, then no difference weighting is necessary. Many measures might be critical. For quality, it might be the parts per million of nonconformances. For service, it might be the percentage of orders filled on time. For speed, it might be the throughput cycle time of an organization. For cost, it might be the cost reduction or inflation offset. For innovation, it might be the percent of sales generated by new products. There are as many measures as there are companies—yield, delivery, throughput, cycletimes, ideas submitted, productivity, and so on. For an excellent treatise on measures, I refer readers to Will Kaydos' fine book, *Measuring, Managing, and Maximizing Performance* (Productivity Press, 1991).

VALUE: THE NEW MANTRA—A FINAL REMINDER

In the 1960s and early 1970s, efficiency and output at low-cost were the popular business mantras. In the late 1970s and 1980s, quality became the mantra, only to be supplanted in the 1990s with service. All of the approaches and solutions proffered by the so-called experts dealt with one or two of these. Through it all, people have made up the essential common denominator for success. The new mantra combines all of these into a single word: *value*. Find the shape of your business that will create value and deliver it consistently, better than the competition, and the market will be yours. Fail, and you will be another case study in the business schools of tomorrow. In conclusion, remember:

- Whatever shape worked to get you where you are will not work to keep you there or get you where you need to be. This is why the ability to shape-shift is essential.
- No organization can downsize its way to long-term prosperity; it can only "grow" its way there, continuously shifting shape as it does.
- People working together in interdependent relationships (partnerships) make everything happen.
- Value creation, as pictured in the mind of the customer, is the only reason businesses exist.
- Only continuous change can create sustainable competitive advantage.
- Whoever can shape-shift to create and consistently deliver the best value will win, and be able to stay around to play again, and again, and again. Will that be you and your organization?

PART FOUR

Where Next?

"WE APPEAR TO BE RACING TOWARD A PROTEAN, FREE-LANCE ECONOMY IN WHICH A TYPICAL COMPANY WILL CONSIST OF A SMALL CORE OF LONG-TERM EMPLOYEES (TO MAINTAIN ENDURING RELATIONSHIPS WITH SUPPLIERS, DISTRIBUTION CHANNELS, AND CUSTOMERS) SURROUNDED BY AN EVER INCREASING CLOUD OF CONTRACTORS, SEMI-PERMANENT EMPLOYEES, AND COMPANY-TO-COMPANY RELATIONSHIPS."

—Michael S. Malone, The Virtual Corporation

"IT IS LIFE'S INVITATION TO FREEDOM, CREATIVITY, AND MEANING THAT WELCOMES US BACK. IF WE CAN BE IN THE WORLD IN THE FULLNESS OF OUR HUMANITY, WHAT ARE WE CAPABLE OF? IF WE ARE FREE TO PLAY, TO EXPERIMENT AND DISCOVER, IF WE ARE FREE TO FAIL, WHAT MIGHT WE CREATE?...WHAT COULD WE ACCOMPLISH IF WE WORKED WITH LIFE'S NATURAL TENDENCY TO ORGANIZE?

—Margaret J. Wheatley, Leadership and the New Science—Learning about Organization from an Orderly Universe.

19.

The Natural
Laws of Business

Our mission: To boldly go where no man has gone before...
—Gene Roddenberry, creator of
Star Trek

CHARTING THE COURSE

There were a lot of good lessons in the *Star Trek* television series presented in the guise of science fiction. In that spirit, in this final chapter, I will take us on a flight of fancy to ponder where new ideas might come from or go to—or already reside, waiting to be discovered.

"THIS IS NEW SCIENCE"

I will periodically use excerpts from author Meg Wheatley's book *Leadership and the New Science—Learning About Organization from an Orderly Universe* (Berret-Koehler, 1992) as a platform for where my thoughts are headed. But I begin with this comment she made in a recent *Executive Excellence* (Provo, UT) newsletter:

> There is no such thing as survival of the fittest, only survival of the fit. This means that there is no one answer that is right, but many answers that might work. Life explores all sorts of combinations content to find anything that works.

255

Several other noted authors and authorities have begun to draw parallels between the natural sciences and business or economic systems. Biological Scientist Stuart Kauffman, a scientist and senior fellow of the Santa Fe Institute, believes there may be some broad underlying law, like the law of gravity, that connects all of the behaviors of the world. In his words, "...this is new science, and bears careful study." When we find this "law," it will seem so obvious, we will be amazed we didn't see it before. His book, *At Home in the Universe* (Oxford University Press, 1995), is rich with support for his thoughts, and continues the theme of many scientists before him. Kauffman is one of the leaders of the new study of complexity and chaos theory as applied to businesses and economic systems.

Stuart Pimm, the leading ecologist and evolutionary biologist believes that there is much in parallel between the behavior of species in their environment and the world of economics. Author Roger Lewin echoes many of the views of Pimm and Kauffman, and describes them skillfully in *Complexity—Life at the Edge of Chaos* (Macmillan, 1992).

James Moore's recent business book *The Death of Competition— Leadership & Strategy in the Age of Business Ecosystems* (Harper Collins, 1996) further reinforces these beliefs. If I had not been convinced of the principles evident in the Prologue, "The Parable of the Forest and Trees," these works would have helped convince me. With that in mind, let us "boldly go" to places not often visited in management and business books.

Seeing the Shape

This book has chronicled a journey from the understanding of value, where we started, to the changes needed to assure the creation and consistent delivery of the best value, through people working together in organizations. The continuing journey has been contingent upon our ability to shape-shift the business and do it faster and better than our competitors. Where do we go from here and how do we chart a course? Did the ancient Indians (Native Americans) who originally settled this land know something we are just discovering? Their belief in "shape-shifters" of many types is scattered through the mythology and legends of every tribe.

The parable I used at the beginning of the book illustrated the startling similarity between the shape and behavior of a natural ecosystem and a business and market economy system. The lessons from nature are too clear and dramatic to ignore. In business, as in nature, stability leads to stagnation and death. Instability, while sometimes chaotic, creates new growth and opportunity. Often we are too close to our ecosystem to see the shape that is evolving. Forests not only live and die as in the parable. They also "move" across the land swept by the wind borne seeds following the death of the old and growth of the new. The scope and pace of this movement is obscured by our relatively smaller perspective and short lifetime compared to the decades or centuries it might take for a forest to move.

Consider how James Moore puts it, in his book:

The most creative and aggressive companies exploit these wider territories transforming the landscape with new ecosystems. The dominant new ecosystems will likely consist of networks of organizations stretching across several different industries, and they will joust with similar networks spread across still other industries.

Now let us consider some ways to chart a course for the future. This course will be based on the beliefs that an organization is a living organism that is seeking meaning—a reason for being—and is capable of adapting, evolving, learning, and surviving in a stressful, chaotic environment.

THE BEST CONTROL IS UNCONTROL

Complex codependent natural systems behave in predictable ways. Unfortunately, we seldom see the similarity of nature to our business systems. It is easy to see some dependent relationships, but difficult or impossible to connect others to the actions and reactions that precipitated them. Often, we do not learn from our errors, because the cause and effect are too far separated in time and place. In those situations, the ultimate control is "uncontrol," with intelligent feedback. The old-school shape of management based on command and control is failing as rapidly as the systems that are being strangled by "overcontrol." As in nature, to have power, we must give it away. "Servant leadership" only begins to touch the periphery of the issue, but is the right mindset. When human values such as integrity and honesty are prevalent, the need for controls, such as policies and procedures, is significantly reduced if not obviated entirely. Thus the ultimate control truly becomes uncontrol!

The decisions of how and when to intervene are undoubtedly difficult ones to make, whether in parenting, managing a business, or in nature. It appears that letting go works better than holding on. As Stuart Pimm's studies have confirmed, natural biosystems, once destroyed cannot be reconstructed exactly; new systems will evolve and adapt. Likewise, organizations cannot be rebuilt exactly as they were—nor should they be, for the environment will also have changed. Tom Koulopoulos, of the Delphi Group, speaks of corporate instinct, and likens it to the instinct that animals and humans develop from exposure to situations, information, and culture.

Our challenge, stated so profoundly by Stuart Kauffman, is to find the laws that govern all this. As he says, "This is very new science and there is much to be studied and learned."

Research has proven that coevolution rewards a win-win strategy whenever there is not a zero-sum market. (Are there really any zero-sum markets? Or just zero-sum thinking?) Reveal the strategy, and competitors adapt. Then the market grows. Author Stephen Covey's "abundance mentality" is a market reality! It is usually far wiser to bake a bigger pie, and take the same-size piece than to fight (often to the death) for a bigger piece of the same pie among equally matched competitors. Frequently, the competitor that bakes the bigger pie also seizes a bigger piece by virtue of being there first. This is the very premise of Hamel and Prahalad's comment about "getting to the future first," in *Competing for the Future.*

A Few Natural Laws of Business

Getting to the future first makes economic sense only if there is a course charted and a shape defined to match. Several important points on this topic have been offered by Harvard professor Chris Bartlett and London Business School's Sumantra Ghoshal. Writing in the *Sloan Management Review*, they state, "...to develop the ability of continuous self-renewal, its [the company's] real battle lies not in reorienting the strategy, restructuring the organization, or revamping the systems, but in changing the individual organization members' behaviors and actions." True, changing the individual behaviors must come first, but this step alone is insufficient. Unless there is an appropriate overall shape of the business in place, the actions may not yield the desired results. The chance is too great to take. The following examples provide helpful markers on this new course to the future.

Teams Today, Game Tomorrow

The celebrated creative design firm IDEO Product Development has no bosses and no job titles. Teams form, work is organized into projects, until completed, they the teams disband. There are no permanent job assignments. IDEO has five principles of brainstorming as described by Tia O'Brien in "IDEO - encourage wild ideas" (*Fast Company*, April–May 1996):

- Stay focused on the topic.
- Encourage wild ideas.
- Defer judgment.
- Build on the ideas of others.
- One conversation at a time.

IDEO also has a popular slogan that describes its new speedy mentality: "Fail often to succeed sooner." This leading-edge company is now working with Samsung, the Korean conglomerate, and Steelcase, the office furniture giant, to convert these revolutionary shape-shifting practices into products.

Muddling Through

Hewlett-Packard's "muddled teams" concept (described in *Fortune* by Stratford Sherman, in "Secrets of HP's Muddled Team," March 18, 1995) is essentially akin to a repertory company shaping itself to meet the needs of the situation. This process could not even occur in most companies because the need and desire for control and progress reporting on a regular quantitative basis would kill or cripple the efforts. By agreeing to levels of improvement previously thought impossible, the HP team leaders "bought" the freedom to design new processes through an uncontrolled and near-chaotic team process.

When asked how often they reported to the corporate management at HP, coleader Julie Anderson said, "Not very often, if we could avoid it. It was very hard to honestly represent the situation in those early days in a way that would mean anything to people from outside the team. They would ask how things were going. We would say, 'Well, fine; you know, we're still working on it.'" This response in most companies would bring down hordes of auditors or corporate staff to "meddle" while arriving at their "measurements." While I believe in the management maxim "what gets measured gets done," some efforts defy measurement in the normal sense.

A Natural Organization

Visa International under the leadership of Dee Ward Hock may be one of the foremost examples of what I call a natural organization. In his article, "The Trillion Dollar Vision of Dee Hock" (*Fast Company*, October-November 1996), M.Mitchell Waldrop describes how Hock did things in ways that no one previously had the courage and foresight to do. By his own admission, everything he had read and studied and convinced him that the command and control mentality in management had gone too far from its roots in the military and religious hierarchies. Although this mentality may have adequately supported the Industrial Revolution companies as they were forming, it had become a limitation and a deterrent to progress. Hock believed that he must create an organization that was different. And he created one that truly was different in many ways. But I want to dwell on the difference not so much in the structure, as in the behavior of the organization and how it related to its environment.

Hock realized that because Visa had far-flung operations and multicultural employees, there is no one way of doing things that could be dictated by corporate headquarters and be successful. He said, "It was beyond the power of reason to design an organization to deal with such complexity, and beyond the reach of the imagination to perceive all the conditions it would encounter....The organization had to be based on biological concepts to evolve; in effect, to invent and organize itself."

That Hock's thinking was ahead of his time is indisputable. As Visa grew and developed in the 1970s and 1980s, Hock was able to test his beliefs in the real-world "laboratory" of the company. And, they worked! A decade later, Hock shared his thoughts with the scientists at The Santa Fe Institute. His ideas and their work on the edge of chaos were right in tune with each other. While scientists from the institute were working on chaos, Hock was thinking about order. Thus, he coined the term for this kind of organization as "chaordic."

Hock learned that Visa couldn't be designed from the top down, because the diversity in banks and payment systems were too great to anticipate all the variations. Rather, he found a way for this huge organization to distribute power in a very natural way—according to the needs of the environment and situation—a "natural organization."

Hock also confirmed the necessity of defining the company's purpose. "[U]nless we can define a purpose for the organization that we can all believe in, we might as well go home. The purpose has to be an authentic statement of what the organization is about, not some platitude cooked up by a consultant." Hock went on to build a "community" around the purpose and principles of the organization. From there, the structure and concept of the organization could begin to evolve. He used his ideas to build a multibillion dollar, multinational business, validation enough for these concepts. However, he is not finished. He says, "The concepts...will take a century or more to mature. What we have here is a baby....We can have a vision of what it will eventually be, but we won't see that vision in our lifetime. That's the fun of it, the mystery. I warn people: Don't start thinking about this lightly; it'll put a burr under your mental saddle. It will call into question all your beliefs about organizations and management. You'll never think about them in the same way again."

Can there be any doubt that we are onto something big and powerful here? The repertory company approach described earlier is being used successfully in several highly respected companies. The concept of corporate instinct is a viable explanation of how great companies continue to do the right things. There are many "natural laws" that seem to apply to business at least as well as they do to the natural sciences, so let's consider a few of them.

THE NATURAL LAWS OF BUSINESS

1. When You Measure Something, You Alter It

In my training as an engineer/scientist, I learned that anytime you measure something, you alter what you measured by the measurement. (This was referred to as Heisenberg's principle.) The challenge became to alter the things as little as possible so the measurement would be valid. The same situation exists in management. Measure the number of teams and the tendency is to form (and often ignore) them. The result is victory by definition. Measure the return on net assets, and that is what will be optimized. Measure growth, and growth will be emphasized. Measure EVA (economic value added) and that parameter will be maximized. Add rewards to these measures and the effect is amplified. This is a useful principle, but a dangerous one. Measurement of any one or two dimensions of any aspect of a business can lead to changing the subtle balance between all the parts of a complex system.

Nature teaches us this over and over. We think we can measure fragile ecosystems, only to discover that the measurement has altered that which we were trying to measure. The interaction between the parts of systems is one of the most difficult aspects to measure, but its is also where the impact is greatest. There is a similar complexity effect in business, too. Meg Wheatley says it this way: "Indeed, it is no longer meaningful to talk of the constituent electrons individual properties as these continually change to meet the requirements of the whole. This is an intriguing image for organizations. It is not difficult to recognize the waves we create in organizations, how we move, merging with others, forming new wholes, being forever changed in the process." In earlier chapters about reward systems, consider the effects of this natural law. The measures on which those rewards are based will surely follow this law and be altered. The lesson is, be sure what you want to happen is what the measures reflect. This is just one small example of the power of using natural laws to predict the likely direction of future events and influence the outcome. Getting to the future first just became microscopically easier.

2. In Complexity, Chaos Can Lead to Order

The subhead of this section sounds contradictory but it is not. One of the standard doctrines of management I heard throughout my entire career was "no surprises." No boss likes surprises. They imply lack of control; and being out of control is the step prior to being out of work. How many times have we heard the phrase, "He lost control" of his business, organization, department, or whatever. This was usually spoken in explanation of a pending or announced departure of a manager. How can we rationalize this new reality of complexity and chaos to being in control? We cannot. The good news is, we *need* not. Visa's success under Dee Hock, IDEO's radically free structure, Oticon's success with the "less is more" theory of control and structure, and Hewlett-Packard's muddled team efforts give us both hope and confidence that this principle is as true in business as it is in nature.

Complexity theory, liberally translated (with apologies to the serious scientists) says that chaos, left to itself, will find order. The complex patterns generated by fractals (those shapes that occur from repetitive interactions of simple nonlinear equations) are essentially simple patterns replicated over and over, just as the images in a kaleidoscope are multiple reflections of a few basic shapes. What looks like chaos is order in disguise. Both Kauffman's work and Lewin's writing document that the most progress is made in the boundary zone at the edge of (but not into the realm of) chaos. This is probably an accurate metaphor for everyday behavior at most of the Silicon Valley growth companies.

Creative teams like those at IDEO and HP, left to their own devices, gravitate toward solutions—and those solutions are better, faster, and more creative than the ones created by a control-oriented organization. If we can stand far enough away, we can "tell the forest from the trees." This metaphor, although around for long time, is like the boiling frog story. It's wrong—it's backward. We must not only focus our attention on the whole from a distance, but from the inside where all the wonderful complexity exists. Both are required; neither alone is sufficient. The challenge is not to control the system, but to understand how it responds and how we can interact with it. Fractals are complex in appearance but come from repeated applications of simple patterns. The simple form, repeated many times becomes complex, but its roots are still simple. So are the solutions to business problems, in many cases.

Like the problem-solving process of asking why over and over, the complexity can be peeled back layer by layer. We seek complex solutions and by doing so make our problems more complex than they were initially. This continuous feedback cycle lies at the root of many complex issues. Do something, and then adjust for the error. Ready, aim, fire—do it again, and again. Knowledge grows by having information repeatedly cycled over and over searching for the simple pattern that emerges. Just as certainly as Deming's statistical analysis exposed the heart of variation, complexity theory can yield its own set of simple organizational solutions—if only we don't "tamper" with it too much in search of control.

3. Diversity Plus Curiosity Equals New Development (Innovation)

We educate the curiosity out of children by replacing it with rote memorization. Then we test them to be sure the process is complete before we allow them to attend our finest colleges and universities. Childlike curiosity is one of the great generators of new ideas. Why do we try to kill it? Because it is threatening. Curiosity is unstructured and surprises people, and we have been trained in "no surprises." Innovation is often fostered from excursions into places that might at first seem irrelevant. Take this chapter for example. What business did I have reading about and talking about biological sciences, chaos theory, and species survival when I was writing a business book? The answer, of course, is that there were relevant lessons to be learned.

New knowledge often comes from unexpected sources. Newton's apple falling from the tree an explanation of gravity. 3M's failure to produce the right kind of adhesive led to Post-It Notes. Accidents combined with child-like curiosity lead us to wonder why and not to accept the conventional wisdom. Finding the root of the fractal and seeing it as a simple form is like discovering the root of a problem which was simple, made complex only by our conditioning.

Let me relate a business story of my own to illustrate this. At the Huffy Bicycle factory, a frame brazing problem was perplexing everyone. One station of what were believed to be four identical brazing lines was producing high levels of bad joints, which caused entire bike frames to be rejected. Teams of engineers came up with all sorts of possible causes: the temperature of the torch, the metallurgy of the brazing alloy, the geometry of the frame joint were all rigorously evaluated, to no avail. Then, out of simple curiosity, a team of hourly brazing operators asked a simple question: What could cause this kind of problem? Using a simple cause/effect diagram, they hypothesized that airflow in the area must be causing the problem. Engineers rejected this possibility and again began to evaluate the torch and nozzle design, gas temperature and flow—to no avail. Then, one day, one of the operators walked over to one of the electric floor fans used to cool the hot area of the plant and turned it in a slightly different direction. The problem was solved. Complex solutions failed, but simple curiosity worked. When asked why she moved the fan, the operator replied, "It was the only part of the airflow system in the area I could easily change."

Information is created anew every time we bring people together. Diversity of perspective adds to this richness. To reprise Bartlett and Ghoshal's opinion cited earlier, organizations will only change if the people within them change. Simple? Yes. Obvious? Maybe. Easy? Not at all—but imperative for success and survival. Creativity can be relearned, at least to some extent, if the environment in which it can exist is the challenge of management.

4. The Ultimate Control is Un-Control

This is one of the hardest of the natural laws to accept and follow. We are helpless, it seems. Yet our own actions often put us into this condition. Sadly, we do not always learn from experience; we repeat our mistakes; we tamper and overcontrol. Meg Wheatley observes, "Anytime we see systems in apparent chaos, our training urges us to interfere, to stabilize and shore things up." Then we wonder why our organizations cannot adapt to changing markets or competition or technology fast enough. We step on diversity and kill curiosity in search of safe stability, but true stability leads to stagnation and death. Natural systems live only because they never achieve complete equilibrium. In chemistry, a reaction which reaches equilibrium stops.

Even if we have the knowledge with us for centuries we ignore it. Lao Tzu, 2,600 years ago, wrote in the *Tao Teh King*:

- Intelligent control appears as uncontrol or freedom, and for that reason it is genuinely intelligent control.
- Unintelligent control appears as external domination, and for that reason it is really unintelligent control.
- Intelligent control exerts influence without appearing to do so.
- Unintelligent control tries to influence by making a show of force.

In an article in the *Sloan Management Review* titled "Rebuilding Behavioral Context: Turn Process Reengineering into People Rejuvenation" (Fall 1995, pp. 11–23), Christopher Bartlett and Sumantra Ghoshal describe this phenomenon:

What (outstanding companies like 3M, Intel, Corning, KAO) have in common is a carefully nurtured, deeply embedded corporate work ethic that triggers the individual-level behaviors of entrepreneurship, collaboration, and learning that are the foundation of organizational renewal. It is a subtle complex characteristic we call the behavioral context.

Fundamental values and a shared vision are powerful forces. In spite of the disloyalty spawned by relentless waves of downsizing, employees who are treated like partners, and are instilled with this sense of purpose require little control. Their behaviors are controlled by self-discipline and understanding—the inherent sense of what is right and wrong; what is congruent with the mission, vision, values, and purpose. These things shape their behavior. Not control, but uncontrol leads them to excel, individually and as a group. A repertory company's sense of community acts in the same way, through its internal and external networks. There is a similarity in the members' perspectives, yet a diversity of their roles that lead to the highest and best performances.

There is an almost palpable feeling about a place where this exists. It is "in the air." Some believe there is an invisible "aura" around certain people, especially the people who are the natural leaders. I know there is an aura about organizations that are performing at this high level of activity. This is constructive, purpose-directed uncontrol that becomes the most powerful form of control. This is one of the most powerful forces in the universe.

Wheatley again (emphasis added):

> [I]f we can trust the workings of chaos, we will see that the domi- nant shape of our organizations can be maintained if we retain clarity about the purpose and direction of the organization. If we succeed in maintaining focus, rather than hands-on control, we also create the flexibility and responsiveness that every organiza- tion craves.

Give this kind of organization intelligently conceived and communicated stretch goals, and they perform beyond anyone's wildest expectations. Supportive, trustworthy, self-confident, and personally secure leadership is necessary for this kind of organization. The leaders must also be sure the safety nets are in place so that mistakes will not be fatal either to careers or the organization. Failures are great learning experiences if they are not fatal, either to the people or companies who make them. The best organizations are like fractals in their consistency and predictability of behavior. The con- sistency, perhaps born in their sense of purpose builds the confidence of their partners. Their complexity is built up of simple, fundamental values and ways of doing business that are constant with their purpose and mission.

5. Organizations Cannot Be Rebuilt Exactly

Attempts to reconstruct natural systems, such as the prairies that once swept across great expanses of our country, have not succeeded. That does not mean great expanses of grass cannot be planted and grow. It simply will not replicate the natural system that existed there before and thus will fall victim to many more forces that it never evolved the immunity or adapt- ability to survive. Weather patterns are different now, for example, as is soil bacteria and insect life. Predators, both plant and animal, are different. Even as much as we try to rebuild exactly the same, it cannot be. Companies and organizations are the same way. New ones may be built. Old ones torn apart by ruthless "slash and burn" turnaround experts are gone forever. The people are one of the major constituencies of these organisms, but it is more than the people. Even if the same people were reassembled, they would be different. They would have new knowledge, new perspec- tives, new viewpoints. The environment would be different; the competition would be different. So, how could things turn out the same? They could not and do not. That does not imply failure, just a very different path to success.

It is important for leaders and followers alike to realize this. Otherwise their expectations will be unrealistic. The good old days are gone forever. Concentrate on making some good *new* days.

6. Continuous Change Gives Life and Opportunity

It cannot be said often enough: Change is the one immutable fact of life. Knowledge grows. We grow (hopefully); we know more and the world around us changes and knows more, too. Like the evolving natural systems, we evolve, we learn, we adapt. The information available to us is expanding at unprecedented rates. Alone it is like a huge well of the freshest water. Drink from it, and at times it seems like it is pumped through a fire hose. Add human insight to information, and it turns into a magical potion called knowledge. This knowledge is the potion which can yield success in the uncharted and dangerous realms we must traverse en route to the future. Combine this knowledge with experience and we achieve that elusive quality called wisdom.

In the past, we were taught that land, labor, and capital were the determinants, the ingredients, the factors of economic success, and each could only have a single owner. This is where information, the newest and fourth great economic factor, is different. It is available to all. The well is not restricted. All can drink from it, and by sharing it, the well becomes deeper and fuller. Success comes to those who can do the most with their knowledge and wisdom. Thus the need to be a shape-shifter.

What we were once, we can never be again. What worked then will not work now. Finding the right shape to create and deliver the right, best value is essential. In chaotic change is enormous opportunity. One solution chosen by many is a remnant of the past. Growing by knowing how to draw on the incredible diversity of solutions is the new sustainable competitive advantage. Simply getting bigger is not the solution.

TREES CANNOT GROW TO THE SKY BUT FORESTS CAN GROW TO THE HORIZON

Bigger is not necessarily better, although many corporations are scrambling to get bigger, to leverage their size by merger and acquisition. The current movement to "get bigger" has spawned megamergers and numerous strategic alliances. Disney buys Cap Cities/ABC. The railroads buy up each other until only a handful survive. IBM buys Lotus. Boeing buys McDonnell Douglas. Banks merge or are acquired almost weekly. On and on. Some of these are real synergistic partnerships. Others are simply attempts to join forces to beat competition in the short term without regard to long-term success. Again, getting bigger is not the answer. Bigness may lead to clout, but not the flexibility necessary to accommodate change and provide greater value for the customer. The challenge of combining the "DNA" of two companies that previously were bitter competitors is a daunting one. Success is rare.

Value is increased only if or when the giants consolidate compatible administrative functions into super-silos to reduce nonvalue-added costs. Size can help if it spawns cross-VCU collaboration, but does it? VCUs are home to their own DNA strands. Bigness may add only ponderous slowness and bureaucracy with more desire for control. More people must agree, approve, be at risk, control, and take action. Most of the large acquisitions and mergers have reduced company value instead of increasing it. Many of them fail miserably. Recent research by Mercer Management Consulting confirms that the performance of megamergers has fallen far short of projections, and often have failed to support the debt incurred in the transaction. Integration (or lack thereof) is one of the major causes of failure.

The extensive emphasis earlier on the integrative approach to Shape-Shifting is confirmed by these findings. Will Microsoft's buying binge yield more success or just more complexity and bulky, disconnected DNA strands? A few kinds of mergers seem to work—leveraged buildups in fragmented industries, combination of direct competitors to dominate a market, or those artfully done by highly refined acquisitors such as GE, Newell, and Dover. The rest suffer, struggle, or simply come apart! Mixing species in nature fails, and only the fittest, most adaptable survive. The same is true in business.

Bigness works only if the value-creating units (VCUs) remain small, fast, and flexible. Remember Toffler's phrase "changing dinosaurs into micro-dinosaurs." Remember the rule about the richness of innovation borne of combining diversity and curiosity? Recall the similarities between natural systems and business or economic systems? Sound strategies based on well thought-out concepts and implemented with consistency lead to the shapes of success in business.

CONCLUSION: THE NEW ORGANIZATIONAL MODEL

My goal in this book is to challenge everyone to become one of the shape-shifters, to tolerate, indulge in, and even encourage the sometimes chaotic meanderings that are the precursors to successful shape-shifting! Assemble the talent. Help it choose and identify with a vision and values and a meaningful sense of purpose. Build a shape of the business that fits the desired shape of value to use as the road map. Revise it constantly. Treat the people—employees, valued suppliers, customers, special professional and personal partners—like true partners. Set tough, stretch goals. Then let the people go, support them—and expect results!

SET COURSE AND ENGAGE

Where do we go from here? That is one of those questions that probably finds its answer somewhere in the shape of systems in nature. We can be sure of one thing. Whatever shape allowed us to achieve our current success will not be the right shape to keep us successful in the future. Times change. Customers' value perceptions and needs change. Stability is stagnation and death. Big trees cannot grow to the sky—nor can big companies! In complexity and chaos is opportunity and the chance to live anew. Unless we constantly strive to understand the changing perception of value with its emotional or situational underpinnings, we are destined to extrapolate the past instead of adapt to the future. To do so is to certainly fail.

To shape-shift continuously is the only course to sustainable advantage. To build new organizational models that capitalize on the talents and learning potential of people is the only way to succeed. To integrate the power of technology and information with human insight is to enhance adaptability and speed learning. To use integrative models of shape-shifting ensures that all parts of the extended organization will be involved in a powerful sense of purpose. To use the power of partnerships, culture, and participation, while integrating the structure and processes is to provide the greatest chance of success. To plan and execute well, with perseverance and commitment is to enhance those chances for success. To realize which are the core competencies and capabilities, and that they are embedded in the people and culture is essential. To determine how their shape must change is to enable the future.

To boldly go where few have gone before is to invite chaos and entertain success. Are you ready? A beautiful, unstable, chaotic, opportunity-filled world lies out there, full of examples of ways to succeed. Will you boldly go to discover that world? Can you become one of the shape-shifters?

INDEX

269